英文精読教室

第6巻

ユーモアを味わう

柴田元幸 編・訳・註

研究社

英文精読教室
第 6 巻
ユーモアを味わう

PRINTED IN JAPAN

はじめに

　昨 2021 年 4 月に刊行を始めたこの『英文精読教室』、幸い一定数の読者の
ご支持をいただいて、今回の 5・6 巻配本まで漕ぎつけることができました。
「物語を楽しむ」「他人になってみる」「口語を聴く」「性差を考える」「怪奇
に浸る」「ユーモアを味わう」と、各巻いちおうテーマ別に分かれていますが、
アンソロジーを作るときの常として、とにかく面白い作品を並べる、という
ことを最優先したラインナップになっています。この巻も、トマス・ハーディ
のような古典的作家から、サローヤンのようなモダン・クラシック、さらに
は謎の現代作家ジャック・ネイプスまで、新旧時代を取り混ぜて選び、なる
べく多様な英語に触れられるようにする、ということもある程度意識しまし
たが、まあいつものように「学ぶ」よりも「楽しむ」を優先した作りになっ
ています。原文で英語の小説を読む楽しみを味わいたいけれど、独力で読む
のはちょっと厳しい、という読者の方々のお役に立てれば、編・訳・註釈者
としては本望です。

　翻訳するとき、べつに強く意識しているわけではないのですが、一歩引い
て考えてみると、なんとなく、まだ英語原文で小説などを楽しんで読むこと
はできなかったけれど、さりとてどんな翻訳でも受け入れる素直さはもう
残っていない、自分にとっても他人にとっても一番うっとうしいころの自分
（高 2・高 3 あたり？）を読者として（ほんとになんとなく、ですが）想定
して訳している気がします。この対訳・註釈本を作るにあたっても、だいた
いそれと同じように、この単語は簡単なはずなのになかなか覚えられなくて

何度も辞書を引いたっけなあ、とか、たしかこのフレーズは 50 年くらい前に辞書の説明を読んだけどいまひとつピンとこなかった気がするなあ、とかかつての自分の顔色を頭の中で窺いながら、多くの読者にとって「大きなお世話」ではなく「小さな親切」となることを願いつつ註釈を作成しました。語やフレーズの「感じ」を摑むには何と言っても的確な例文が鍵なので、すぐれた一連の辞書からの例文をかなり多く挙げています。もちろん常時いちいちそれにお付き合いいただく必要はなく、「いまは話の続きが知りたいんだよ」と思うときはどんどん話自体を読み進めてください。註はあくまで離陸のための補助です。

　全 6 巻のシリーズですが、第 1 巻から順に読む必要はありません。ご自分が惹かれるテーマから手にとっていただければと思います（註に関しては、あとの巻の註釈には、これは第〇巻のどこそこにも出てきた、という記述がありますが、初めの方の巻で、これはあとで第〇巻にも出てくる、と「先回り」することはありません）。各巻の中でも、作品を掲載順に読む必要はありません。この巻はまず SF の鬼才フィリップ・K・ディックのごく短い痛快な作品からウォームアップ的に始まり、あとは時代順に並んでいます。各作品の難易度を 1 〜 3 で示してありますから（1 が一番易しい）、読む際の目安にしてください。ご自分の読みが妥当かどうかを確認してもらえるよう、右側のページには対訳を盛り込みました。少し語学的に敷居が高い、と思える作品に関しては（あるいは、原文だけで読むのはまだ少ししんどい、という場合は）、まず対訳を読んでもらってから原文に向かう、というやり方もあると思います。

　それぞれお好きな形で楽しみ、あわよくばついでに学んでいただけますように。

編訳註者

英文精読教室
第 6 巻
ユーモアを味わう

目次

The Eyes Have It
Philip K. Dick

目はそれを持っている

フィリップ・K・ディック

難易度2
★ ★ ☆

フィリップ・K・ディック
(Philip K. Dick, 1928-1982)

　現実と幻覚、事実と記憶、人間とレプリカなどの対比（もしくはその欠如）を通して、現実とは何か、人間とは何かを鋭く問う作品を数多く発表したアメリカの最重要 SF 作家。ここに収めた超短篇 "The Eyes Have It" は *The Man in the High Castle*（1962）で一応の成功を収めるずっと以前の 1953 年、雑誌 *Science Fiction Stories* に発表された。

It was quite **❶**by accident I discovered **❷**this incredible invasion of Earth by **❸**lifeforms from another planet. **❹**As yet, I haven't done anything about it; I can't think of anything to do. I wrote to the Government, and they sent back a pamphlet on the repair
5 and maintenance of **❺**frame houses. Anyhow, the whole thing **❻**is known; I'm not the first to discover it. Maybe it's even **❼**under control.

I was sitting in **❽**my easy-chair, **❾**idly turning the pages of a paperbacked book someone had left on the bus, when I came
10 across **❿**the reference **⓫**that first put me on the trail. For a moment I didn't respond. **⓬**It took some time for the full import to sink in. After I'd **⓭**comprehended, it seemed odd I hadn't noticed it **⓮**right away.

The reference was clearly to **⓯**a nonhuman species of incredible
15 properties, **⓰**not indigenous to Earth. A species, I **⓱**hasten to point

---

The Eyes Have It: 慣用句 "The ayes have it"（賛成多数により可決。aye は yes の意）というフレーズのもじり。

❶ by accident: たまたま

❷ this incredible invasion: この信じがたい侵略

❸ lifeform(s): 生物

❹ As yet: いままでのところは

❺ frame house(s): 木造家屋

❻ is known: 世間に知れわたっている

❼ under control: 制御されて

❽ my easy-chair: いつも座っている安楽椅子

❾ idly: 手持ちぶさたに

❿ the reference: 言及

⓫ that first put me on the trail: first は for the first time の意。trail は動物などが残していった、追跡の手掛かりとなる「跡」の意で、put ... on the trail

8

　別惑星からの生命体による、この信じがたい地球侵入を私が発見したのはまったくの偶然であった。いまのところまだ何の行動も取っていない。何をしたらいいか、思いつかないのだ。政府に手紙を書いたところ、木造家屋の修理と維持に関するパンフレットを送り返してきた。いずれにせよ、この件は世に知られている。私が最初の発見者ではない。もうすでに対策が講じられたかもしれない。

　いつもの安楽椅子に座って、誰かがバスに忘れていったペーパーバックの本をパラパラめくっていたら、最初の手掛かりとなった言及に出くわしたのである。私はしばし、何の反応もしなかった。その意義がしみ込んでくるのに、しばらく時間がかかったのだ。いったん把握すると、すぐに気づかなかったことが不思議だった。

　それは明らかに、人間以外の、信じがたい性質を持つ、地球自生ではない種への言及であった。急いでつけ加えれば、この種は通常、普通の人間に扮

で「～を手掛かりへと導く」。

⓬ It took some time for the full import to sink in: その重要性（import）が十分に沈み込むのにしばらくかかった。sink in は情報や教訓が「しっかり頭に入る」の意味でよく使う。*The enormity of what I had done didn't sink in until I saw the other driver's dead body.*（相手の運転手の死体を目にして初めて、私は自分の犯した罪のひどさを実感した。『動詞を使いこなすための英和活用辞典』）

⓭ comprehend(ed): 理解する

⓮ right away: すぐに。第 2 巻 p. 40, l. 16 に "Right away I saw she had had the whole thing rebuilt"（なかに入ったとたん、姉が全体を建て替えたことがわかった）の形で既出。

⓯ a [...] species of incredible properties: 信じがたい特性を持つ種

⓰ not indigenous to Earth: 地球土着ではない

⓱ hasten to point out: 急いで指摘する

out, ❶customarily masquerading as ordinary human beings. Their
❷disguise, however, became ❸transparent ❹in the face of the
following observations by the author. It was at once obvious the
author knew everything. Knew everything — and was ❺taking it
5 in his stride. ❻The line (and I tremble remembering it even now)
read:

    … *his eyes slowly* ❼*roved about the room.*

    ❽Vague chills ❾assailed me. I tried to picture the eyes. Did they
roll like ❿dimes? ⓫The passage indicated not; they seemed to move
10 through the air, not over the surface. ⓬Rather rapidly, apparently.
No one in the story was surprised. ⓭That's what tipped me off. No
sign of amazement at such an ⓮outrageous thing. Later the matter
was ⓯amplified.

    … *his eyes moved from person to person.*

---

❶ customarily masquerading as ...: 通例〜に扮装している

❷ disguise: 変装

❸ transparent: 嘘や変装について使うと「見えみえ」の意味になる。

❹ in the face of the following observations: 以下の発言 (observations) か
ら見て、発言とつき合わせると

❺ taking it in his stride: take ... in (one's) stride で「〜を苦もなくこなす、受
けとめる」の意。*She took all these misfortunes in (her) stride.*（彼女は
すべての不運をくじけることなく切り抜けた。『コンパスローズ英和辞典』）

❻ The line ... read:「その一行には〜と書いてあった」。この意味の read は、第
5 巻 p. 182, ll. 9–10 に "These always gave the title of his play and then
they used to read as follows"（いつもかならず劇の題があって、それから
こう書いてあった）の形で既出。

❼ *rove(d)*: さまよう、動き回る

❽ Vague chills: 漠然とした悪寒

❾ assail(ed): 〜を襲う

している。しかし、著者による以下の記述によって、彼らの変装は透けて見えてしまう。著者が何もかも知っていることは瞬時に明らかであった。すべてを知りながら、ひるまずに受けとめている。その一行は（思い出すといまでも震えてしまう）こうあった――

・・・・・・彼の目は部屋の中をゆっくりさまよった。

漠たる寒気が私を襲った。私はその目を思い描こうとした。それらは10セント硬貨のように転がったのか？　文章からするとそうではなさそうだ。床面を転がったのではなく、宙を動いていったようだ。それもどうやら、かなり迅速に。物語の中の誰も驚かなかった。それで私も真相が見えてきた。かように常軌を逸した出来事に、何の驚きも示していないのだから。やがて事態は拡大した。

・・・・・・彼の目は人から人へと移っていった。

⓾ dime(s): 10 セント硬貨
⓫ The passage indicated not: この not の使い方は、たとえば *"Do you think it'll rain tomorrow?" "I think not."*（「明日、雨が降ると思う？」「いや、降らないと思う」）などと同じ。
⓬ Rather rapidly, apparently: どうやらかなり速く。apparently は第 3 巻 p. 188, ll. 8-9, *"The man's wife and children were watching, apparently."*（男の女房と子供たちはどうやら一部始終を見ていたらしい）などで述べたように「どうやら」であって「明らかに」ではない。
⓭ That's what tipped me off: tip ... off で「～に（事実・真相などを）感じさせる、勘づかせる」。
⓮ outrageous: とんでもない、法外な
⓯ amplified <amplify: ～を増幅する、拡大する

❶ There it was in a nutshell. The eyes had clearly come apart from the rest of him and were **❷**on their own. My heart **❸**pounded and **❹**my breath choked in my windpipe. I had **❺**stumbled on an accidental mention of a totally unfamiliar race. Obviously **❻**non-

5 Terrestrial. Yet, to the characters in the book, it was perfectly natural — which suggested they belonged to the same species.

And the author? A slow suspicion burned in my mind. The author was **❼**taking it rather *too easily* in his stride. Evidently, he felt this was quite a usual thing. He made absolutely no attempt to

10 conceal this knowledge. The story continued:

… **❽***presently his eyes* **❾***fastened on Julia.*

Julia, being a lady, **❿**had at least the breeding to feel indignant. She is described as **⓫**blushing and knitting her brows angrily. At this, I sighed with relief. They weren't *all* non-Terrestrials. The

15 narrative continues:

… *slowly, calmly, his eyes examined every inch of her.*

---

❶ There it was in a nutshell: "There he is!" で「いたぞ、あそこだ！」となるように、There … is/was は探していた物や人、重要な物や人が確かにそこにある、というニュアンス。in a nutshell は、何か複雑な問題が簡潔に説明されている事態を言い表わすのに使う。*Okay, that's our proposal in a nutshell. Any questions?*（さ、以上が我々の提案の肝です。質問は？ *Longman Dictionary of Contemporary English*）

❷ on their own: on one's own で alone の意味なので、要するにその前の had […] come apart from the rest of him と言っていることは同じ。

❸ pound(ed):（心臓が）ドキドキと打つ

❹ my breath choked in my windpipe: 息が気管で詰まった

❺ stumble(d) on …: ～に偶然出くわす

❻ non-Terrestrial: 地球外の。Steven Spielberg の映画 *E.T. the Extra-*

12

この一言で決まりだった。目は明らかに、彼の体から分離して、独自に動いていたのである。私の心臓は高鳴り、息は気管で詰まった。まったく未知の種族にたまたま言い及んだ例に私は行きあたったのだ。間違いなく、地球大気圏外生物。とはいえ、本の中の登場人物にとっては、まったく自然な存在のようだ。ということはつまり、彼らも同じ種に属しているのではないか。

ならば、著者は？　ゆっくりと、私の意識の中でひとつの疑念に火が点いていった。どうも著者は、あまりにもひるまずにすべてを受けとめている。明らかに、これをまったくの日常茶飯事と感じているのだ。知っているということを、少しも隠そうとしていない。物語はさらに続いた──

　……まもなく彼の目がジュリアに貼りついた。

ジュリアはレディであり、少なくともこれに憤慨するような育ちである。彼女は顔を赤らめ、怒りに眉をひそめた、との描写があった。これを読んで私はほっとため息をついた。みんながみんな、地球大気圏外生物ではないのだ。物語は続く──

　……ゆっくり、落ち着きはらって、彼の目がジュリアの隅々まで吟味した。

Terrestrial (1982) で知られる語 extra(-)terrestrial と同義。

❼ taking it rather *too easily* in his stride: take ... in (one's) stride は p. 10, ll. 4-5 に "Knew everything—and was taking it in his stride"（すべてを知りながら、ひるまずに受けとめている）の形で既出。

❽ *presently*: シェークスピアの時代には「ただちに」の意だが、現代では「やがて」「まもなく」。

❾ fasten(ed) on ...: 通常は視線が何かに「釘付けになる」の意だが、文字どおりには「〜に貼りつく」。

❿ had at least the breeding to feel indignant:（こうした無礼に）憤りを感じるだけの育ちのよさ（the breeding）があった

⓫ blushing and knitting her brows angrily: 赤面し、怒って眉に皺を寄せ

❶Great Scott! But here the girl turned and **❷**stomped off and the matter ended. **❸**I lay back in my chair gasping with horror. **❹**My wife and family **❺**regarded me in wonder.

"What's wrong, dear?" my wife asked.

5   I couldn't tell her. Knowledge like this was too much for the ordinary **❻**run-of-the-mill person. I had to keep it to myself. **❼**"Nothing," I gasped. I leaped up, **❽**snatched the book, and hurried out of the room.

10 In the garage, I continued reading. There was more. Trembling, I read **❾**the next revealing passage:

… he put his arm around Julia. Presently she asked him if he would remove his arm. He immediately did so, with a smile.

It's not said what was done with the arm after the fellow had
15 removed it. Maybe it was left standing **❿**upright in the corner. Maybe it was thrown away. I don't care. In any case, the full

---

❶ Great Scott!: こいつは驚いた！

❷ stomped off: すごい剣幕で立ち去った

❸ I lay back in my chair gasping with horror: 第 4 巻 p. 214, l. 2 の "'Oh no!' gasp Tooka and Etsuyo"（「わぁ大変！」トオカとエツヨが息を呑む）に関する註❷で触れたように、gasp は文脈によって「ハッと息を呑む」「息も切れぎれに喋る」「喘ぐ」などの訳語が充てられるが、ここは「喘ぐ」か。

❹ My wife and family: 私の妻子

❺ regard(ed): 〜をじっと見る

❻ run-of-the-mill: ありふれた

❼ "Nothing," I gasped: こちらの gasp は「息も切れぎれに言った」「喘ぐように言った」か。

❽ snatched the book: 本をひっつかんだ

　何ということ！　だがここで娘はくるっと回れ右し、カンカンに怒って立ち去り、この件は終わりを告げた。私は椅子の背に倒れ込み、恐怖に喘いだ。私の妻と子供たちは驚きの表情で私を見た。

「どうしたの、あなた？」妻が訊いた。

　彼女には言えなかった。こんなことを知らされるのは、ごく普通の人間には荷が重すぎる。私一人のこととしてとどめておくしかない。「何でもない」私は喘ぎあえぎ言った。そしてパッと飛び上がり、本を乱暴に摑んで、あたふたと部屋から出ていった。

　ガレージで続きを読んだ。話はまだあった。震えながら、次の意味深長な一節を読んだ——

　……彼は片腕をジュリアの体に回した。程なく彼女は、その腕、外してくださらないかしらと言った。彼は即座に、にっこり笑いながら、言われたとおりにした。

　外したあと、男が腕をどうしたかは書かれていない。隅に立てかけておいたのだろうか。放り投げたのか。どちらでもいい。いずれにせよ、意味はしっ

❾ the next revealing passage: revealing は「示唆に富む、隠された物事を明かす」。*a revealing insight into her life*（彼女の生活の内奥をうかがわせる洞察。『ロングマン英和辞典』）

❿ upright: まっすぐに

meaning was there, **❶**staring me right in the face.

Here was a race of creatures **❷**capable of removing portions of their anatomy at will. Eyes, arms — and maybe more. **❸** Without batting an eyelash. My knowledge of biology **❹** came in handy, at
5 this point. Obviously they were simple beings, **❺**uni-cellular, some sort of primitive **❻**single-celled things. **❼**Beings no more developed than starfish. **❽**Starfish can do the same thing, you know.

I read on. And came to **❾**this incredible revelation, **❿**tossed off coolly by the author **⓫**without the faintest tremor:

10   *… outside the movie theater we split up. Part of us went inside, part* **⓬***over to the cafe for dinner.*

⓭ Binary fission, obviously. Splitting in half and forming two **⓮** entities. Probably each lower half went to the cafe, **⓯** it being

---

❶ staring me right in the face: *I was so ashamed that I couldn't look her in the face.* (私は恥ずかしくて彼女の顔をまともに見ることができなかった。『コンパスローズ英和辞典』）などと同じ用法。right は強調。

❷ capable of removing portions of their anatomy at will: anatomy は辞書でまず出てくる定義は「解剖（学）」だが、このように（解剖学的観察の対象となる）身体そのものについて使うことも多い。at will: 自在に

❸ Without batting an eyelash: まばたき一つせず、平然と

❹ came in handy: 役に立った。come in handy は知識や道具についてよく使われる。*A hacksaw always comes in handy for cutting plastic pipes.* (ビニールパイプを切るには弓のこがつねに役立つ。*Longman Dictionary of Contemporary English, Corpus*)

❺ uni-cellular: 単細胞の

❻ single-celled: 1 行上の uni-cellular と同じ。

❼ Beings no more developed than starfish: せいぜいヒトデくらいしか進化していない生物

❽ Starfish can do the same thing, you know: ヒトデの腕は切れやすく、再生しやすい。一本の腕から完全な個体が再生される例もあるという。

かりそこにあって、私を正面から見据えていた。

　つまりこれは、体のさまざまな部分を意のままに取り外しできる生物なのである。目、腕——まだほかにも外せるのかもしれない。まばたき一つせずに。ここで私の生物学の知識が役に立った。明らかにこれは、単純な、単細胞の原生動物である。ヒトデ程度にしか進化していない。ヒトデも同じことができるのである。

　私は先を読んだ。そしてこの信じがたい公言を、著者が少しもおののくことなく、さもあっさりと行なっている箇所に行きあたった——

　……映画館の外で私たちは二つに分かれた。私たちの一部は中に入り、一部は夕食を食べにカフェに向かった。

　明らかに、二分裂。二つに分かれて、二個の個体を形成するのだ。おそらくカフェの方が遠いのでそれぞれの下半分がそちらに行き、上半分たちが映

❾ this incredible revelation: revelation は p. 14, l. 11 の "the next revealing passage"（次の意味深長な一節）の revealing と同じ発想で、何か大きな事実が明かされること、または明かされたその内容。*I was surprised by the revelation that our neighbor is a murderer.*（隣人が殺人犯だとわかって驚いた。『コンパスローズ英和辞典』）

❿ tossed off coolly: toss off ... は何かをざっと述べたり書いたりすること。*I tossed off a few letters.*（手紙を何通かさっと書き上げた。『ロングマン英和辞典』）

⓫ without the faintest tremor: 少しも震えることもなく。coolly とすでに形容したことのダメ押しという感じ。

⓬ *over to the cafe*: over はそこへ行くのに何かを越えていく、ある程度距離があるというニュアンス。*Please take this teapot over to the table.*（このティーポットをテーブルに持っていってください。『コンパスローズ英和辞典』）

⓭ Binary fission: 二分裂（一個体がほぼ等しい二つの新個体に分裂する）

⓮ entities <entity: 個体

⓯ it being farther: since it [=the cafe] was farther (than the movie theater)

farther, and the upper halves to the movies. I read on, hands shaking. **❶**I had really stumbled onto something here. **❷**My mind reeled as I made out this passage:

    ... I'm afraid there's no doubt about it. **❸** *Poor Bibney has lost his*
5 *head again.*

    Which was followed by:

    ... and Bob says **❹***he has utterly no guts.*

    ❺ Yet Bibney got around as well as the next person. The next person, however, **❻**was just as strange. He was soon described as:

10   *... totally lacking in brains.*

❼There was no doubt of the thing in the next passage. Julia, whom I had thought to be the one normal person, **❽**reveals herself as also being an alien lifeform, similar to the rest:

---

❶ I had really stumbled onto something here: stumble on ... は p. 12, ll. 3-4 に "I had stumbled on an accidental mention of a totally unfamiliar race." (まったく未知の種族にたまたま言い及んだ例に私は行きあたったのだ) の形で既出。

❷ My mind reeled as I made out this passage: 次の一節を読んで私の頭は混乱した。reel(ed):（頭が）混乱する、動揺する。make out ...:〜を読みとる。make out は第 1 巻 p. 194, ll. 1-3 に "A log burning in the fireplace was the only source of light, by which I could make out a number of hunched figures sitting around the room." (暖炉で燃えている一本の丸太が唯一の光源で、その光を頼りに見てみると、背を丸めた人影がいくつか、部屋のあちこちに散らばっているのがわかった) の形で既出。

❸ *Poor Bibney has lost his head again*: lose one's head は普通「冷静さを失う」の意。

❹ *he has utterly no guts*: have no guts はむろん普通は「根性がない」の意だが、gut の字義どおりの意味は「はらわた」。

画館に行ったのだろう。私は両手をぶるぶる震わせながら先を読んだ。何という大発見か。次の一節を読むと、くらくらしてきた──

　……あいにくだが間違いない。気の毒にビブニーは、また頭がどこかに行ってしまったんだ。

　そして次は──

　……奴には全然肝がないとボブは言ってる。

　だがビブニーは隣の者と変わらず普通にやっている。一方隣の者だって、ビブニーに負けず奇怪なのだ。彼はじきにこう描写される──

　……脳味噌がまったくない。

　次の一節で、疑いは完全に消えた。唯一ノーマルな人間だと思えたジュリアも、やはりほかの者たちと変わらず外来の生命体であることを露呈するのだ──

❺ Yet Bibney got around as well as the next person: get around は「（病人・老人などが）（不自由なく）歩く、動き回る、出歩く、出かける」。*He can barely get around with the aid of cane.*（彼は杖を頼りにかろうじて歩ける。『動詞を使いこなすための英和活用辞典』）as well as the next person: 普通は「誰にも劣らず」などと訳すが、ここは前後とのかねあいから字義どおりに訳すしかない。

❻ was just as strange: 同じくらい奇妙だった。just は単なる強調だが、just 抜きで was as strange と言うとやや座りが悪い。

❼ There was no doubt of the thing: この the thing はこうした奇怪な事態全体を指す。

❽ reveals herself as …: 自分が〜であることを明かす、示す

... **❶**quite deliberately, Julia had given her heart to the young man.

It didn't **❷**relate **❸**what the final disposition of the organ was, but I didn't really care. It was evident **❹**Julia had gone right on living in her usual manner, like all the others in the book. Without
5 heart, arms, eyes, brains, **❺**viscera, dividing up in two **❻**when the occasion demanded. Without **❼**a qualm.

... **❽**thereupon **❾**she gave him her hand.

I **❿**sickened. **⓫**The rascal now had her hand, as well as her heart. **⓬**I shudder to think what he's done with them, by this time.

10 ... he took her arm.

⓭Not content to wait, **⓮**he had to start dismantling her on his own. **⓯**Flushing crimson, I **⓰**slammed the book shut and leaped

---

❶ quite deliberately, Julia had given her heart to the young man: deliberately はなかなか日本語一語で定義しにくいが、たとえば Longman Dictionary of Contemporary English では 1) done in a way that is intended or planned（意図・計画されたやり方で）; 2) done or said in a slow careful way（ゆっくり・慎重なやり方・言い方で）とある。ここもその両方がある感じ。give one's heart to ... は普通は「〜が心から好きになる」の意。ただしたとえばボブ・ディラン初期の代表曲 "Don't Think Twice, It's All Right" (1963) には "I give her my heart but she wanted my soul"（彼女に心を捧げても彼女は魂を欲しがった）という一節があり、「心を与える」という具体的なイメージを捨てるべきではない。

❷ relate: 〜を物語る

❸ what the final disposition of the organ was: その器官（the organ）の最終的な処置（disposition）はどのようなものだったか。要するに、心臓を結局どうしたのか、ということ。

❹ Julia had gone right on living in her usual manner: right は p. 14, l. 16 - p. 16, l. 1 の "In any case, the full meaning was there, staring me right in the face."（いずれにせよ、意味はしっかりそこにあって、私を正面から見据えていた）の right と同じ強調の役割。

はっきり意識的に、ジュリアは心臓を若者に委ねた。

最終的にこの器官がどう処理されたかは語られていなかったが、私にはどうでもよかった。ジュリアがそのまま、本に出てくるほかの者たち同様、普通に生きつづけたことは明らかであった。心臓も、腕も、目も、脳味噌も、はらわたもなしに、必要とあらば二つに分裂して。何の不安もなく。

……そうして彼女は若者に自らの手を差し出した。

私はムカムカしてきた。悪党はいまや彼女から心のみならず、手まで奪った。いまに至るまでに、こいつがそれをどうしたか考えると、思わず身震いしてしまう。

……男は彼女の腕を取った。

大人しく待つこともせず、自分から彼女を解体しにかかったのだ。顔が真っ赤になるのを感じながら私は本を乱暴に閉じ、飛び上がった。だがそれでも、

❺ viscera: viscus（内臓・はらわた）の複数形。「生々しさ」が感じられる言葉で、visceral として形容詞にすると「内臓に訴えるかのように生々しい」という意味。

❻ when the occasion demanded: 状況が要求すれば

❼ a qualm: 不安、懸念

❽ *thereupon*: その結果

❾ *she gave him her hand*: give ... one's hand で普通は「～との結婚を承諾する」の意。

❿ sicken(ed): 吐き気を催す

⓫ The rascal: 悪党

⓬ I shudder to think ...: この一文だけ現在形になっていることに注意。「～を考えると（いまも）ぞっとする」

⓭ Not content to ...: ～することに甘んじず、～では満足せず

⓮ he had to start dismantling her on his own: この have to ... は「～しなければならない」ではなく、少し大げさにいえば「よりによって、けしからぬことに、～という暴挙に走る」という意。dismantling <dismantle: ～を解体する。on his own:（腕や心臓が差し出されるのを待たずに）自分で

⓯ Flushing crimson: 顔を深紅に染めて

⓰ slammed the book shut: 本をバタンと閉じた

to my feet. **❶**But not in time to escape one last reference to **❷**those carefree bits of anatomy **❸**whose travels had originally thrown me on the track:

 … her eyes followed him all the way down the road and across the
5 *meadow.*

 I rushed from the garage and back inside the warm house, as if the **❹** accursed things were following *me*. My wife and children were playing Monopoly in the kitchen. I joined them and played **❺**with frantic fervor, brow feverish, teeth chattering.

10 **❻**I had had enough of the thing. I want to hear no more about it. Let them come on. Let them invade Earth. I don't want to **❼**get mixed up in it.

 ❽I have absolutely no stomach for it.

---

❶ But not in time to ...: だが〜するには間に合わなかった

❷ those carefree bits of anatomy: これら自由気ままな (carefree) 身体 (anatomy) の部分 (bits)

❸ whose travels had originally thrown me on the track: そもそも (originally) それらの移動 (travels) が私を追跡へと駆り立てたのだった。on the track (〜を追跡して) は p. 8, l. 10 の "the reference that first put me on the trail" (最初の手掛かりとなった言及) の on the trail とほぼ同じ。travel は第 1 巻 p. 156, ll. 5-6 の "His eyes traveled over the case, poking, testing, looking for flaws."(目がスーツケースを眺めまわし、あちこち押したりつついたりして、あらを探している) での動詞形もそうだが、「旅」「旅する」という日本語よりずっと意味が広く第 5 巻 p. 151 の註**❽**でも述べたとおり、「移動」「移動する」に近い。

❹ accursed: 呪わしい

もうひとつ最後の、自由に動く例の身体のパーツへの言及から逃れられはしなかった。思えばまず初めに、この種の言及に出会って、私も真相に勘づきはじめたのである——

　……彼女の目が、彼を追って道路をずっと下っていき、草原を越えていった。

　あたかも呪わしい生物たちに自分が追われているかのように、私はガレージを飛び出し、暖かい家の中に帰った。妻と子供たちはキッチンでモノポリーをしていた。私もその仲間に入り、狂おしい熱意とともにゲームに興じた。額は熱を帯び、歯はガタガタ鳴った。

　もうこんな話はうんざりだ。これ以上聞きたくない。来るなら来るがいい。地球を侵略するがいい。関わるのはごめんだ。

　私にはそんなことに耐える腹はない。

❺ with frantic fervor, brow feverish: 半狂乱の情熱とともに、額も熱く
❻ I had had enough of the thing: この the thing は p. 18, l. 12 に "There was no doubt of the thing in the next passage."（次の一節で、疑いは完全に消えた）の形で既出。
❼ get mixed up in ...: 〜に関わりあいになる
❽ I have absolutely no stomach for it: have no stomach for ... で「〜に気が向かない」の意。*I have no stomach for a fight.*（けんかをするつもりはない。『研究社 新英和中辞典』）

ちなみに

　このように「比喩的な表現を文字どおりに捉える」ことでグロテスクな笑いを生むという手口は Poe も得意とした。"Loss of Breath"（1835）は文字どおり息をどこかになくしてしまう男の話だし、"Never Bet the Devil Your Head"（1841）は "I'll bet the Devil my head"（悪魔に首を賭けてもいい）が口癖の男が本当に悪魔に首をとられてしまう話。そもそも代表作 "The Fall of the House of Usher"（1839）にしても、「アッシャー家の没落」という比喩的な（より普通の）意味に、結末でアッシャー屋敷が倒壊し池に呑まれることによって「アッシャー家の崩壊」という文字どおりの意味が加わることになる。

Old Andrey's Experience as a Musician
Thomas Hardy

アンドリー爺さんの楽師体験

トマス・ハーディ

難易度 2
★ ★ ☆

トマス・ハーディ
(Thomas Hardy, 1840-1928)

イギリスの小説家・詩人。*The Return of the Native*（1878），*Tess of the d'Urbervilles*（1891）など重厚で、どちらかといえば深刻な長篇小説で知られる書き手だが、短篇小説では意外に軽妙な側面も見せる。ここでは作品集 *Life's Little Ironies*（1894）から、音楽を楽しく活かした二篇を選んだ。

*❶*I was one of the quire-boys at that time, and we and the players were to appear at ❷ the manor-house as usual that Christmas week, to play and sing in ❸ the hall to ❹ the Squire's people and visitors (❺among 'em being the ❻archdeacon, ❼Lord
5 and Lady Baxby, and I don't know who); afterwards going, as we always did, to have a good supper in ❽the servants' hall. ❾Andrey knew this was the custom, and meeting us when we were starting to go, he said to us: ❿"Lord, ⓫how I should like to join in that meal of beef, and ⓬turkey, and ⓭plum-pudding, and ⓮ale, that ⓯you
10 happy ones ⓰be going to just now! One more or less will make no

---

❶ I was one of the quire-boys at that time …: ここに取り上げたのは、*Life's Little Ironies* の中の、小品を集めたセクション 'A Few Crusted Characters' (crusted は「古めかしい」) に収められた 'Old Andrey's Experience as a Musician' と 'Absent-Mindedness in a Parish Choir' の二篇。便宜上、前者をひとまずの共通タイトルに使わせてもらった。どちらも、村を長年離れていた末に戻ってきた男に、彼がいないあいだに村でどんなことがあったか村人たちが代わるがわる物語る、という体裁を採っている。ここで語っている 'I' は Mr Profitt なる名前の学校教師。quire: choir（聖歌隊）の古い別綴り。
❷ the manor-house: 領主の邸宅
❸ the hall: 現代では hall といえば「玄関」だったり「廊下」だったりするわけだが、こういう領主様がまだ幅を利かせている文脈では「お屋敷」（すなわち前行の the manor-house と同義）あるいはその「大広間」の意になる。
❹ the Squire: 地主
❺ among 'em: among them
❻ archdeacon: 英国国教会の「大執事」。*Longman Dictionary of Contemporary English* の定義は 'a priest of a high rank in the Anglican Church who works under a bishop'。とにかく「偉い人」だと思っておけば十分。
❼ Lord and Lady Baxby: Lord は侯爵 (marquess) や伯爵 (earl) などの位を持つ貴族につける敬称。Lady も単に「ご婦人」ではなく、Lord の夫人に対する敬称。
❽ the servants' hall:「使用人部屋《大邸宅で使用人が食事をしたり休息したりする比較的大きな部屋》」(『研究社 新英和大辞典』)

「当時私は聖歌隊の一員で、そのクリスマスの週、私たち聖歌隊と楽隊はい
つものとおり地主様のお屋敷に行って地主様の御家族とお客様たちを前に広
間で歌い、演奏することになっていた（お客様には大執事様、バクスビー卿
と奥様、まだまだほかにもいらっしゃった）。終わったらいつもどおり、召
使い部屋で美味しいごちそうにあずかることになっている。そういうならわ
しだとアンドリーも知っていて、そろそろ出かけようという私たちのところ
に寄ってきて、こう言った。『ああ、お前たちが羨ましい――わしも牛、七面鳥、
プラムプディング、エールを御相伴したいものだ！　一人くらい増えようが
減ろうが地主様にとって違いはあるまい。わしは歌う男の子として通るには
年を食いすぎておるし、歌う女の子として通るにはあごひげが長すぎる。ご

❾ Andrey knew this ...: 作中ではこの人物は Andrew と呼ばれているが、タイ
　　トルに合わせて Andrey と直した。この前のセクションではこの人物の息子の
　　物語が語られ、親子とも名は同じ Andrey だったと述べられている。
❿ "Lord, how I should like ...": この Lord は貴族の称号ではなく、「ああ」「おお」
　　などと訳される感嘆の言葉。
⓫ how I should like to ...: should は現代人の耳にはやや古風。How I'd like to
　　... と短縮して言うのが普通だろうし、I'd は何の略かと問われれば I would とた
　　いていの人は答えるだろう。
⓬ turkey: 感謝祭のご馳走といえば七面鳥、クリスマスのご馳走といえばやはり
　　七面鳥。
⓭ plum-pudding:「刻んだスエット・干しブドウ・砂糖漬け果実皮・小麦粉・パ
　　ン粉・黒砂糖・卵・香辛料・ブランデーなどをプディング型に詰めて蒸した菓
　　子」（『リーダーズ英和辞典』）。Christmas pudding とも呼ぶくらいで、伝統
　　的にクリスマスの菓子。Charles Dickens の A Christmas Carol (1843) でも、
　　Mrs Cratchit が作ったプラム・プディングが出てくる場面はちょっとしたハイ
　　ライトである。
⓮ ale: かつてはホップを入れる・入れないで beer と区別されたが、現在ではビー
　　ルと同じと考えてとりあえず間違いではないらしい。
⓯ you happy ones: お前ら幸福な者たち
⓰ be going to: are going to。このようにこの小説内の話し言葉は時おり破格だ
　　が、ほとんどの場合文脈から判断できると思う。

difference to the Squire. I am too old to ❶pass as a singing boy, and too ❷bearded to pass as a singing girl; can ❸ye lend me a fiddle, ❹neighbours, ❺that I may come with ye as ❻a bandsman?"

'Well, we didn't like to ❼be hard upon him, and lent him an
5 old one, though ❽Andrey knew no more of music than the Giant o' Cernel; and ❾armed with the instrument he walked up to the Squire's house with the others of us at ❿the time appointed, and went in boldly, his fiddle under his arm. He made himself as natural as he could in opening ⓫the music-books and moving
10 the candles to the best points for throwing light upon ⓬the notes; and all went well till we had played and sung ⓭"While shepherds watch", and "Star, arise", and "Hark the glad sound". Then the Squire's mother, a tall ⓮gruff old lady, who was much interested in church-music, said quite ⓯unexpectedly to Andrey: " ⓰My man, I

---

❶ pass as ...: 〜として通る。たとえば 20 世紀前半のアメリカで passing とい えば黒人が白人として「通す」ことを言った。

❷ bearded: あごひげが生えた

❸ ye: you

❹ neighbour(s): 聖書の 'Thou shalt love [...] thy neighbour as thyself'（己 のごとく汝の隣(となり)を愛すべし。*St. Luke*, 10: 27）などと同じで、文字どおり近 所の住人という意味に加えて、「同胞」「仲間」という含みもある。

❺ that I may ...: 私が〜できるよう。このシリーズで何度か触れたように、現代 英語なら so I can ... となるところ。

❻ a bandsman: 楽団員

❼ be hard upon ...: 〜に辛くあたる

❽ Andrey knew no more of music than the Giant o' Cernel: the Giant o' Cernel は通例 the Cerne Abbas Giant と呼ばれる、ドーセット州の村 Cerne Abbas 近郊の丘陵に描かれた巨人の絵（高さ 55 メートル）。「アンドリー が音楽を知らぬこと、サーネルの巨人のごとし」。要するに「なんにも知らない」 ということをユーモラスに言っている。

近所の皆さんよ、どなたかわしにフィドルを貸してくださらんか、そうすりゃわしも楽師としてあんた方と一緒に行ける』

　ま、あんまり殺生なことも言いたくないので、アンドリーが音楽のお字も知らないとわかってはいたが、私たちは古いフィドルを貸してやることにした。かくして爺さん、楽器もしっかり手に入れ、言われた時間に私たちと一緒に地主様のお屋敷に出かけ、フィドルを小脇に抱えて堂々中に入っていった。楽譜を開いて、音符にしっかり光が当たるよう蠟燭を動かすときも精一杯それらしくふるまい、みんなで『羊飼いに見守られ』『高く上がれ、星よ』『聞け悦ばしき音を』を歌い奏でたところまでは万事うまく行った。ところがそこで、地主様の母上、これが背の高いつっけんどんな年配のご婦人で、教会音楽に興味津々というお方なのだが、出し抜けにアンドリーに向かって、『ちょっとあんた、あんた一人だけ楽器弾いてないじゃないの。どういうわけ』

❾ armed with …: 〜で武装して
❿ the time appointed: 指定された時間
⓫ the music-books: 楽譜帳。'music' だけでも「楽譜」の意になる。*Have you brought your music?*（楽譜をお持ちになりましたか。『研究社 新英和大辞典』）
⓬ the notes: 音符
⓭ "While shepherds watch": 通例 'While shepherds watched their flocks by night'（羊飼いたちが夜に群れを見守るなか）で始まるクリスマス・キャロル。以下、"Star, arise" は 'O Morning Star! Arise ere day is broken'（おお朝の星よ！　昇れ、日が訪れる前に）、"Hark the glad sound" は 'Hark, the glad sound! The Savior comes'（聴け、悦ばしき音を！　主は来ませり）で始まるキャロル。Hark, the glad sound! の日本語訳詩「もろびとこぞりて」は、別の曲 'Joy to the World' のメロディと結びつけられて知られている。
⓮ gruff: ぶっきらぼうな
⓯ unexpectedly: 思いがけなく
⓰ My man: 目下の者に呼びかけるときの言葉。

see you don't play your instrument with the rest. How is that?"

'Every one of the quire was **❶**ready to sink into the earth with
❷ concern at **❸** the fix Andrey was in. We could see that he **❹** had
fallen into a cold sweat, and **❺**how he would get out of it we did
5 not know.

'"I've had a misfortune, **❻**mem," he says, **❼**bowing as meek as a
child. "Coming along the road I fell down and **❽**broke my bow."

'"O, I am sorry to hear that," says she. "Can't it be mended?"

'"O no, mem," says Andrey. "**❾**'Twas broke **❿**all to splinters."

10 '"I'll see what I can do for you," says she.

'And then it seemed **⓫** all over, and we played **⓬** "Rejoice, ye
drowsy mortals all", **⓭**in D and two sharps. But **⓮**no sooner had we
got through it than she says to Andrey:

'"**⓯**I've sent up into the attic, where we have some old musical
15 instruments, and found a bow for you." And she hands the bow

---

❶ ready to sink into the earth: 日本語の「穴があったら入りたい」と似た発想。

❷ concern: 心配、懸念

❸ the fix Andrey was in: fix は「困った立場、苦境」。in, into と合わせて使う。
I'm really in a (fine) fix.（本当にやっかいなことになった。『コンパスローズ
英和辞典』）

❹ had fallen into a cold sweat:「どっと冷や汗をかく」は現代では break out
in a cold sweat という言い方が一般的。

❺ how he would get out of it:「それからどうやって抜け出るか」の「それ」
は a cold sweat のこと。had fallen *into* a cold sweat という表現がすぐ前
にあるので、out of ... がごく自然に出てくる。

❻ mem: ma'am (madam) の変形。

❼ bowing as meek as ...: この bow は「お辞儀する」で、発音は /báʊ/。
meek: 従順に

❽ broke my bow: こっちの bow は弦楽器の「弓」で、発音は /bóʊ/。

とおっしゃった。

　アンドリー進退きわまれり、と私たち聖歌隊もオロオロし、穴を掘って消えてしまいたい気分だった。見れば本人も脂汗をかいている。いったいどう切り抜けるのか、見当もつかなかった。

『奥様、実はあいにく』とアンドリーは子供みたいにしおらしくお辞儀しながら言った。『ここへ伺う途中転んで弓を折ってしまいまして』

『あらまあ、それは気の毒に』とご婦人はおっしゃった。『修繕できないのかい？』

『いえそれが奥様、ばらばらに砕けてしまいまして』

『何かしてあげられないか、考えてみよう』と御母堂はおっしゃった。

　やれやれ一段落、と思って私たちは『歓喜せよ、汝ら眠たき者たちよ』をシャープ二つのニ長調で演奏した。ところが、終わりまで来たとたん、御母堂がアンドリーにおっしゃるには、

『屋根裏に古い楽器がいろいろあるんで見に行かせたらね、弓が出てきた

❾ 'Twas broke: it was broken
❿ all to splinters: ばらばらに
⓫ all over: ここは「万事休す」よりも「一件落着」。
⓬ "Rejoice, ye drowsy mortals all": 通例 'Awake, ye drowsy mortals all'（目覚めよ、眠たき者らよ）で始まるキャロルのバリエーションか。mortals:「いずれ死ぬ定め」という含みをこめた意味での「人間」。
⓭ in D and two sharps: ニ長調に # が２つあることを言っているのか。
⓮ no sooner had we got through it than ...: no sooner had A done B than C did D で「A が B するやいなや C が D した」の意。ここでは語りも乗ってきていわば実況中継的になってきているので、C did D の部分が she says to Andrey と現在形になっている。get through ... で仕事や困難を「切り抜ける」。
⓯ I've sent up into the attic: この send は send for the doctor で「医者を呼びにやる」などと同じで、何かの目的で「誰かを送り出す」の意。the attic: 屋根裏

to poor **❶**wretched Andrey, who didn't even know **❷**which end to take hold of. "Now we shall have **❸**the full accompaniment," says she.

'Andrey's face looked as if it were **❹**made of rotten apple as he
5 stood in the circle of players in front of his book; for if there was one person in **❺**the parish that everybody was afraid of, 'twas this **❻** hook-nosed old lady. However, by keeping a little behind the next man he managed to **❼** make pretence of beginning, **❽** sawing away with his bow without letting it touch the strings, **❾**so that it
10 looked as if he were **❿**driving into the tune with **⓫**heart and soul.
⓬ 'Tis a question if he wouldn't have got through all right if one of the Squire's visitors (**⓭**no other than the archdeacon) hadn't

---

❶ wretched: 哀れなる。第 1 巻に収めた Ursula K. Le Guin, 'The Ones Who Walk Away from Omelas' では、町の人々全員が幸せになるために一人惨めな境遇を強いられている子供にこの形容詞が充てられている。'They know that if the wretched one were not there sniveling in the dark ...' (彼らは知っている。もしあのみじめな子が闇の中でメソメソ泣いていなかったら……) [p. 140, ll. 12-13]

❷ which end to take hold of: どっちの端 (end) をつかむべきなのか

❸ the full accompaniment: 完全な伴奏

❹ made of rotten apple: apple を一個のリンゴではなくリンゴの「果肉」と考えれば rotten の前に a がないのも納得が行くが、まあ普通は a rotten apple と言う。

❺ the parish:「1 つの教会 (church) と 1 人の牧師 (parson) を有する区域で英国では行政上の最小単位」(『コンパスローズ英和辞典』)。伝統的にイギリスの「地域」を考える上できわめて重要な区分。

❻ hook-nosed: わし鼻の

❼ make pretence of ...: 〜のふりをする。pretence はアメリカ英語では pretense。

❽ sawing away with his bow: 弓を使ってガンガン弾いて。saw は元来「のこ

よ』。そうして御母堂は弓を渡してくださったが、哀れアンドリーはどっち
の側を持ったらいいかもわかりゃしない。『これで全員揃った演奏が聞ける
ね』と御母堂はおっしゃった。

　楽師たちの輪に入り、楽譜を前にして立ったアンドリーの顔ときたら、ま
るっきり腐ったリンゴみたいに見えた。何しろここいらへんで、誰もが恐れ
ている人物が一人いるとしたら、それはこのカギ鼻をした年配のご婦人だっ
たのだから。けれどアンドリーは、隣の男のややうしろにいるよう努めつつ、
弾きはじめたような格好をしてみせ、弓を弦に触れずに上下させて、いかに
も全身全霊、演奏に打ち込んでいるように見せかけた。あれでもし、地主様
のお客の一人が（そう、ほかならぬ大執事様だった）アンドリーがフィドル

ぎりを挽く」。

❾ so that: なので、だから。本シリーズでも頻出。第4巻 p. 110, ll. 6-8, 'My
mother has uncharacteristically spent nearly an hour on my hair that
morning, plaiting and replaiting so that now my scalp tingles.'（母はそ
の朝、私の髪を三つ編みにするのに母らしくもなく一時間近くかけて何度も何
度も編み直したので、私の頭皮はいまチクチクしている）など。

❿ driving into the tune: そのメロディを奏でることに全身全霊を傾けている感
じ。

⓫ heart and soul:「身も心も」と同様の決まり文句。

⓬ 'Tis a question if he wouldn't have got through all right if ...: if が2つ
出てくるが、一つ目は「〜かどうか」（whether）で、二つ目は「もし〜なら」。
したがって 'Tis a question if は「〜であるかどうかは疑問だ、微妙だ」。get
through ...（切り抜ける）は p.30, ll. 12-13 に 'But no sooner had we got
through it than ...'（ところが、終わりまで来たとたん……）と、it を伴った形
で既出。「もし〜していたら、彼が無事切り抜けられなかったか、微妙なところだ」

⓭ no other than ...: ほかならぬ〜、よりによって〜。none other than とも言う。
The man was none [no] other than his father.（その男性はほかでもない
彼の父親だった。『コンパスローズ英和辞典』）

noticed that he held the fiddle ❶upside down, ❷the nut under ❸his chin, and ❹ the tail-piece in his hand; and they began to crowd round him, thinking 'twas some new way of performing.

'This ❺revealed everything; the Squire's mother ❻had Andrey
5 turned out of the house as ❼a vile impostor, and ❽there was great interruption to the harmony of the proceedings, the Squire ❾declaring ❿he should have notice to leave his cottage ⓫that day fortnight. However, when we got to the servants' hall there sat Andrey, ⓬who had been let in at the back door by the orders of
10 the Squire's wife, ⓭after being turned out at the front by the orders of the Squire, and nothing more was heard about his leaving his cottage. But Andrey never performed ⓮in public as a musician after that night; and now he's ⓯dead and gone, poor man, as we all shall be!'
15

'I had quite forgotten the old choir, with their fiddles and ⓰bass-

❶ upside down: さかさまに
❷ the nut: バイオリンなどの「上駒」。ネックと糸巻きの境の部分。
❸ his chin: あごの先
❹ the tail-piece: nut と反対端の、弦とエンドピンとをつなぐ部分。しいて日本語にすれば「緒止め板」。
❺ reveal(ed): ～を明らかにする、暴く
❻ had Andrey turned out of the house: turn A out of B で「A を B から追い出す」。これに have A + 過去分詞（A を～させる）が組み合わさっている。
❼ a vile impostor: 邪悪な詐欺師
❽ there was great interruption to the harmony of the proceedings: 直訳すれば「進行の調和に大きな中断（interruption）が入った」。
❾ declaring <declare: ～と宣言する
❿ he should have notice ...: he は Andrey。直接話法に直せば、地主は 'He

をさかさに持って、上駒をあごの下に当てて緒止板を手に握ってることに気づかなかったら、あるいは一晩、無事に切り抜けられたかもしれん。だが皆さんこれをご覧になって、こいつはきっと何か新しい演奏方法にちがいないと考え、アンドリーのまわりに群がってきた。

　これですべてバレてしまった。下劣なペテン師、と地主様の御母堂はアンドリーを罵って屋敷から叩き出し、彼奴は二週間後の今日立ちのいてもらうと地主様もおっしゃるものだから、和やかな雰囲気もすっかり途切れてしまった。ところが、私たちが召使い部屋に行くと、なんとアンドリーがそこに座っている。聞けば、地主様の御命令で表玄関から追い出されたものの、地主様の奥様の御命令で裏口から入れていただいたとのこと。立ちのき話もそれっきり立ち消えになった。だがアンドリーはその後二度と楽師として人前に出ることはなかった。哀れその彼ももうこの世にいない……」

「聖歌隊か、忘れてたなあ、フィドルもバスビオールもいたなあ」と、久し

---

shall have notice ...' というようなことを言った（shall は「～させるぞ」と、語り手の意思を表す）。notice はこのように誰かを追い出す・首にする等の通告にも、あるいは借り手が出ていく・辞める等の通告にも使う。

⓫ that day fortnight: その日から 2 週間で

⓬ who had been let in at the back door: let ... in で「～を中に入れる」。

⓭ after being turned out at the front: turn out は l. 5 に既出。

⓮ in public: 人前で

⓯ dead and gone: dead なら gone に決まっているわけだが、「すでに世を去った」という響きの決まり文句。第 5 巻 p. 262, ll. 12-13 に 'even when his mother was dead and gone and he himself was old and alone'（母親が死んでしまい彼自身も老いて独り身になってからもなお）の形で既出。

⓰ bass-viol(s): ヴィオラ・ダ・ガンバの英語名。現代の楽器で言えばチェロに相当。

viols,' said ❶the home-comer, ❷musingly. 'Are they still going on the same ❸as of old?'

'❹Bless the man!' said Christopher Twink, ❺the master-thatcher; '❻why, they've been done away with these twenty year.
5 A young ❼teetotaller plays the organ in church now, and plays it very well; though 'tis not quite such good music as in old times, because the organ ❽is one of them that go with a winch, and the young teetotaller says ❾he can't always throw the proper feeling into the tune without ❿wellnigh working his arms off.'

10   'Why did they make the change, then?'

'Well, partly because of fashion, partly because the old musicians ⓫got into a sort of scrape. A terrible scrape 'twas too — wasn't it, John? I shall never forget it — never! They ⓬lost their

---

❶ the home-comer: 11 歳でこの地を離れ、35 年ぶりに戻ってきた Mr Lackland なる人物。
❷ musingly: 物思いにふけるように
❸ as of old: 昔のように
❹ Bless the man!: 文字どおりには「この男に神の祝福あれ！」(God bless the man!) だが、「いいや、とんでもない！」という響き。
❺ the master-thatcher: 屋根葺き屋の親方
❻ why, they've been done away with these twenty year: 第 2 巻 p. 46, l. 11 の '"Why, sure," said Mrs. Jelinek'(「そうよ、そうよねえ」とミセス・ジェリネクが言った）で述べたように、why は驚き・承認・抗議・戸惑い等、さまざまな感情を伝える。ここでは軽い驚き（そうか、長年離れていた人はそんなことも知らないわけだ！）。they've been done away with: do away with … で「〜を廃止する」。year の複数が years になっていないが、これはハーディの小説では（つまりヴィクトリア朝イングランドの庶民の会話を再現した小説では）よく見かける。このあと p. 40, l. 11 に出てくる 'nine couple of dancers' なども同様。

ぶりにこの地に帰ってきた男がなつかしそうに言った。「いまも変わらずに
やってるのかい？」

「いやいや、廃止されてもう 20 年になるよ！」と、屋根葺き職人の親方ク
リストファー・トウィンクが言った。「いまじゃ酒一滴飲まん若い奴が教会
でオルガンを弾いていて、実にうまいものさ。でもまあ昔みたいにいい音楽っ
てわけには行かない。何せこのオルガンってのがウインチで回すやつでな、
メロディに思いを込めようにも腕がもげちまいそうだ、と酒一滴飲まん若い
奴は言ってる」

「じゃあなんで楽隊をやめたんだ？」

「ま、ひとつには流行り廃りってこともあるが、もうひとつ、楽隊連中が騒
動を起こしてね。いやあ、大した騒動だったよな、ジョン？　あれは忘れら
れんね──絶対忘れられん！　あいつらはね、教会の人間としての面目をな

❼ (a) teetotaller: 絶対禁酒主義者。total（完全な）の意味を強調すべく頭文字
のＴ（tee）を前につけて出来た語とされる。

❽ is one of them that go with a winch: 現代の標準的な英語でいえば is one
of those (organs) which work with a winch か。a winch: ウインチ、クラ
ンク

❾ he can't always throw the proper feeling into the tune without …:
throw は感情などを「盛り込む」。ここは can't, without と否定語が二つあっ
てややこしいが、直訳は（何しろウインチを回す速さで演奏のテンポが決まる
ので）「ほとんど腕がほぼもげてしまうことなしに、しかるべき感情をメロディ
に盛り込むことはかならずしもできない」。

❿ wellnigh: almost

⓫ got into a sort of scrape: get into … はよくない状態に「なる、巻き込まれ
る」。scrape は「窮地」。

⓬ lost their character: この character は「評判、名声」。

character as ❶officers of the church as complete as if they'd never had any character at all.'

'That was very bad for them.'

'Yes.' The master-thatcher ❷attentively regarded past times as if
5 they lay ❸about a mile off, and went on: —

❹*Absent-Mindedness in a Parish Choir*

'It happened on Sunday after Christmas — the last Sunday
10 ever they played in Longpuddle church ❺gallery, ❻as it turned out, though they didn't know it then. As you may know, sir, the players formed a very good band — almost as good as ❼the Mellstock parish players that were led by the Dewys; and ❽that's saying a great deal. There was Nicholas Puddingcome, the leader,
15 with the first fiddle; there was Timothy Thomas, the bass-viol man; John Biles, ❾the tenor fiddler, ❿Dan'l Hornhead, with the

---

❶ officer(s) of the church: 教会に正式（official）に属している人間、という感じ。

❷ attentively: 心を集中して

❸ about a mile off: 一マイルほど離れたところに

❹ *Absent-Mindedness*: うわの空の有様

❺ gallery: 回廊

❻ as it turned out: 結果的にはそうなったのだが

❼ the Mellstock parish players that were led by the Dewys: Mellstock は ハーディが自分の生まれた村 Stinsford に基づいて作った架空の村。初期の長 篇 *Under the Greenwood Tree*（1872）では、Dewy 家の三代にわたる男 たちが聖歌隊の中心となっている。

❽ that's saying a great deal: 「それは多くを語っている」とは、メルストック の聖歌隊に迫るというのは大したことなのだ、という含み。

くしたのさ——はじめから面目のかけらもなかったみたいに、きれいさっぱり！」

「そりゃあいけないねえ」

「そうとも」。屋根葺きの親方は、あたかも過去の日々が一マイルばかり離れたあたりに広がっているかのようにじいっと遠くに目をやり、話を続けた——

聖歌隊の粗忽

「クリスマスのあとの日曜のことだった。これがロングパドルの教会の回廊で奴らが演奏した最後の日曜になったわけだが、そのときはそんなことわかりゃしない。あんたもご存じだろうが、連中は実にいい楽隊だった。ジューイ親子率いるメルストック教区の楽隊にだってひけをとらない。大したもんだ。リーダーは第一フィドルのニコラス・パディンカム。バスビオールはティモシー・トマス。テナーフィドルはジョン・バイルズ。セルパンがダヌル・

❾ the tenor fiddler: tenor fiddle はヴィオラに相当。
❿ Dan'l: Daniel

❶ serpent; Robert Dowdle, with the ❷ clarionet; and Mr Nicks, with the oboe — all ❸ sound and powerful musicians, and ❹ strong-winded men — ❺ they that blowed. For that reason they were very much ❻ in demand Christmas week for little ❼ reels and dancing
5 parties: for they could ❽ turn a jig or a hornpipe out of hand as well as ever they could turn out ❾ a psalm, and ❿ perhaps better, not to speak irreverent. In short, one half-hour they could be playing a Christmas carol in the Squire's hall to the ladies and gentlemen, and drinking ⓫ tay and coffee with 'em as ⓬ modest as saints; and
10 the next, at ⓭ The Tinker's Arms, ⓮ blazing away like wild horses with ⓯ the "Dashing White Sergeant" to nine couple of dancers and more, and swallowing ⓰ rum-and-cider hot as ⓱ flame.

'Well, this Christmas they'd been out to one ⓲ rattling randy

❶ serpent: セルパン。「16-18 世紀のヘビ状に湾曲した低音管楽器」(『研究社 新英和中辞典』)。チューバに近い。
❷ clarionet: clarinet
❸ sound: (心身が) 健全な
❹ strong-winded: 逆に short-winded であれば「すぐ息が切れる」。
❺ they that blowed: those who blew. 管楽器担当の連中、ということ。
❻ in demand: 需要がある
❼ reel(s): リール。スコットランドで生まれた軽快な舞踏。次の dancing parties とともに、教会の厳かな音楽とは対照的なものとして挙がっている。
❽ turn a jig or a hornpipe out of hand: turn はすぐあとでも turn out a psalm という形で出てきていて、曲を「ひねり出す」という感じ。jig も hornpipe も教会に睨まれそうな舞曲。out of hand: 即座に
❾ a psalm: 賛美歌
❿ perhaps better, not to speak irreverent: 前行で賛美歌と同じくらいダンス音楽も上手い、と言ったわけだが、ここで perhaps better と来て「いや、ひょっとしたらダンス音楽の方が上かも」——と言うと教会音楽を貶めることになるので、not to speak irreverent で「いや、不敬な (irreverent) ことを言う

40

ホーンヘッド、クラリネットがロバート・ダウドル。そしてオーボエがミスター・ニックス。みんながっちりたくましく、管楽器吹きは肺活量たっぷりだ。おかげでクリスマスの週には、ちょっとしたリールやらダンスパーティやらに引っぱりだこだった。何しろ讃美歌もお手のものだが、ジグやホーンパイプも即座に弾いてのけて、こういっちゃ何だが讃美歌よりもっといいくらいだった。地主様のお屋敷の広間で紳士淑女を前にクリスマスカロルを30分演奏して、聖者みたいに大人しく紅茶やコーヒーを御相伴したかと思えば、次の30分には鋳掛け屋亭で九組だかそこらの踊り手を前に、荒馬みたいに激しく「颯爽たる白き軍曹」を弾きまくり吹きまくり、炎みたいに熱いラムのリンゴ酒割りをガブ呑みしてるってわけだ。

　で、そのクリスマス、連中は毎晩毎晩どんちゃん騒ぎに呼び出されて、ほ

わけじゃないんだが」。

⑪ tay: tea

⑫ modest: 謙虚な、慎み深い

⑬ The Tinker's Arms: いかにも教会とは対照的な、大衆的な場という響きの名。現実にも Arms という語はきわめて多くのパブの名前に入っている。「紋章」（a coat of arms）の意。tinker は「（旅回りの）鋳掛け屋、よろず修繕屋」。

⑭ blazing away: blaze は元来「燃え立つ」の意なので、いかにもガンガン演奏している感じ。

⑮ the "Dashing White Sergeant": 同名のダンスも出来ているくらいポピュラーな曲。Dashing は「颯爽とした」、Sergeant は「軍曹」。

⑯ rum-and-cider: ラム酒とリンゴ酒のカクテル。現代アメリカで cider と言えばアルコールを含まないリンゴ果汁だが、イギリスの伝統的な飲み物としての cider は酒で、アルコール度はビールと同程度。

⑰ flame: 炎

⑱ rattling randy: 威勢のいいどんちゃん騒ぎ

after another every night, and had got ❶next to no sleep at all. Then came the Sunday after Christmas, their fatal day. 'Twas so ❷mortal cold that year that they could hardly sit in the gallery; for though ❸the congregation down in the body of the church had ❹a stove to
5　keep off ❺the frost, the players in the gallery had nothing at all. So Nicholas said at ❻morning service, when ❼'twas freezing an inch an hour, "❽Please the Lord I won't stand this ❾numbing weather no longer: this afternoon we'll have something in our ❿insides to make us warm, ⓫if it cost a king's ransom."

10　　'So he brought ⓬a gallon of hot brandy and beer, ⓭ready mixed, to church with him in the afternoon, and by keeping the jar ⓮well wrapped up in Timothy Thomas's bass-viol bag it kept drinkably warm till they wanted it, which was just a ⓯thimbleful in ⓰the Absolution, and another after the Creed, and the remainder at the
15　beginning o' the sermon. When they'd had the last ⓱pull they felt quite comfortable and warm, and as the sermon went on — most

---

❶ next to ...:（否定語とともに）ほとんど〜。*I bought it for next to nothing.*（ただ同然の値段で買った。『研究社 新英和大辞典』）
❷ mortal: ものすごく、とても（標準的には mortally）
❸ the congregation down in the body of the church: 下の教会主要部（the body）にいる会衆
❹ a stove: 現代アメリカでは主に料理用の「レンジ」の意だが、元来は日本語の「ストーブ」と同じく暖房器具であることの方が主。
❺ the frost:（霜が降りるほどの）寒さ
❻ morning service: この service は「礼拝」。
❼ 'twas freezing an inch an hour: freeze は「霜がつもる」。
❽ Please the Lord: これは信心深さの表明ではない。鼻息も荒く、息巻いている感じ。

とんど一睡もしていなかった。そうしてクリスマスのあとの日曜日、あの破滅の日が来たんだ。その年はとにかくおそろしく寒くて、とてもじゃないが回廊なんかでじっとしちゃおれん。下の礼拝席に座った連中はストーブがあって寒さをしのげるけれど、回廊の楽隊には何もないんだ。で、一時間に一インチ霜がつもるかっていう朝の礼拝でニコラスが言うに、『こんなひでぇ天気、もう我慢できねぇ。昼過ぎには、王様の身代金払っても腹に何かあったかいのを入れるぞ』。

　というわけでニコラスは午後の回、熱いブランデーとビールを混ぜたやつを一ガロン持って教会に現われ、飲みたくなるときまで冷めないようティモシー・トマスのバスビオールのケースにしっかりくるんで入れておいた。ま、そんなにたくさん飲むわけじゃない――〈罪の赦し〉のときに一口、〈クレド〉で一口、残りを説教のはじまりに。だがそうやって飲み終えるとすっかり暖まって気持ちもくつろいだものだから、説教が続くうちに――しかもあいに

❾ numbing: 麻痺させる（ような）

❿ insides: 腹（の中）

⓫ if it cost a king's ransom: cost は標準的な現代英語では costs。a king's ransom（王の身代金）は「大金」を意味する成句。

⓬ a gallon: ガロン（イギリスでは4クォート、約4.5リットル）

⓭ ready mixed: あらかじめ混ぜた

⓮ well wrapped up: しっかりくるんだ状態に

⓯ thimbleful:（酒などの）ごく少量。thimble は日本の「指ぬき」に近いが、ただし先は閉じているので指がぬけはしない。

⓰ the Absolution ... the Creed ... the sermon:「罪の赦し」「クレド（使徒信条）」そして説教、と礼拝の手順がなぞられている。

⓱ pull:（酒などの）ひと飲み

unfortunately for 'em it was a long one that afternoon — they fell asleep, ❶every man jack of 'em; and there they slept on as ❷sound as rocks.

''Twas a very dark afternoon, and by the end of the sermon all
5 you could see of the inside of the church were the ❸ pa'son's two candles ❹ alongside of him in ❺ the pulpit, and his ❻ spaking face behind 'em. The sermon being ended at last, the pa'son ❼gie'd out the Evening Hymn. But no quire ❽ set about sounding up the tune, and the people began to turn their heads to learn the reason
10 why, and then Levi Limpet, a boy who sat in the gallery, ❾nudged Timothy and Nicholas, and said, "Begin! begin!"

'"Hey? what?" says Nicholas, ❿ starting up; and the church being so dark and his head so ⓫muddled ⓬he thought he was at the party they had played at all the night before, and ⓭away he went,
15 bow and fiddle, at "⓮The Devil among the Tailors", the favourite

---

❶ every man jack of 'em: 「だれも彼も皆」の意の成句。of 'em (of them) はなくても同じ。

❷ sound: (眠りが) 深く

❸ pa'son's <parson: 牧師。p. 32 の註❺で述べた the parish (教区) を統括する役割。

❹ alongside of ...: ～と並んで

❺ the pulpit: 説教壇

❻ spaking: speaking

❼ gie'd out: gave out <give out:「(礼拝式で会衆のために)〈賛美歌〉の歌詞を読み上げる」(『研究社 新英和大辞典』)

❽ set about ...: ～に取りかかった

❾ nudge(d): 注意を引くために、人をひじなどで突く

❿ starting up: パッと起き上がって。このstartは「始める」ではなく「ハッとする」。第5巻 p. 84, ll. 12-14 の 'I started up, looked from that door, and saw

くその日の説教はいつになく長かった——楽隊は一人残らず眠ってしまった。岩みたいに、ぐっすりと。

　その午後はえらく暗くて、説教が終わるころにはもう、教会の中で見えるのは、説教壇に立つ牧師様のかたわらに置いた二本の蠟燭と、その向こうにある牧師様の顔だけだった。で、説教がようやっと済んで、牧師様が晩の讃美歌の歌詞を唱え出した。ところが楽隊はいっこうにメロディを奏でない。どうしたのかと思ってみんなが首を回した。で、楽隊と一緒に回廊に座ってたリーヴァイ・リンペットって小僧がティモシーとニコラスをつついて、『音楽！　音楽！』とささやいた。

　『え、何？』とニコラスががばっと身を起こしながら言った。だがとにかく教会は暗いし頭はぼうっとしてるしで、てっきりここは昨夜一晩中演奏したパーティの会場だと思っちまって、フィドルを抱え弓を手に『悪魔と仕立て

this Some one else standing by the red light near the tunnel'（ハッと飛び上がって扉から見てみると、その誰か別の人間がトンネル近くの警告灯の脇に立っていて）など、何度か既出。

❶ muddled: 混乱した

❷ he thought he was at the party they had played at all the night before: 一見 at がひとつ多いように思えるが、'he was at the party' と 'they had played at the party all the night before' が組み合わさっているので、これで間違いではない。

❸ away he went, bow and fiddle: 弓とフィドルを手に取り、颯爽と弾きはじめた

❹ The Devil among the Tailors: 有名な曲の名でもあり、その曲に合わせたダンスの名でもあり、かつパブによく置かれていた、9本のピンと1個の木の球から成るゲームの名でもある。

jig of our neighbourhood at that time. The rest of the band, being in the same state of mind and ❶nothing doubting, followed their leader with all their strength, ❷according to custom. They ❸poured out ❹that there tune till ❺the lower bass notes of "The Devil among
5 the Tailors" made ❻the cobwebs in the roof shiver like ghosts; then Nicholas, seeing nobody moved, shouted out ❼as he scraped (❽in his usual commanding way at dances when the folk didn't know the ❾figures), " ❿Top couples cross hands! And when I make the fiddle ⓫squeak at the end, every man kiss his ⓬pardner under the
10 ⓭mistletoe!"

'The boy Levi was so frightened that he ⓮bolted down the gallery stairs and ⓯out homeward like ⓰lightning. The pa'son's hair ⓱fairly ⓲stood on end when he heard the evil tune ⓳raging through the church, and thinking the quire had gone crazy he held
15 up his hand and said: "Stop, stop, stop! Stop, stop! What's this?"

---

❶ nothing doubting: 何も疑わず（doubting nothing）

❷ according to custom: 習慣どおり

❸ poured out ...: ～をあふれ出させた

❹ that there tune: there が余計なように思えるが、that there ... で that ... とほとんど変わらず「その、そこの～」の意。*that there man*（あの人＝that man there.『リーダーズ英和辞典』)

❺ the lower bass notes: 低い音。note は p. 28, ll. 9-10 では楽譜に記された音符一つひとつを意味したが（'moving the candles to the best points for throwing light upon the notes'〔音譜にしっかり光が当たるよう蠟燭を動かし〕）、ここでは演奏されたメロディー音一音のこと。

❻ the cobwebs: 蜘蛛の巣

❼ as he scraped: ギイギイ弾きながら。scrape は何かをこすったり、軋らせたりすることを意味するが、ここではさらに広がって「弾きまくる」。

❽ in his usual commanding way: いつもの、有無を言わせぬ口調で

屋たち』をガンガン弾きはじめた——当時ここいらへんで一番人気のあった
ジグだ。ほかの連中も頭は同じありさまだったから、つゆとも疑わず例によっ
て目一杯リーダーのあとを追った。『悪魔と仕立て屋たち』を力の限り弾き
まくり吹きまくり、その低音の響きで天井にかかった蜘蛛の糸が幽霊みたい
に震えたほどだった。そのうちにニコラスが、誰も動かないのを見て、フィ
ドルをかき鳴らしながら、ダンスでみんなが踊り方を知らないときにいつも
やるように叫んだ——『先頭のカップル、手を交叉させて！　最後に俺の
フィドルがキイッと鳴ったら、男はみんなヤドリギの下でパートナーにキス
する！』

　小僧のリーヴァイはすっかり怯えてしまい、回廊から階段を駆け降りて、
稲妻みたいにそのまま家まで飛んで帰った。邪悪なメロディが教会中に響き
わたるのを聞いて牧師様も髪を逆立たせ、楽隊が錯乱したのだと思って片手
を上げて『やめろ、やめろ、やめろ！　やめろ、やめろ！　何の真似だ？』

❾ figures: ダンスのひと連なりの動きのこと。

❿ Top couples: 各列一番前のカップル

⓫ squeak: キーキー鳴る。l. 6 の scrape よりさらに「キーキー度」が高い。

⓬ pardner: partner. 実はイギリスの文章よりアメリカの西部劇でよくお目にか
　かる。

⓭ mistletoe: やどりぎ。クリスマスの装飾に用いられ、その下では女性にキスを
　してもよいとされる。

⓮ bolted down the gallery stairs: 回廊の階段を飛ぶように降りた

⓯ out homeward: ここも bolted からつなげて読む。

⓰ lightning: 稲妻

⓱ fairly: かなり、相当に

⓲ stood on end: 直立した

⓳ raging through the church: rage は「猛威をふるう、荒れ狂う」。

Old Andrey's Experience as a Musician

But they didn't ❶hear'n for the noise of their own playing, and the more he called the louder they played.

'Then the folks came out of their ❷pews, ❸wondering down to the ground, and saying: "❹What do they mean by such ❺wickedness! ❻We shall be consumed like Sodom and Gomorrah!"

'And the Squire, too, came out of his pew ❼lined wi' green baize, where lots of lords and ladies visiting at the house ❽were worshipping along with him, and went and stood in front of the gallery, and shook his fist in the musicians' faces, saying, "What! In ❾this reverent edifice! What!"

'And at last they heard'n through their playing, and stopped.

'"❿Never such an ⓫insulting, disgraceful thing — never!" says the Squire, who couldn't ⓬rule his passion.

'"Never!" says the pa'son, who had come down and stood beside him.

'"⓭Not if the Angels of Heaven," says the Squire (⓮he was

---

❶ hear'n: hear him. このあとl. 11 に出てくるheard'n も同じくheard him。
❷ pew(s): (教会の) 座席
❸ wondering down to the ground: wonder は「驚く」、down to the ground は「徹底的に」。
❹ What do they mean: どういうつもりだ
❺ wickedness: 邪悪さ
❻ We shall be consumed like Sodom and Gomorrah!: 旧約聖書にあるとおり、ソドムもゴモラも人間の邪悪な行ないゆえに神によって滅ぼされた (*Genesis*, 18, 19)。consume(d): 〜を焼きつくす
❼ lined wi' green baize: line はこういう生地関連の話では「〜に裏地をつける」の意になることも多いが、ここは教会の会衆席について言っているので、「〜に沿って広げる、並べる」の意。baize は通例緑色の粗いラシャ。
❽ were worshipping <worship: 礼拝する

48

と叫んだ。だけど自分たちの演奏の音にかき消されてその声は奴らの耳に届かず、牧師様が叫べば叫ぶほど演奏もますますやかましくなった。

やがて礼拝者たちも席を立って外に出て、すっかり驚き呆れて口々に『ぜんたいどういう了簡だ、あんな邪な真似して！　私らみんな、ソドムとゴモラみたいに焼き尽くされちまうぞ！』などと言っていた。

そうして地主様も、緑のベースを敷いた、屋敷に訪ねてきている領主様やその奥様たちと一緒に礼拝していた席から出てきて、回廊の前に立ち、楽師たちの顔に向けてげんこつを振り回して『何なんだ！　この神聖な建物で！何なんだ！』とわめいた。

そうしてやっと奴らにも音楽に混じって声が届き、みんな演奏をやめた。『こんな無礼な、浅ましい話は聞いたことがないぞ！』と、憤懣やるかたない地主様は言った。

『聞いたことがない！』と、説教壇から降りてきて地主様と並んで立った牧師様も言った。

『天から天使たちが降りてきたって』と地主様は言った。この方もそれなり

❾ this reverent edifice: この神聖な建物。edifice は大きくて厳かな建物について言う。

❿ Never such an ...: There has never been such an ...

⓫ insulting, disgraceful: 無礼な、嘆かわしい

⓬ rule his passion: 癇癪を抑える

⓭ Not if the Angels of Heaven ...: ここまで読んだだけで、「たとえ天の天使たちが〜したとしても、絶対に〜ない」という展開になることは予想がつく（つまり、文頭にある Not は文の後半の内容を否定するだろうという見当がつく）。

⓮ he was a wickedish man, the Squire was: the Squire was a wickedish man とそんなに変わらないが、この方が実際に語っている感じ、思いつくままに言葉をくり出している感じが増す。wickedish は「wicked っぽい」で、まあ邪は邪だが大したことはない、という含み。

49

a wickedish man, the Squire was, though now ❶for once he happened to be on the Lord's side) — "not if the Angels of Heaven come down," he says, "❷shall one of you villainous players ever ❸sound a note in this church again; for the insult to me, and my
5 family, and my visitors, and the pa'son, and ❹God Almighty, that you've ❺a-perpetrated this afternoon!"

'Then the unfortunate church band ❻came to their senses, and remembered where they were; and 'twas ❼a sight to see Nicholas Puddingcome and Timothy Thomas and John Biles ❽creep down
10 the gallery stairs with their fiddles under their arms, and poor Dan'l Hornhead with his serpent, and Robert Dowdle with his clarionet, all looking as little as ❾ninepins; and ❿out they went. The pa'son might have ⓫forgi'ed 'em when he learned the truth o't, but the Squire would not. That very week he ⓬sent for ⓭a barrel-organ

---

❶ for once: 今度ばかりは。*Just for once, let me treat you.*（一度くらいは、おごらせてよ。『コンパスローズ英和辞典』）
❷ shall one of you villainous players ...: ここが p. 48, l. 16 とこのページ l. 2 の 'Not if the Angels of Heaven ...' の Not によって否定される部分。つまりおそらく「お前ら villainous players の誰一人として……ない」という方向に落ち着くことがここまで読めば見当がつく。villainous: 悪人の
❸ sound a note: 音を響かせる
❹ God Almighty: 全能の神
❺ a-perpetrated <perpetrate:（悪事・犯罪など）を犯す。語頭の a- はボブ・ディランの曲のタイトルに 'The Times They Are A-Changin'（「時代は変わる」）などのように、歌でよくお目にかかるが、語調を整えるのが主な役割で、意味は特にない。
❻ came to their senses: 正気に戻った
❼ a sight: 見物（みもの）
❽ creep: 這うように進む

に邪なところはあったんだが、いまばかりは神の側に立っていた。『天から天使たちが降りてきたって、お前ら悪党楽師の誰一人、二度とこの教会で一音たりとも出させるもんか。お前らは今日ここで、私と、私の家族と、私のお客様方と、牧師様と、全能なる神様を侮辱したんだぞ！』

　まもなく、哀れ教会楽隊の面々も正気に返り、自分たちがどこにいるかを思い出した。そりゃあ見物だったね──ニコラス・パディンカム、ティモシー・トマス、ジョン・バイルズ、みんな弦楽器を小脇に抱えてこそこそ階段を降りていき、セルパンを持ったダヌル・ホーンヘッド、クラリネットを持ったロバート・ダウドル、みんなナインピンズのピンみたいに縮こまってこそこそと教会から出ていった。あとで真相を知って、まあ牧師様だけならお許しになったかもしれんが、地主様はそうは行かなかった。もうその週のうちに、

❾ ninepins: ナインピンズ、九柱戯。今のボウリングの原型。
❿ out they went: they went out よりリアルな語り口。
⓫ forgi'ed: forgiven
⓬ sent for ...: 〜を取り寄せた。この send は、p. 30, ll. 14-15 で彼の母が口にした 'I've sent up into the attic, where we have some old musical instruments'（屋根裏に古い楽器がいろいろあるんで見に行かせたらね）と同じ発想。
⓭ a barrel-organ: 18〜19 世紀にイギリスの教会で使用された手回しオルガン。教会音楽においては一種過渡的な存在であり、それまでの楽隊に取って代わり、のち鍵盤のついたオルガンに取って代わられた。あらかじめ金属のロールに賛美歌が記録されていて、誰かがウインチを安定したリズムで回さねばならず、良き音楽を生み出すのはなかなか大変だったようである（Elna Sherman, 'Music in Thomas Hardy's Life and Work', 1940 による）。

that would play ❶two-and-twenty new psalm-tunes, ❷so exact and particular that, ❸however sinful inclined you was, you could play nothing but psalm-tunes ❹whatsomever. He had a really ❺respectable man to turn the winch, as I said, and the old players
5 played no more.'

❶ two-and-twenty: 少し古い英語では語調のためにこうして一の桁と十の桁を ひっくり返すことがよくある。

❷ so exact and particular: きわめて正確にして几帳面

❸ however sinful inclined: however sinfully inclined（どれだけ罪深い方に傾 いていても）

❹ whatsomever: whatsoever. 否定語に添えられて強調を強める。whatsoever であれば第 2 巻 p. 150, ll. 4-5, 'a jury of his peers had acquitted George Wilson Dunn of any wrongdoing whatsoever'（自分と同様の地位の人々 から成る陪審によって、ジョージ・ウィルソン・ダンはいかなる罪も犯してい ない、と無罪放免されたのである）の形で既出。

❺ respectable: 第 5 巻 p. 188, ll. 2-3 の 'These respectable bourgeois'（こ のまっとうなブルジョワ夫婦）で触れたように、「まともな」「ちゃんとした」

新しい讃美歌 22 曲を自動演奏するバレルオルガンを注文なさった。この演奏というのが実にきっちり緻密にして正確で、どんなに罪深い人間でも讃美歌以外何も弾けやしない。で、さっき言ったようにウィンチを回す係にとことん堅物の人間を雇い、昔からの楽師たちはもう演奏しなくなったんだ」

ということ。

ちなみに

　トマス・ハーディは生涯音楽を愛した。ヴェルディやワーグナーも
愛聴したが、幼いころから慣れ親しんだ音楽への愛着も失わなかった。
この小説で描かれているような、教会で歌われる賛美歌、もっとくだ
けた場で演奏されるダンス音楽、その両方をハーディはつねに楽しみ、
作品にもしばしば登場させた。祖父も父も音楽に長けていて、ひとこ
ろは楽隊を組んで、まさに教会では教会音楽を奏で、ダンスの場では
踊るための音楽を提供していたという。

The Man with the Heart in the Highlands
William Saroyan

心が高地にある男

ウィリアム・サローヤン

難易度 1
★ ☆ ☆

ウィリアム・サローヤン
(William Saroyan, 1908-1981)

アメリカの小説家・劇作家。カリフォルニア州フレズノに生まれ、その地を主たる舞台に、アルメニア系アメリカ人共同体の生活をシンプルな英語で温かく描いた。

"The Man with the Heart in the Highlands" はサローヤンの初期の代表的な短篇で、1936 年に刊行された短篇集 *Three Times Three* に収録された。

I n 1914, when I was ❶not quite six years old, an old man ❷came
down San Benito Avenue playing a solo on ❸ a bugle and
stopped in front of our house. I ran out of the yard and stood at ❹the
curb waiting for him to start playing again, but he wouldn't do it. I
5 said, ❺I sure would like to hear you play another tune, and he said,
Young man, could you get a glass of water for an old man whose
heart is not here, but in the highlands?

What highlands? I said.

❻The Scotch highlands, said the old man. Could you?

10 What's your heart doing in the Scotch highlands? I said.

My heart is ❼grieving there, said the old man. Could you bring
me a glass of cool water?

Where's your mother? I said.

My mother's in Tulsa, Oklahoma, said the old man, but her
15 heart isn't.

Where *is* her heart? I said.

---

❶ not quite ...: 完全に〜ではない
❷ came down San Benito Avenue: down はすでにこのシリーズで何度か出
てきたとおり、坂を下るということとは限らず、中心から離れるという響き。
たとえば第 1 巻 p. 36, ll. 11-12 には "His mother laughed, and following
him to the door, watched him down the road"（母親があははと笑い、玄
関まで息子を送り出して、道路を歩いていくのを見送った）とあった。San
Benito Avenue はフレズノにある通り（正式には San Benito Street）で、
サローヤンはこの通りの 2226 番地で少年時代の決定的な数年間を過ごした。
❸ a bugle: （軍隊の）らっぱ
❹ the curb: 車道と歩道の境に並んだ敷石。日本語の「道端」という感覚に近い。
❺ I sure would like to ...: こうした口語的な喋り方では、surely より sure の方
が圧倒的に自然。

　一九一四年、僕がまだ六歳にもなっていないとき、年とった男の人が一人で軍隊ラッパを吹きながらサンベニート・アベニューをやって来て、僕たちの家の前で止まった。僕は庭から駆け出して、歩道の縁に立ち、男の人がまた吹き出すのを待ったが、いっこうにはじめそうもなかった。ぜひもう一曲聞きたいんですけど、と僕が頼むと男の人は言った。坊や、水を一杯持ってきてくれるかね、心がここになく、高地にある男に？

　コウチって、どこの？　と僕は言った。

　スコットランドの高地だよ、と年とった男の人は言った。持ってきてくれるかい？

　おじさんの心、スコットランドの高地で何してるの？

　私の心はそこで悲しみに暮れているのさ。冷たい水、持ってきてくれるかい？

　おじさんのお母さんはどこにいるの？

　私の母親はオクラホマのタルサにいる。でも母の心はタルサにはない。

　お母さんの心、どこにあるの？

❻ The Scotch highlands:「高地」といえば誰でもまずスコットランドを思い浮かべるが、その連想を広めたのは、スコットランドの国民的詩人 Robert Burns (1759-1796) の有名な詩 "My Heart's in the Highlands" (1789)。書き出しは "My heart's in the Highlands, my heart is not here, / My heart's in the Highlands, a-chasing the deer"（わが心は高地にあり　ここにはあらず／わが心は高地にありて　鹿を追う）。この詩に曲もついている。

❼ grieving <grieve:（深く）悲しむ

In the Scotch highlands, said the old man. I am very thirsty, young man.

❶ How come the members of your family are always leaving their hearts in the highlands? I said.

5   That's the way we are, said the old man. ❷ Here today and gone tomorrow.

Here today and gone tomorrow? I said. ❸ How do you figure?

Alive one minute and dead the next, said the old man.

Where is your mother's *mother?* I said.

10   ❹ She's up in Vermont, in a little town called White River, but her heart isn't, said the old man.

Is her poor old ❺ withered heart in the highlands too? I said.

❻ Right smack in the highlands, said the old man. ❼ Son, I'm dying of thirst.

15   ❽ My father came out on the porch and ❾ roared like a lion that has just awakened from evil dreams.

---

❶ How come the members of your family are always leaving their hearts in the highlands?: How come …? は Why …? と意味は同じだが Why …? と違い疑問文の語順をとらない。第 4 巻 p. 64, l. 9 に "But—how come we never saw you before?"（だけど――どうしていままで誰もあんたのこと見かけなかったのよ？）の形で既出。My heart is in … という言い方に加えて、leave one's heart in … という言い方も、1953 年に書かれた、「想い出のサンフランシスコ」の邦題で知られるポピュラーソング "I Left My Heart in San Francisco"（サンフランシスコに心を置いてきた）で広まった。

❷ Here today and gone tomorrow: 人がすぐにいなくなってしまうこと、世の移ろいやすいことなどを言う決まり文句。

❸ How do you figure?: どうしてそう思うのか、どうしてそうだとわかるのか

❹ She's up in Vermont: up は「北の方」という含み。

スコットランド高地にあるんだよ。ねえ坊や、私はものすごく喉が渇いてるんだ。

どうしておじさんの家族はみんな、高地に心を置いてきてしまうの？

そういうふうに生まれついてるんだよ。今日いたかと思えば、明日はもういない。

今日いたかと思えば、明日はもういない？　どういうこと？

いま生きてると思っても、次の瞬間にはもう死んでるってことさ。

おじさんのお母さんのお母さんはどこにいるの？

ヴァーモントのね、ホワイトリバーっていう小さな町にいるよ、でも心はそこにない。

くたびれた、しなびた心がやっぱり高地にあるわけ？

ばっちり高地にあるとも。なあ、私は喉が渇いて死にそうなんだよ。

僕の父さんが玄関に出てきて、邪悪な夢から覚めたばかりのライオンみたいに吠えた。

---

❺ withered: しぼんだ

❻ Right smack in the highlands: smack in the ... または smack in the middle of the ... といった形で「もろ〜に」「〜のど真ん中に」といった意味になる。Right は強調。

❼ Son: 大人が若者や子供に呼びかけるときによく使う。

❽ My father came out on the porch: porch は第 4 巻 p. 82, ll. 6-7 でも触れたように、「軒先」「玄関」と考えていい場合も多い（玄関の両横の空間も含み、もっと広いが）。"She looked out to see Arnold Friend pause and then take a step toward the porch, lurching."（顔を上げると、アーノルド・フレンドは動きを止め、それから一歩玄関ポーチの方へよたよたと踏み出した）

❾ roar(ed): 吠える

Johnny, he roared, ❶get the hell away from that poor old man.
Get him ❷a pitcher of water before he falls down and dies. ❸Where
in hell are your manners?

❹Can't a fellow try to find out something from a traveler ❺once
5 in a while? I said.

Get the old gentleman some water, said my father. ❻God damn
it, don't stand there ❼like a dummy. Get him a drink before he falls
down and dies.

You get him a drink, I said. ❽You ain't doing nothing.

10 Ain't doing nothing? said my father. ❾Why, Johnny, you know
God damn well I'm getting a new poem arranged in my mind.

❿How do you figure I know? I said. You're just standing there
on the porch with your sleeves rolled up. How do you figure I
know?

15 Well, ⓫you ought to know, said my father.

Good afternoon, said the old man to my father. Your son has

---

❶ get the hell away from ...: 〜からさっさと離れろ

❷ a pitcher: 水差し

❸ Where in hell are your manners?: in hell 抜きで、行儀の悪い子供を叱る標
   準的な言い方。

❹ Can't a fellow try to ...: Can't I try to ... と言うよりも一般論を述べている感
   じ。

❺ once in a while: 時には、たまには

❻ God damn it: 早くもこのページ 3 度目の swear words（汚い言葉）。

❼ like a dummy: 馬鹿みたいに

❽ You ain't doing nothing: 上品な言い方に直せば You are not doing anything.

❾ Why, Johnny, you know God damn well ...: why は p. 36, l. 4 の "why,

　ジョニー、いい加減にしなさい、と父さんは吠えた。その人がぶっ倒れて死んじまう前にピッチャーに水を入れてきてやりなさい。礼儀ってものがあるだろうが。

　少しくらい話を聞いたっていいじゃないか、せっかく旅の人が来たんだから、と僕は言った。

　この方に水持ってきてあげなさい、と僕の父さんは言った。ったく、いつまでもぽさっとつっ立ってるんじゃない。ぶっ倒れて死んじまう前に水持ってきてあげなさい。

　父さん持ってくればいいじゃないか、と僕は言った。どうせ何もしてないんだから。

　どうせ何もしてない？　おいおいジョニー、お前だって知ってるだろう、父さんがいま頭の中で詩を構想してるってこと。

　どうして僕にわかると思うのさ。父さんただ、腕まくりして玄関に立ってるだけじゃないか。僕にわかるわけないよ。

　いやそれは、わかるべきなんだよ、と父さんは言った。

　ご機嫌よう、と年とった男の人は僕の父さんに言った。息子さんから伺っ

they've been done away with these twenty year"（いやいや、廃止されてもう 20 年になるよ！）で触れたとおり、驚き・承認・抗議・戸惑い等、さまざまな感情を伝える。
❿ How do you figure I know?: p. 58, l. 7 の "How do you figure?" と同じ発想。
⓫ you ought to know: ought to ... は should ... とほぼ同義だが、should ... よりも「そうするのが当然だ」という響きがやや強い。

been telling me how clear and cool the climate is in these parts.

(❶Jesus Christ, I said, ❷I never did tell this old man anything about the climate. ❸Where's he getting that stuff from?)

Good afternoon, said my father. Won't you come in for a little
5 rest? ❹We should be honored to have you at our table for ❺a bit of lunch.

Sir, said the old man, I am starving. I shall ❻come right in.

Can you play ❼*Drink to Me Only with Thine Eyes?* I said to the old man. I sure would like to hear you play that song on the bugle.
10 That song is my favorite. I guess I like that song better than any other song in the world.

Son, said the old man, when you ❽get to be my age you'll know songs aren't important, bread is ❾the thing.

Anyway, I said, I sure would like to hear you play that song.
15 The old man went up on the porch and shook hands with my father.

---

❶ Jesus Christ, I said: 息子も負けずに swear words を活用している。I said とあるが、口に出したのではなく、心の中で言っただけ。

❷ I never did tell ...: I never told ... よりやや否定感が強いが、そんなに変わらない。

❸ Where's he getting that stuff from?: stuff はきわめて意味が広く、漠然と「もの」「こと」を指すことも多いが、ここは「下らないこと」「ナンセンス」のニュアンスが含まれている。*None of your stuff!*（へらず口をきくな、たわごとを言うな。『研究社 新英和大辞典』）

❹ We should be honored to ...: 〜できれば光栄に存じます

❺ a bit of ...: ちょっとした〜

❻ come right in: すぐ中に入る

❼ *Drink to Me Only with Thine Eyes*: 古いイギリスの歌で、19 〜 20 世紀

てたんですよ、このあたりは気候もよくて涼しいんだって。

（何言ってんだこの人、と僕は思った。僕、気候のことなんか一言も言って
ないぞ。どこからそんなもの引っぱり出してきたんだ？）

　ご機嫌よう、と僕の父さんは言った。よかったら上がって少し休んでいか
れませんか？　昼食をご一緒いただけたら光栄ですよ。

　ええ、もうお腹が空いて死にそうなんです、と年とった男の人は言った。
すぐ上がらせていただきますよ。

　ねえ、「瞳で乾杯しておくれ」吹ける？　と僕は男の人に言った。あの歌、
ぜひラッパで聞きたいなあ。一番好きな歌なんだよ。世界中のほかのどの歌
よりも好きだなあ。

　あのな坊や、と男の人は言った。君も私の歳になったらわかるさ、歌なん
て大事じゃないんだと。肝腎なのはパンさ。

　とにかくさ、あの歌ぜひ吹いてほしいんだけど。

　男の人は玄関先まで上がって僕の父さんと握手した。

My name is Jasper MacGregor, he said. I am an actor.

I am ❶mighty glad to ❷make your acquaintance, said my father. Johnny, get Mr. MacGregor a pitcher of water.

I went around to the well and poured some cool water into a
5 pitcher and took it to the old man. He drank the whole pitcherful ❸in one long swig. Then he looked around at the landscape and up at the sky and away up San Benito Avenue where the evening sun was beginning to go down.

❹I reckon I'm five thousand miles from home, he said. Do you
10 think we could eat a little bread and cheese to ❺keep my body and spirit together?

Johnny, said my father, run down to ❻the grocer's and get a loaf of French bread and ❼a pound of cheese.

Give me the money, I said.

15 Tell Mr. Kosak to ❽give us credit, said my father. ❾I ain't got a penny, Johnny.

---

❶ mighty: すごく。アメリカ口語。
❷ make your acquaintance: あなたと知り合いになる
❸ in one long swig: 一気にぐいぐい飲んで
❹ I reckon: reckon は the day of reckoning などといえば物々しく「最後の審判の日」の意になるが、このようなアメリカ口語の文脈では think とほぼ同じ。
❺ keep my body and spirit together: keep body and soul together（なんとか生きていく）という言い方のバリエーション。
❻ the grocer's: 食料雑貨店
❼ a pound of cheese: 1 ポンドは 453.6 グラムなので、0.5 キロと覚えておけばまあだいたい間に合う。
❽ give us credit: つけで売ってくれる
❾ I ain't got a penny: 俺は 1 セントも持っていない。ain't は p. 60, l. 9 に "You

ジャスパー・マグレガーと申します、と男の人は言った。役者をしており
ます。

お近づきになれて嬉しいですよ、と父さんは言った。ジョニー、ミスタ・
マグレガーにお水を持ってきてさし上げなさい。

僕は井戸に回っていって冷たい水をピッチャーに汲み、男の人のところに
持っていった。男の人はピッチャーの水をぐいぐい一気に飲み干した。それ
から周りの景色を見回し、空を見上げ、夕陽が沈みかけたサンベニート・ア
ベニューの先を見やった。

ここは故郷から五千マイル離れているなあ、と男の人は言った。みんなで
少しばかりパンとチーズとか食べられますかねえ、そうすりゃ私も、も少し
命をつなぎ止めておけるんですが。

ジョニー、と僕の父さんは言った。店に行ってフランスパン一本とチーズ
一ポンド買ってきなさい。

お金ちょうだいよ、と僕は言った。

つけにしてくれってミスタ・コーサックに言いなさい。父さんは一セント
も持ってないよ、ジョニー。

---

ain't doing nothing"（どうせ何もしてないんだから）の形で aren't の代わり
に出てきたが、ここでは haven't の代わり。卑俗に響くということではまった
く同じ。penny（単数）/ pence（複数）はアメリカの通貨単位ではないが、1
セント貨に限っては penny とも言う。

He won't give us credit, I said. Mr. Kosak **❶**is tired of giving us credit. He's **❷**sore at us. He says we don't work and never pay our **❸**bills. We **❹**owe him forty cents.

❺Go on down there and **❻**argue it out with him, said my father.
5 You know that's your job.

He won't **❼** listen to reason, I said. Mr. Kosak says he doesn't know anything about anything, all he wants is the forty cents.

Go on down there and make him give you a loaf of bread and a pound of cheese, said my father. You can do it, Johnny.

10 Go on down there, said the old man, and tell Mr. Kosak to give you a loaf of bread and a pound of cheese, son.

❽Go ahead, Johnny, said my father. **❾**You haven't yet failed to leave that store with **❿** provender, and you'll be back here in ten minutes with food **⓫**fit for a king.

15 **⓬**I don't know, I said. Mr. Kosak says we are trying to **⓭** give him the merry run around. He wants to know what kind of work

---

❶ is tired of ...: 〜にうんざりしている

❷ sore at ...: 〜に怒って

❸ bill(s): 請求書。pay the bills と言えば「生活費を稼ぐ」に近い成句。

❹ owe him forty cents: 彼に 40 セント借りている

❺ Go on down there: Go there とほぼ変わらないが、リズムがいかにも口語的になる。

❻ argue it out <argue ... out: 〜についてとことん話し合う。*You don't agree with me? All right, let's argue it out.*（きみはぼくの考えに賛成じゃないのか？ よし、徹底的に議論しようじゃないか。『動詞を使いこなすための英和活用辞典』)

❼ listen to reason: 理屈に耳を傾ける

❽ Go ahead: 許可を与えるときなどにも使うが（「どうぞご自由に」という感じ）、

66

つけてもらえないよ、と僕は言った。もうつけはうんざりだってミスタ・コーサックは言ってる。僕たちのこと、怒ってるんだ。働きもしないで、借りも返さないって。あの人に四十セント借りてるんだよ。

行って理を説いてやりなさい、と父さんは言った。それがお前の役目なんだから。

あの人、理なんか聞かないよ。私には難しいことは何もわからん、四十セントが欲しいだけだ、そう言うんだよ。

いいから行ってパン一本とチーズ一ポンドもらってきなさい。お前ならできるよ、ジョニー。

行ってきなさい、と年とった男の人も言った。行ってミスタ・コーサックに言うんだ、パン一本とチーズ一ポンドをくださいって。

さあジョニー、と僕の父さんは言った。お前いままで一度も、手ぶらであの店から帰ってきたことないじゃないか。今日だって十分もしたら、王さまにふさわしい食べ物抱えて戻ってくるさ。

どうかなあ、と僕は言った。お前らごまかすんじゃないってミスタ・コーサックに言われるんだよ。お前さんの父さんいったいどんな仕事してるん

ここでは「さあ、行きなさい」と促している。
❾ You haven't yet failed to ...: まだ一度も〜できなかったことはない
❿ provender: 食べ物
⓫ fit for a king: これで「立派な」「豪華な」の意の成句。fit は「ふさわしい」。
⓬ I don't know:「知らない」ではなく「うーん、どうかなあ」。
⓭ give him the merry run around: give ... the runaround（〜に言い逃れをする、〜の言うことをはぐらかす）のバリエーション。

you are doing.

Well, go ahead and tell him, said my father. I have nothing to ❶conceal. I am writing poetry. Tell Mr. Kosak I am writing poetry night and day.

5 Well, all right, I said, but ❷I don't think he'll be much impressed. He says you never go out like other ❸unemployed men and look for work. He says you're lazy and ❹no good.

You go on down there and tell him he's crazy, Johnny, said my father. You go down there and tell that fellow your father is one of
10 the greatest unknown poets living.

❺He might not care, I said, but I'll go. I'll do my best. Ain't we got nothing in the house?

Only popcorn, said my father. We been eating popcorn four days ❻in a row now, Johnny. ❼You got to get bread and cheese if
15 you expect me to finish that long poem.

I'll do my best, I said.

---

❶ conceal: 〜を隠す
❷ I don't think he'll be much impressed: それほど感心しないと思う。I'm impressed と言えば「それはすごいですね」という意。
❸ unemployed: 失業した
❹ no good: 人間について使うと「ろくな人間ではない」の意。
❺ He might not care: どうでもいいと思うかもしれない
❻ in a row: 立て続けに。第 3 巻 p. 90, ll. 6-7 に "about nine of us in a row had just been tied in knots by Maglie"（9 人ばかり続けてマグリーにキリキリ舞いさせられて）という形で既出。
❼ You got to: you've got to = you have to

だって。

　なら言ってやればいい、父さんは隠すことなんか何もないぞ。父さんは詩を書いているんだ。ミスタ・コーサックに言ってやれ、夜も昼も詩を書いてますって。

　わかったよ、でもあんまり感心してくれないと思うなあ。お前の父さんはほかの失業者みたいに仕事を探しに行かない、怠け者のろくでなしだ。そう言うんだよ。

　あんたは頭がおかしいんだって言ってやれ、ジョニー、と父さんは言った。あの男に言ってやれ、僕の父さんは今日最高の知られざる詩人の一人なんだって。

　それがどうしたって顔すると思うけど、と僕は言った。でもとにかく行くよ。精一杯やってみるよ。うちには何もないの？

　ポップコーンだけだ、と父さんは言った。もう四日間ずっとポップコーンしか食べてないんだぞ、ジョニー。いま書いてる長い詩、父さんに書き上げさせようと思ったら、パンとチーズ手に入れてきてくれないと。

　精一杯やってみるよ、と僕は言った。

Don't take too long, said Mr. MacGregor. I'm five thousand miles from home.

I'll run all the way, I said.

If you find any money on the way, said my father, remember
5 we go fifty-fifty.

All right, I said.

I ran all the way to Mr. Kosak's store, but I didn't find any money on the way, ❶not even a penny.

I went into the store and Mr. Kosak opened his eyes.

10 Mr. Kosak, I said, if you were in China and ❷didn't have a friend in the world and no money, ❸you'd expect some Christian over there to give you a pound of rice, wouldn't you?

What do you want? said Mr. Kosak.

I just want to talk a little, I said. You'd expect some member of
15 ❹the Aryan race to ❺help you out a little, wouldn't you, Mr. Kosak?

❻How much money you got? said Mr. Kosak.

---

❶ not even a penny: 「1 セント貨」の意味での penny は p. 64, ll. 15-16 に "I ain't got a penny, Johnny"（父さんは 1 セントも持ってないよ、ジョニー）の形で既出。

❷ didn't have a friend in the world: in the world は否定を強めて「まったく〜でない」という意味になるが、ここではもっと文字どおり、「この世に一人の友もいない」というイメージもしっかりある。

❸ you'd expect some Christian over there to …: そこにいるキリスト教徒が誰か、〜してくれると期待しますよね。expect は「期待する」ではなく「予期する」だと何度か述べてきたが（たとえば第 5 巻 p. 150, ll. 2-3, "You have no time to run from a face you do not expect"〔予想していない顔から逃げようと思ってももう手遅れだ〕）、ここは「期待する」が適切。ただし、「希望を持つ」というニュアンスではなく、「当然のこととして期待する」という含み。

あまり時間かからんようにな、とミスタ・マグレガーは言った。わしは故郷から五千マイル離れてるんだから。

行き帰りずっと走るよ、と僕は言った。

途中で金を拾ったら、忘れるなよ、父さんと山分けだからな、と父さんが言った。

わかった、と僕は言った。

ミスタ・コーサックの店まで僕はずっと走っていったが、途中でお金は拾わなかった。一セントも。

僕が店に入っていくと、ミスタ・コーサックが目を開けた。

ミスタ・コーサック、と僕は言った。もしあなたが中国にいて、一人の友だちもいなくてお金もなかったら、そこにいるクリスチャンが一ポンドの米を分けてくれればって思いますよね？

何が欲しいんだ？　ミスタ・コーサックは言った。

少し話がしたいだけですよ、と僕は言った。誰か白人が救いの手をさしのべてくれたらって思いますよね、そうでしょうミスタ・コーサック？

君、金はいくら持ってるんだ？　ミスタ・コーサックは言った。

❹ the Aryan race: アーリア人種。ナチスが「ユダヤ人でない白人」の意味で使って以来、何とも使いにくい言葉になっている。この作品は 1936 年発表なので、いわばギリギリ。

❺ help you out: help out は誰かを手助けする、誰かに力を貸すというニュアンス。*When we were first married, my parents helped us out with the rent.*（私たちが結婚したてのころ、私の親が家賃を援助してくれた。『動詞を使いこなすための英和活用辞典』）

❻ How much money you got?: How much money have you got?

It ain't a question of money, Mr. Kosak, I said. I'm talking about being in China and needing the help of the white race.

❶I don't know nothing about nothing, said Mr. Kosak.

❷How would you feel in China that way? I said.

I don't know, said Mr. Kosak. What would I be doing in China?

Well, I said, you'd be visiting there, and you'd be hungry, and not a friend in the world. You wouldn't expect a good Christian to ❸turn you away without even a pound of rice, would you, Mr. Kosak?

❹I guess not, said Mr. Kosak, but you ain't in China, Johnny, and neither is your ❺Pa. You or your Pa's got to go out and work sometime in your lives, so ❻you might as well start now. ❼I ain't going to give you no more groceries ❽on credit because I know you won't pay me.

Mr. Kosak, I said, you misunderstand me: I'm not talking about a few groceries. I'm talking about ❾all them heathen people

---

❶ I don't know nothing about nothing: 「正しい」文法に従うなら I don't know anything about anything または I know nothing about anything だが、この言い方にいかにも「何も知らんもんね」という感じの味わいがあることは確か。

❷ How would you feel in China that way?: that way は l. 2 の being in China and needing the help of the white race を指す。

❸ turn you away: turn ... away で「～を退ける、～への援助を拒む」。*Don't turn me away. I desperately need your help.*（断らないでくれ。きみの助けが何としても必要なんだ。『動詞を使いこなすための英和活用辞典』）

❹ I guess not: I guess I wouldn't expect a good Christian to turn me away ...

❺ Pa: 庶民的な響きの「父ちゃん」「お父ちゃん」。

❻ you might as well start now: ならいま始めたっていいじゃないか。might as well ... は「まあ大した違いではないが、一応こっちの方がいいのでは」と

72

　お金の問題じゃありませんよミスタ・コーサック、と僕は言った。中国にいて、白人の助けを必要としてるって話なんです。

　私には難しいことは何もわからんね、とミスタ・コーサックは言った。

　中国でそうなったらどんな気持ちがすると思います？

　さあね。私が中国なんか行って何するのかね？

　そうですねえ、あなたは中国を訪問していて、お腹を空かせていて、友だちは一人もいない。善良なクリスチャンがあなたのこと、米一ポンドもくれずに追い返すなんて思わないでしょう？

　まあそうだろうな、だけど君は中国になんかいないんだよジョニー、そして君のパパも同じだ。君だか君のパパだかが、いつかは世間に出て働かなくちゃいけない。だったらいまさっさと始めたらどうだ。もうこれ以上君たちにつけで食べ物を渡したりしない。どうせ払わないに決まってるんだからね。

　ミスタ・コーサック、それは誤解というものです。僕はちょっとばかりの食べ物の話なんかしてるんじゃないんです。あなたが中国にいて周りじゅう

いうニュアンス。第 2 巻 p. 40, ll. 13-14 に "Finally she grunted: 'Might as well go on inside. It's cold out here.'"（そしてとうとううなるように言った。「まあとにかくなかへ入ろうじゃないの。こんな寒いところにいてもしょうがないから」）の形で既出。

❼ I ain't going to give you no more groceries: 折り目正しい英語で言えば I'm not going to give you any more groceries. groceries は「食料雑貨品」。

❽ on credit: つけで。credit は p. 64, l. 15 に "Tell Mr. Kosak to give us credit"（つけにしてくれってミスタ・コーサックに言いなさい）の形で既出。

❾ all them heathen people: 標準的な英語なら all those heathen people。普通であれば those と言うところが them になる例は、第 3 巻 p. 26, l. 6 に "I read one of them paragraphs over again, so as to be certain"（念のためもう一度、一段落だけ読み直した）の形で既出。heathen は「キリスト教徒でない」ということ。

around you in China, and you hungry and dying.

This ain't China, said Mr. Kosak. You got to go out and make your living in this country. Everybody works in America.

Mr. Kosak, I said, ❶suppose it was a loaf of French bread and a
5 pound of cheese you needed to keep you alive in the world, would you hesitate to ask a Christian ❷missionary for these things?

Yes, I would, said Mr. Kosak. I would be ashamed to ask.

Even if you knew you would give him back two loaves of bread and two pounds of cheese? I said. Even then?

10 Even then, said Mr. Kosak.

Don't be that way, Mr. Kosak, I said. That's ❸defeatist talk, and you know it. Why, the only thing that would happen to you would be death. You would die ❹out there in China, Mr. Kosak.

I wouldn't care if I would, said Mr. Kosak, you and your Pa
15 have got to pay for bread and cheese. Why don't your Pa go out and get a job?

❶ suppose it was ... you needed to keep you alive: 生きつづけるのに〜が必要なのだとしたら。you needed の前に that を補うとわかりやすいかもしれない。
❷ (a) missionary: 宣教師
❸ defeatist talk: 敗北主義者の物言い
❹ out there in China: out がなくてもさして意味は変わらないし、out there の二語がなくてもそんなに変わらないが、あることで中国が遠いことがいわば確認されているような響き。

異教徒に囲まれて、お腹を空かせて死にかけてるっていう話なんです。

ここは中国じゃないぞ。この国じゃ自分で生計を立てなきゃいかんのだ。アメリカではみんな働くんだよ。

ミスタ・コーサック、たとえばあなたが生き延びるためにフランスパン一本とチーズ一ポンドが必要だとしますよね、それでそこにクリスチャンの宣教師がいたら、パンとチーズをくださいって頼むのをためらいますか？

ああ、ためらうとも。頼むなんて恥だと思うだろうよ。

いずれ自分がパン二本、チーズ二ポンドにして返すとわかっていても？それでも頼まない？

それでも頼まないね、とミスタ・コーサックは言った。

そんなこと言っちゃ駄目ですよ、ミスタ・コーサック、と僕は言った。そういうのは負け犬の言いぐさですよ、そうでしょう。そうなったらもう死ぬしかなくなっちゃうじゃありませんか。あなたははるか中国で死ぬんですよ、ミスタ・コーサック。

死のうが死ぬまいが知ったこっちゃないね。パンとチーズが欲しけりゃ君と君のパパとで金を払わなきゃならんのだ。なんで君のパパは仕事を探しに行かないんだ？

Mr. Kosak, I said, how are you, ❶anyway?

I'm fine, Johnny, said Mr. Kosak. How are you?

❷Couldn't be better, Mr. Kosak, I said. How are the children?

Fine, said Mr. Kosak. Stepan is beginning to walk now.

5 That's great, I said. How is Angela?

Angela is beginning to sing, said Mr. Kosak. How is your grandmother?

She's feeling fine, I said. She's beginning to sing too. She says she would rather be an opera star than queen. How's Marta, your
10 wife, Mr. Kosak?

Oh, ❸swell, said Mr. Kosak.

I cannot tell you how glad I am to hear that all is well at your house, I said. I know Stepan is going to be a great man some day.

I hope so, said Mr. Kosak. I am going to ❹send him straight
15 through high school and ❺see that he gets every chance I didn't get. I don't want him to open a grocery store.

---

❶ anyway: それはともかく

❷ Couldn't be better: これ以上よくはありえない＝最高だ

❸ swell: 素晴らしい、素敵な。古風なアメリカ英語。

❹ send him straight through high school: 高校に行かせて一気に（休学させたりもせず）卒業させる

❺ see that he gets every chance: この see は単に「見る」ではなく、see (to it) that ... で「～するよう取り計らう、気をつける」。*See that all the doors are locked before you go to bed.*（寝る前にドアの鍵が全部かかってるのを確かめて。『コンパスローズ英和辞典』）

ところでミスタ・コーサック、お元気ですか？

元気だよ、ジョニー。君はどうかね？

最高に元気ですよ、ミスタ・コーサック。お子さんたちはお元気ですか？

元気だよ。ステパンは歩きはじめた。

そりゃすごい。アンジェラは？

アンジェラは歌いはじめた。君のお祖母さんは元気かね？

元気ですよ。お祖母ちゃんも歌いはじめたんです。女王になるよりオペラの歌姫の方がいいって言ってます。奥さんのマータさんはいかがです？

うん、元気一杯だとも、とミスタ・コーサックは言った。

それはよかった、ほんとに嬉しいですよ、ご家族みんなお元気だと伺って。ステパンはいずれきっと立派な人になりますよ。

だといいがな。高校まで行かせようと思ってるんだ、私が得られなかったチャンスをちゃんと得られるように。食料品店の親父にはなってほしくないからね。

❶I have great faith in Stepan, I said.

What do you want, Johnny? said Mr. Kosak. And how much money you got?

Mr. Kosak, I said, you know I didn't come here to buy
5 anything. You know I enjoy a quiet ❷philosophical chat with you ❸ every now and then. Let me have a loaf of French bread and a pound of cheese.

You got to pay cash, Johnny, said Mr. Kosak.

And Esther, I said. How is your beautiful daughter Esther?

10 Esther is all right, Johnny, said Mr. Kosak, but you got to pay cash. You and your Pa are the worst citizens in this whole ❹county.

I'm glad Esther is all right, Mr. Kosak, I said. ❺Jasper MacGregor is visiting our house. He is a great actor.

I never heard of him, said Mr. Kosak.

15 And a bottle of beer for Mr. MacGregor, I said.

I can't give you a bottle of beer, said Mr. Kosak.

❶ I have great faith in Stepan: have faith in ... で「〜の力、才能を信じている」。
❷ philosophical: 哲学的な
❸ every now and then: ときどき
❹ county: 郡
❺ Jasper MacGregor is visiting our house: この visit は「〜の家に滞在する」。

ステパンならきっと大丈夫ですよ。

何が欲しいんだ、ジョニー？　金はいくら持ってるのかね？

ミスタ・コーサック、おわかりでしょう、僕はべつに何かを買いに来たわけじゃないんです。時おりあなたとこうして、哲学的なお喋りを静かに交わすのが楽しいんです。フランスパン一本とチーズ一ポンドください。

現金で払わなくちゃ駄目だよ、ジョニー。

それとエスター。美しいお嬢さんエスターは元気ですか？

エスターなら大丈夫だよ、ジョニー。現金で払わなくちゃ駄目だよ。君と君のパパはこの郡で最低の住民だな。

エスターが大丈夫と聞いて嬉しいですよ、ミスタ・コーサック。ジャスパー・マグレガーがうちにお客に来てるんです、偉い役者なんですよ。

聞いたことないね、とミスタ・コーサックは言った。

あとミスタ・マグレガーにビール一本も、と僕は言った。

君にビール一本やるなんて、できるわけないだろ。

Certainly you can, I said.

I can't, said Mr. Kosak. I'll let you have one loaf of **❶**stale bread, and one pound of cheese, but that's all. What kind of work does your Pa do when he works, Johnny?

5 My father writes poetry, Mr. Kosak, I said. That's the only work my father does. He is one of the greatest writers of poetry in the world.

When does he get any money? said Mr. Kosak.

He never gets any money, I said. **❷**You can't have your cake
10 and eat it.

I don't like that kind of a job, said Mr. Kosak. Why doesn't your Pa work like everybody else, Johnny?

He works harder than everybody else, I said. My father **❸**works twice as hard as the average man.

15 Well, that's fifty-five cents you owe me, Johnny, said Mr. Kosak. I'll let you have **❹**some stuff this time, but never again.

---

❶ stale: （食べ物が）古くなった
❷ You can't have your cake and eat it: 決まり文句。「お菓子を食べてしまって、
　 しかも持っていることはできない」（両方ともいい思いはできない）
❸ works twice as hard as the average man: 並の男の二倍一生懸命働く
❹ some stuff: stuff は漠然と「もの」あるいは「食べ物」。

　いやいやできますとも。

　できないよ。古いパン一本とチーズ一ポンドはやろう、でもそれで全部だ。君のパパ、働くときはどんな仕事するのかね、ジョニー？

　僕の父さんは詩を書くんです、ミスタ・コーサック。父さんの仕事はもっぱらそれです。現代における最高の詩人の一人ですよ。

　いつになったら金が入るのかね？

　金は入らないんです。そこまで都合よくできてないんです。

　そういう仕事はよくないと思うね。なんで君のパパはほかの連中みたいに働かないんだ？

　誰よりも一生懸命働いてますよ。並の人間の二倍働いてます。

　いいか、これで五十五セントの貸しだぞ、ジョニー。今回はまあ渡してやるが、もうこれっきりだからな。

Tell Esther I love her, I said.

All right, said Mr. Kosak.

Goodbye, Mr. Kosak, I said.

Goodbye, Johnny, said Mr. Kosak.

5　　I ran back to the house with the loaf of French bread and the pound of cheese.

My father and Mr. MacGregor were in the street waiting to see if I would come back with food. They ran ❶half a block toward me and when they saw that it was food, they waved back to the house

10 where my grandmother was waiting. She ran into the house to set the table.

I knew you'd do it, said my father.

So did I, said Mr. MacGregor.

He says we got to pay him fifty-five cents, I said. He says ❷he

15 ain't going to give us no more stuff on credit.

That's his opinion, said my father. What did you talk about,

❶ half a block: 四つ角から四つ角までが a block。第2巻 p. 182, ll. 16-17 に "He walked a few blocks to a nearby bus stop."（何ブロックか歩いて、次のバス停まで行った）の形で既出。

❷ he ain't going to give us no more stuff on credit: 行儀よく言えば he isn't going to give us any more food on credit.

エスターに伝えてください、僕が愛してるって、と僕は言った。

わかった、とミスタ・コーサックは言った。

さよなら、ミスタ・コーサック。

さよなら、ジョニー。

僕はフランスパン一本とチーズ一ポンドを抱えて家に駆け戻った。

僕の父さんとミスタ・マグレガーは表に出て、僕が食べ物を持って帰ってくるのをいまかいまかと待っていた。二人とも半ブロック僕の方に駆けてきて、食べ物があるのを見るや、お祖母さんが待っている家の方に手を振って合図した。お祖母さんはテーブルをセットしに家の中へ駆けていった。

わかってたよ、お前ならできるって、と僕の父さんが言った。

私もだよ、とミスタ・マグレガーが言った。

五十五セント払わなくちゃ駄目だって、と僕は言った。もうこれ以上つけはきかないって。

それはまあ向こうの意見さ、と父さんは言った。何の話をしたんだ、ジョ

Johnny?

First I talked about being hungry and ❶at death's door in China, I said, and then I ❷inquired about the family.

How is everyone? said my father.

5　Fine, I said.

So we all went inside and ate the loaf of bread and the pound of cheese, and each of us drank two or three ❸quarts of water, and after every ❹ crumb of bread had disappeared, Mr. MacGregor began to look around the kitchen to see if there wasn't something 10 else to eat.

That green can up there, he said. ❺What's in there, Johnny?

❻Marbles, I said.

That ❼cupboard, he said. Anything ❽edible in there, Johnny?

❾Crickets, I said.

15　That big ❿jar in the corner there, Johnny, he said. ⓫What's good in there?

---

❶ at death's door: 死にかけている

❷ inquire(d): 訊ねる

❸ quart(s): 液体の単位としては、アメリカでは約 0.95 リットル、イギリスでは約 1.14 リットル。まあ「だいたい 1 リットル」と覚えておけば十分。

❹ crumb: (パンなどの) くず、かけら

❺ What's in there: What's in it が「正しい」ように思えるが、この形も普通に使われる。

❻ Marble(s): ビー玉

❼ cupboard: 食器棚。/kʌbəd/ と発音する。

❽ edible: 食べられる

❾ Cricket(s): コオロギ

❿ (a) jar: (広口の) 壜

ニー？

　はじめは中国でお腹を空かせて死にかけてる話をして、それから家の人たちは元気ですかって訊いたよ。

　みんな元気か？　と父さんは言った。

　うん、と僕は言った。

　というわけで僕たちは家に入ってパン一本とチーズ一ポンドを食べ、一人二、三リットル水を飲み、パン屑の最後のひとかけも消えてしまうと、ほかに何か食べ物はないかとミスタ・マグレガーは台所の中を見回しはじめた。

　あそこの緑の缶、とミスタ・マグレガーは言った。あの中には何があるのかね、ジョニー？

　ビー玉だよ、と僕は言った。

　そこの食器棚。中に何か食べられるものはあるかね、ジョニー？

　コオロギだね。

　そこの隅の大きな甕、ジョニー、何かいいものが入ってるのかね？

❶ What's good in there?: 何かいいものが入っているのか

I got ❶a gopher snake in that jar, I said.

Well, said Mr. MacGregor, ❷I could go for a bit of boiled gopher snake ❸in a big way, Johnny.

You can't have that snake, I said.

5   Why not, Johnny? said Mr. MacGregor. ❹Why the hell not, son? I hear of fine Borneo ❺natives eating snakes and grasshoppers. You ain't got half a dozen fat ❻grasshoppers around, have you, Johnny?

Only four, I said.

Well, ❼trot them out, Johnny, said Mr. MacGregor, and after we
10 ❽have had our fill, I'll play *Drink to Me Only with Thine Eyes* on the bugle for you. I'm mighty hungry, Johnny.

So am I, I said, but ❾you ain't going to kill that snake.

My father sat at the table with his head in his hands, dreaming. My grandmother ❿ paced through the house, singing arias from
15 ⓫Puccini. ⓬As through the streets I wander, she roared in Italian.

How about a little music? said my father. I think the boy would

---

❶ a gopher snake: インディゴヘビ

❷ I could go for a bit of boiled gopher snake: go for ... で「〜を好む」だが、I could go for ... だと「いま〜が食べられたら／飲めたらなあ」といった意味になる。

❸ in a big way: 大いに

❹ Why the hell not, son?: 何で駄目なんだよ？

❺ native(s): 地元民

❻ grasshopper(s): バッタ

❼ trot them out: trot ... out で「〜を出して見せる、披露する」。*Automobile makers are trotting out their new models this month.* (自動車メーカーはどこも今月、新しいモデルを発表する。『動詞を使いこなすための英和活用辞典』)

インディゴヘビ飼ってるんだよ、と僕は言った。

そうかね、とミスタ・マグレガーは言った。私としては、茹でたインディゴヘビなんかも大歓迎だがね。

あのヘビは駄目だよ、と僕は言った。

なんでだね、ジョニー？　なんで駄目なんだ？　ボルネオの立派な現地人は、ヘビやバッタを食べるっていうぞ。君、太ったバッタとかいっぱい飼ってたりしないかね、ジョニー？

四匹だけ、と僕は言った。

じゃあそれ出しなさい、とミスタ・マグレガーは言った。そいつをしっかり腹に入れたら「瞳で乾杯しておくれ」を吹いてあげようじゃないか。私はすごく腹が減ってるんだよ、ジョニー。

僕もだよ、と僕は言った。でもあのヘビは殺しちゃ駄目だよ。

僕の父さんは食卓に座って、両手で頭を抱えて夢を見ていた。お祖母ちゃんは家の中を、プッチーニのアリアを歌いながら歩きまわっていた。私が街を歩けば、とお祖母ちゃんは朗々とイタリア語で歌った。

音楽、少しどうでしょう？　と父さんは言った。この子が喜ぶと思うんで

---

❽ have had our fill <have one's fill: 思う存分食べる

❾ you ain't going to kill that snake: このように be going to は、軽い命令のニュアンスを帯びることがある。*You're not going to do anything about any of it.*（このことにはいっさい手を出してはいけない。『リーダーズ英和辞典』）

❿ pace(d): 歩き回る、行ったり来たりする

⓫ Puccini: プッチーニ(1858-1924)はメトロポリタン歌劇場の招きで1907年、1910年にアメリカを訪れている。

⓬ As through the streets I wander: 通例「私が街を歩けば」と訳される、オペラ『ラ・ボエーム』(*La Bohème*) 英語版の一節。お祖母ちゃんはイタリア語で朗々と歌った（roared）ので、"Quando me'n vo'"。

❶be delighted.

I sure would, Mr. MacGregor, I said.

All right, Johnny, said Mr. MacGregor.

So he got up and began to blow into the bugle and he blew
5 louder than any man ever blew into a bugle and people **❷**for miles
around heard him and got excited. Eighteen neighbors gathered in
front of our house and **❸**applauded when Mr. MacGregor finished
the solo. My father led Mr. MacGregor out on the porch and said,
Good neighbors and friends, I want you to meet Jasper MacGregor,
10 the greatest Shakespearean actor of our day.

The good neighbors and friends said nothing and Mr.
MacGregor said, I remember my first appearance in London in
1867 as if it was yesterday, and he **❹**went on with the story of his
career. Rufe Apley the carpenter said, How about some more
15 music, Mr. MacGregor? and Mr. MacGregor said, Have you got an
egg at your house?

---

❶ be delighted: 喜ぶ
❷ for miles around:「近くも遠くも、そこらじゅうの」といった意味の成句。
❸ applaud(ed): 拍手喝采する
❹ went on with the story of his career: go on with ... で「(しているこ
と)を(やめずに)そのまま続ける」。*Steve went on with his work as we
talked.*（スティーブは私と話しながら仕事を続けていた。『動詞を使いこなす
ための英和活用辞典』）

すよ。

　そうなんですよ、ほんとに、と僕も言った。

　よしわかったジョニー、とミスタ・マグレガーは言った。

　そうしてミスタ・マグレガーは席を立ち、ラッパを吹きはじめた。誰よりも大きな音で彼は吹き、周りじゅう何マイルも人々がそれを聞いて胸を躍らせた。わが家の前に十八人の人が集まって、ミスタ・マグレガーがソロを終えると拍手喝采を贈った。父さんがミスタ・マグレガーを玄関先に連れ出し、言った。ご近所の皆さん、ジャスパー・マグレガーをご紹介します。今日（こんにち）誰よりも偉大なシェークスピア俳優です。

　ご近所の皆さんは何も言わず、ミスタ・マグレガーが口を開いた。いまでも昨日のように覚えていますとも、一八六七年にロンドンで初めて舞台に立ったときのことを。こうしてミスタ・マグレガーは己の生涯を物語った。と、大工のルーフ・アプリーが言った。また少し音楽やってもらえませんかね、ミスタ・マグレガー？　するとミスタ・マグレガーは、あんたの家に卵はあるかね？　と言った。

I sure have, said Rufe. I got a dozen eggs at my house.

❶ Would it be convenient for you to go and get ❷ one of them dozen eggs? said Mr. MacGregor. When you return I'll play a song that will make your heart leap with joy and ❸grief.

5   I'm on my way already, said Rufe, and he went home to get an egg.

Mr. MacGregor asked Tom Baker if he had a bit of sausage at his house and Tom said he did, and Mr. MacGregor asked Tom if it would be convenient for Tom to go and get that little bit 10 of sausage and come back with it and when Tom returned Mr. MacGregor would play a song on the bugle that would change the whole history of Tom's life. And Tom went home for the sausage, and Mr. MacGregor asked each of the eighteen good neighbors and friends if he had something small and nice to eat at his home 15 and each man said he did, and each man went to his home to get the small and nice thing to eat, ❹ so Mr. MacGregor would play

---

❶ Would it be convenient for you to ...: 直訳は「あなたにとって〜するのは都合がいいだろうか」。丁寧にものを頼んでいる感じ。

❷ one of them dozen eggs: them は p. 72, l. 16 - p. 74, l. 1 の all them heathen people around you in China (中国で周りじゅうにいる異教徒たち) の them と同じ。

❸ grief: 深い悲しみ。p. 56, l. 11 に既出の動詞 grieve ("My heart is grieving there"〔私の心はそこで悲しみに暮れているのさ〕) の名詞形。

❹ so Mr. MacGregor would play the song he said would be so wonderful to hear: 基本的には本シリーズ頻出の so A would/could do B (A が B するよう／できるよう) のパターン。the song he said would be so wonderful to hear: he said が挿入されている。「聴くに素晴らしいはずと彼が言った歌」

　ありますとも、とルーフは言った。卵、家に一ダースありますよ。

　その一ダースのうち一個、よかったら取りに行ってもらえるかね？　あん
たが戻ってきたら、あんたの心を喜びと悲しみで舞い上がらせる歌を吹いて
しんぜよう。

　俺もう駆け出してますよ、とルーフは言い、卵を取りに家へ走っていった。

　ミスタ・マグレガーはトム・ベーカーに、あんたの家にソーセージ一切れ
とかあるかねと訊き、ありますとトムが答えるとミスタ・マグレガーは、よ
かったら取りに行ってもらえるかね、あんたが戻ってきたらあんたの人生ま
るごと変えちまう歌を吹いてしんぜようと言った。そうしてトムがソーセー
ジを取りに家へ帰ると、ミスタ・マグレガーはご近所の皆さん一人ひとりに、
何かちょっとした食べ物は家にないかねと訊き、ありますよと相手は答え、
ミスタ・マグレガー言うところの耳に何とも心地よい歌を吹いてもらおうと

the song he said would be so wonderful to hear, and when all the
good neighbors and friends had returned to our house with all the
small and nice things to eat, Mr. MacGregor lifted the bugle to his
lips and played ❶*My Heart's in the Highlands, My Heart is not Here,*
5 and each of the good neighbors and friends wept and returned
to his home, and Mr. MacGregor took all the good things into the
kitchen and our family ❷feasted and drank and ❸was merry: an
egg, a sausage, a dozen ❹green onions, two kinds of cheese, butter,
two kinds of bread, boiled potatoes, fresh tomatoes, a melon, tea,
10 and many other good things to eat, and we ate and ❺our bellies
tightened, and Mr. MacGregor said, Sir, ❻if it is all the same to you
I should like to ❼dwell in your house ❽for some days to come, and
my father said, Sir, my house is your house, and Mr. MacGregor
stayed at our house seventeen days and seventeen nights, and on
15 the afternoon of the eighteenth day a man from the Old People's
Home came to our house and said, I am looking for Jasper

❶ *My Heart's in the Highlands* ...: p. 57, 註❻で触れた、ロバート・バーンズ
の詩で知られる歌。
❷ feast(ed): ごちそうを食べる
❸ was merry: 愉快に過ごした
❹ green onion(s): 葉タマネギ
❺ our bellies tightened: お腹がパンパンに張った
❻ if it is all the same to you: あなたにとって同じことなら＝差し支えなければ
❼ dwell in ...: 〜に居住する
❽ for some days to come: to come はその前に years, days などが来て「来
たるべき〜」。

それぞれちょっとした食べ物を取りに帰り、何かちょっとした食べ物を手に近所の人たち全員がわが家に戻ってくると、ミスタ・マグレガーはラッパを持ち上げて口に持っていき、「わが心は高地に　わが心はここにあらず」を演奏した。ご近所の皆さんの誰もが涙を流しながら家に帰っていき、ミスタ・マグレガーは食べ物をみな台所に持っていって、僕たち一家は御馳走を食べ、飲み、楽しく過ごした。卵、ソーセージ、葉タマネギ一ダース、チーズ二種類、バター、パン二種類、茹でジャガイモ、穫れ立てのトマト、メロン、紅茶、そのほかにもまだたくさん。僕たちは食べ、お腹がきつくなり、ミスタ・マグレガーは言った。もしよろしければ、私このお宅にしばらく住ませていただけませんかね。すると僕の父さんは、私の家はあなたの家ですともと言い、ミスタ・マグレガーはうちにまる十七日泊まっていき、十八日目の午後に、老人ホームの職員がうちへやって来て、ジャスパー・マグレガーという

MacGregor, the actor, and my father said, What do you want?

    I am from the Old People's Home, said the young man, and I want Mr. MacGregor to come back to our place because we are ❶putting on our ❷annual show in two weeks and need an actor.

5   Mr. MacGregor got up from the floor where he had been dreaming and went away with the young man, and the following afternoon, when he was very hungry, my father said, Johnny, go down to Mr. Kosak's store and get a little something to eat. I know you can do it, Johnny. Get anything you can.

10   Mr. Kosak wants fifty-five cents, I said. He won't give us anything more without money.

    Go on down there, Johnny, said my father. You know you can ❸get that fine Slovak gentleman to give you a bit of something to eat.

15   So I went down to Mr. Kosak's store and ❹took up the Chinese problem where I had dropped it, and it ❺was quite a job for me to

---

❶ put(ting) on ...: 〜を上演する、催す
❷ annual: 毎年恒例の、年一回の
❸ get that fine Slovak gentleman to ...: get A to do B で「A に B をさせる、するよう仕向ける」。Slovak: スロバキア人の
❹ took up <take up: (中断した話・授業などを) 再開する、続ける
❺ was quite a job: ひと仕事だった、けっこう大変だった

役者を探してるんですと言い、何の用だね？　と僕の父さんは言った。

　私、老人ホームの者でして、とその若い男の人は言った。ミスタ・マグレガーに戻ってきていただきたいんです、年に一度の芝居を二週間後にやるんで、役者が必要なんです。

　床に寝そべって夢を見ていたミスタ・マグレガーは床から起き上がって若い男と一緒に出ていき、翌日の午後、ひどく腹を空かせた僕の父さんが、ジョニー、ミスタ・コーサックの店に行って何か食べるものをもらって来なさいと言った。お前ならできるさ、ジョニー。何でもいいからもらって来い。

　五十五セント払えってミスタ・コーサックは言ってるんだよ、と僕は言った。お金なしじゃ何もくれないよ。

　いいから行きなさい、ジョニー。お前ならあの立派なスロバキア人の紳士から、きっと何か食べ物もらって来れるさ。

　そこで僕はミスタ・コーサックの店に行き、中国問題をこのあいだ終えた時点から再開し、ずいぶん手こずった末に、鳥の餌を一箱と、メープルシロッ

go away from the store with a box of **❶**bird seed and half a can of maple syrup, but I did it, and my father said, Johnny, **❷** this sort of fare is going to be pretty dangerous for the old lady, and **❸**sure enough in the morning we heard my grandmother singing like a

5 canary, and my father said, How the hell can I write great poetry **❹**on bird seed?

❶ bird seed: (飼っている鳥に与える) 粒餌

❷ this sort of fare: fare はこの場合「食べ物」。

❸ sure enough: 果たして、案の定

❹ on bird seed: 鳥の餌を食べて

プの半分入った缶を手にして店を出た。だいぶ苦労したけれど、とにかく僕
はやり遂げた。僕の父さんは、ジョニー、この手の食べ物は祖母ちゃんには
けっこう危険だぞと言った。果たせるかな、翌朝、お祖母ちゃんがカナリア
みたいに歌うのを僕たちは聞き、そして僕の父さんは言った——鳥の餌なん
かで、どうやって偉大な詩を書けっていうんだ？

ちなみに

本短篇には戯曲バージョンがある。*My Heart's in the Highlands*——
と、今度はバーンズの詩のタイトルをそのまま借りたこの一幕物の戯
曲は、小説刊行から 3 年後の 1939 年にブロードウェイで上演されて
大ヒットした。物語は基本的に小説バージョンと変わらないが、小説
では終始飄々としている父親が、戯曲では出版社から「掲載不可」の
通知とともに詩が送り返されてきたときなど、やや寂しげな顔を見せ
たりもする。

The Debutante
Leonora Carrington

はじめての舞踏会
レオノーラ・キャリントン

難易度 1
★ ☆ ☆

レオノーラ・キャリントン
(Leonora Carrington, 1917-2011)

　イギリスに生まれ、1937 年にシュルレアリスト画家マックス・エルンストに出会ったのを契機に自らもシュルレアリスティックな芸術を製作するようになり、戦後は長年メキシコで画家として活動。執筆に携わったのは主に 1930 年代後半で、ここで取り上げる "The Debutante" は元来フランス語で書かれ（"La debutante"）、作品集 *La Dame ovale* (1939) に収められた。英訳は Kathrine Talbot と Maria Warner、著者が監訳している。

W hen I was a debutante, I often went to the zoo. I went so
often that I knew the animals better than I knew girls of
my own age. Indeed it was in order to get away from people that ❶I
found myself at the zoo every day. ❷The animal I got to know best
5 was a young hyena. She knew me too. She was very intelligent. I
taught her French, and she, in return, taught me her language. In
this way we passed many pleasant hours.

My mother was arranging ❸a ball in my honour on the first of
May. During this time I was in a state of great ❹distress for whole
10 nights. I've always ❺detested balls, especially when they are given
in my honour.

On the morning of the first of May 1934, very early, I went to
visit the hyena.

"❻What a bloody nuisance," I said to her. "I've got to go to my
15 ball tonight."

"You're very lucky," she said. "I'd love to go. I don't know how

---

タイトルの debutante とは社交界にデビューする年頃の女性のこと。イギリス
ではデビュタントは宮廷でお目見えするならわしだったが、1958 年を最後に、
エリザベス女王がこの慣習を廃止した。
❶ I found myself at the zoo every day:「気がついたら動物園にいた」という
ほど「無自覚」感が強いわけではなく、「つい毎日行ってしまった」くらい。
❷ The animal I got to know best: get to ... は p. 62, l. 12 に "when you get
to be my age"（君も私の歳になったら）の形で既出。
❸ a ball in my honour: 私のために開かれる舞踏会。in hono(u)r of ...: ～を祝
して
❹ distress: 苦悩、心労
❺ detest(ed): ～をひどく嫌う
❻ What a bloody nuisance: bloody は言っていることを強調しようと思ったら

100

　社交界にデビュー間近のころ、あたしはしょっちゅう動物園に行った。あんまりしょっちゅう通ったものだから、同い歳の女の子たちより、動物たちの方が親しくなってしまった。そもそも人間から逃げたくて、毎日動物園に通ったのだ。いちばん仲よくなったのは、一匹の若いハイエナだった。ハイエナもあたしのことをわかってくれた。ハイエナはすごく賢かった。あたしは彼女にフランス語を教え、向こうもお返しにハイエナ語を教えてくれた。そんなふうにして、あたしたちは何時間も楽しく過ごした。

　あたしのママは、五月一日にあたしの社交界入りを祝う舞踏会を開こうと、せっせと準備を進めていた。この時期、あたしはもう辛くて辛くて、一晩じゅう眠れなかった。舞踏会なんて、好きだったためしがない。特に、自分のために開かれる舞踏会なんて最悪だ。

　一九三四年五月一日の朝、まだひどく早い時間、あたしはハイエナに会いにいった。

「嫌んなっちゃうよ」とあたしは彼女に言った。「今夜ね、自分の舞踏会に出なくちゃいけないの」

「いいなあ」と彼女は言った。「あたしも行きたいなあ。ダンスはできない

一部のイギリス人にあってはほぼ自動的に出てくる強調語。*Mind your own bloody business!*（てめえの頭のハエでも追え。『研究社 新英和大辞典』）a nuisance: 厄介

to dance, but at least I could make **❶**small talk."

"There'll be **❷** a great many different things to eat," I told her. "I've seen **❸**truckloads of food delivered to our house."

" **❹** And you're complaining," replied the hyena, **❺** disgusted. 5 "Just think of me, I eat once a day, and you can't imagine **❻**what a heap of bloody rubbish I'm given."

I had an **❼**audacious idea, and I almost laughed. "All you have to do is to go instead of me!"

"We don't **❽**resemble each other enough, **❾**otherwise I'd gladly 10 go," said the hyena rather sadly.

"Listen," I said. " **❿** No one sees too well in the evening light. If you **⓫** disguise yourself, nobody will notice you in the crowd. Besides, we're **⓬**practically the same size. You're my only friend, I beg you to do this for me."

15 She **⓭** thought this over, and I knew that she really wanted to accept.

---

❶ small talk: お喋り

❷ a great many different things to eat: different はこのように複数名詞があとに来ると、「違う」というより「いろいろな」。

❸ truckloads of ...: トラック何台分もの〜

❹ And you're complaining: この And は「そして」というよりむしろ「なのに」。*A sailor and afraid of the weather!*（船乗りなのに天気を怖がるとは！ Arthur Conan Doyle, *The Doings of Raffles Haw*, 1891）

❺ disgusted: うんざりして

❻ what a heap of bloody rubbish: a heap は（乱雑に積み重ねられた）山。bloody は p. 100, l. 14 の "What a bloody nuisance" と同じ。rubbish は「ごみ、くず」の意でイギリスでは非常によく使う。

❼ audacious: 大胆不敵な

けど、お喋りくらいできるよ」

「いろんな食べ物が出るんだよ」とあたしは彼女に言った。「トラック何台も、うちに食べ物を届けにきてたもの」

「それで文句言うなんて」とハイエナはうんざりしたように言った。「あたしのこと考えてみてよ、食事は一日一度、それも最低のゴミみたいなんだよ、あんたには想像もつかないよ」

　と、あたしはすごいアイデアを思いついて、もう少しで笑い出してしまうところだった。「あんたがあたしの代わりに出ればいいよ！」

「だってあたしたちそんなに似てないよ。似てりゃ喜んで行くけど」とハイエナが悲しそうに言った。

「大丈夫。夜で暗いんだから、そんなにはっきり見えやしないよ。変装していけば、人込みにまぎれて誰も気づかない。あたしたち背丈だってだいたい同じだし。あんたしか友だちはいないのよ、お願い」

　そう言われて彼女は考え込んだが、内心引きうけたがっていることは明らかだった。

❽ resemble: 〜に似ている

❾ otherwise: そうでなければ（if not）

❿ No one sees too well: 誰もよく見えない

⓫ disguise yourself: 変装する

⓬ practically: ほとんど〜も同然（almost）

⓭ thought this over: think ... over（または think over ...）で「〜をよく考える」。
I sat back in my chair and thought over the events of the past week.（椅子に深々と座り直し、私はこの一週間の出来事をあれこれ考えた。『動詞を使いこなすための英和活用辞典』）

"❶Done," she said all of a sudden.

❷ There weren't many keepers about, it was so early in the morning. I opened the cage quickly, and in a very few moments we were out in the street. I ❸hailed a taxi; at home, everybody was
5 still in bed. In my room I brought out ❹ the dress I was to wear that evening. It was a little long, and the hyena ❺found it difficult to walk in my high-heeled shoes. I found some gloves to hide her hands, which were too hairy to look like mine. By the time the sun was shining into my room, she was able to ❻make her way around
10 the room several times, walking ❼more or less ❽upright. We were so busy that my mother almost opened the door to say good morning before the hyena had hidden under my bed.

"There's a bad smell in your room," my mother said, opening the window. "You must have a ❾scented bath before tonight, with
15 my new bath salts."

"Certainly," I said.

❶ Done: それで決まりだ、了解
❷ There weren't many keepers about, it was so early in the morning: It was so early in the morning that there weren't many keepers about の前後がひっくり返っている。こっちの方が口語的。it was ... の前に because や as が入っていないが、これは普通。I didn't say anything, I was so scared. (何も言わなかった。何しろ怯えていたから) keeper(s): 飼育係。about: あたりに。There was no one about. (あたりにはだれもいなかった。『コンパスローズ英和辞典』)
❸ hail(ed): 〜を呼び止める
❹ the dress I was to wear: 着ることになっているドレス。dress は第4巻 p. 110, ll. 4-5 の "I am wearing a checkeredlike blue-and-green cotton dress" (私はチェックっぽい青と緑の綿のワンピースを着ている) について述

「いいわ」と彼女はきっぱり言った。

　まだ朝も早く、あたりには飼育係もそんなにいなかった。あたしはすばやく檻を開けて、二人でまたくまに街へ出た。タクシーを拾って家に帰ると、まだみんな眠っていた。あたしは自分の部屋に入って、その晩着ることになっているドレスを取り出した。ドレスは少し長めだったし、ハイヒールもハイエナには歩きづらそうだった。手が毛深すぎてあたしの手には見えないので、手袋を出してやった。陽が部屋に差してくるころには、まあ一応まっすぐ立って、部屋のなかを何度か歩きまわれるようになっていた。二人とも熱中していたせいで、ママがお早ようを言いにきたときも、ハイエナがあわててベッドの下に隠れる前にドアを開けられてしまうところだった。

「この部屋、何だか臭うわねえ」とママが窓を開けながら言った。「舞踏会の前に、香り風呂に入らなくちゃ駄目よ、ママがこないだ買ってきたバスソルトを使ってね」

「はあい」とあたしは言った。

べたように、ほとんどの場合「ワンピース」と訳すのが自然だが、ここは何しろデビュタントなので「ドレス」。
❺ found it difficult to ...:（やってみたら）〜するのに苦労した
❻ make her way around the room: make one's way は「進む」の意だが、それが難儀だという含み。
❼ more or less: おおむね
❽ upright: 真っすぐに立って
❾ scented: 香りをつけた

She didn't stay long. I think the smell was too much for her.

"Don't be late for breakfast," she said and left the room.

The greatest difficulty was to find a way of ❶disguising the hyena's face. We spent hours and hours looking for a way, but 5 she always ❷rejected my suggestions. At last she said, "I think I've found the answer. Have you got a maid?"

"Yes," I said, ❸puzzled.

"❹There you are then. ❺Ring for your maid, and when she comes in we'll ❻pounce upon her and ❼tear off her face. I'll wear 10 her face tonight instead of mine."

"It's not ❽practical," I said. "She'll probably die if she hasn't got a face. Somebody will certainly find ❾the corpse, and we'll be put in prison."

"I'm hungry enough to eat her," the hyena replied.

15 "And the bones?"

"As well," she said. "So, ❿it's on?"

---

❶ disguising >disguise: p. 102, l. 12 に "If you disguise yourself, nobody will notice you in the crowd."（変装していけば、人込みにまぎれて誰も気づかないわ）の形で既出。

❷ rejected my suggestions: 私の提案を拒否した

❸ puzzled: とまどって

❹ There you are then: ならそれよ、それで決まりよ。*You just plug it in, push this button, and there you are.*（プラグを入れて、ボタンを押せば OK。*Merriam-Webster Dictionary*）

❺ Ring for your maid: ベルを鳴らしてメイドを呼ぶ。ring for ... は send for ...（～を呼びに人を送り出す）と同じ発想。

❻ pounce upon her: 彼女に飛びかかる

❼ tear off ...: ～を引きはがす

　ママはそそくさと出ていった。臭いに耐えられなかったのだろう。

「朝ご飯に遅れないようにね」とママは立ち去りぎわに言った。

　いちばん厄介だったのは、ハイエナの顔をごまかす手段を考え出すことだった。何時間も二人でさんざん知恵を絞ったけれど、彼女はいつも決まって、私の案を却下するのだった。やがてとうとう、彼女が言った。「わかった、これよ。ねえ、あんた、メイドはいる？」

「うん、いるけど」とあたしはとまどって答えた。

「なら決まりよ。ベルを鳴らしてメイドを呼んでよ。入ってきたら、襲いかかって顔をはぎ取るの。今夜はその顔をつけていくわ」

「駄目よ、そんなの。顔なんか取られたら死んじゃうじゃない。きっと誰かに死体を見つかって、あたしたち牢屋行きだよ」

「あたしお腹すいてるから、まるごと食べちゃえるよ」

「骨は？」

「骨もよ」と彼女は言った。「じゃ、決まり？」

❽ practical: 現実的な、実際的な

❾ the corpse: 死体

❿ it's on: be on で「行なわれる、行なわれる予定である」。*The union says the strike is still definitely on.*（ストライキは必ず決行すると組合は述べている。『ロングマン英和辞典』）

"❶Only if you promise to kill her before tearing off her face. It'll hurt her too much otherwise."

"All right. It's all the same to me."

❷Not without a certain amount of nervousness I rang for Mary,
5 my maid. I certainly wouldn't have done it if I didn't hate having to go to a ball so much. When Mary came in I turned to the wall so as not to see. ❸I must admit it didn't take long. A brief cry, and it was over. While the hyena was eating, I looked out the window. A few minutes later she said, "I can't eat any more. Her two feet ❹are
10 left over still, but if you have a little bag, I'll eat them later in the day."

"You'll find a bag ❺embroidered with ❻fleurs-de-lis in the ❼cupboard. ❽Empty out the handkerchiefs you'll find inside, and take it." She did as I suggested. Then she said, "Turn round now
15 and look how beautiful I am."

In front of the mirror, the hyena was ❾admiring herself in

---

❶ Only if: 〜しさえするなら

❷ Not without a certain amount of nervousness: 一定量の不安なしではなく＝それなりに不安な思いで

❸ I must admit ...: 〜と認めねばならない＝まあたしかに〜だ

❹ are left over still: まだ残っている。leftovers といえば「食べ残し」。

❺ embroidered with ...: 〜を刺繍した

❻ fleur(s)-de-lis: 百合紋章。フランス王室の紋章。文字どおりには flower(s) of lily。

❼ cupboard: 食器棚。p. 84, l. 13 に "That cupboard, he said. Anything edible in there, Johnny?"（そこの食器棚。中に何か食べられるものはあるかね、ジョニー？）の形で既出。

❽ Empty out ...: 〜を全部出す

「顔をはぐ前に殺すって約束してくれたらね。じゃなきゃいくらなんでも、痛すぎるもの」

「いいよ。あたしにはどっちでも同じだよ」

　かなり不安な気持ちで、あたしはメイドのメアリを呼んだ。舞踏会に行くのが嫌で嫌で仕方なくなかったら、絶対そんなことしなかったと思う。メアリが入ってくると、あたしは見ないように壁の方を向いた。たしかに、大して時間はかからなかった。短い叫び声が上がって、それでおしまい。ハイエナが食べているあいだ、あたしは窓の外を見ていた。二、三分して彼女は言った。「もう食べられない。まだ両足が残ってるの。小さい袋か何かあったら、入れといてあとで食べるんだけど」

「そこの戸棚に、百合の紋の刺繍をしたバッグがある。なかのハンカチを空けて使ってちょうだい」。ハイエナは言われたとおりにした。それから彼女は言った。「さ、こっちを向いて。見てよ、あたしきれいになったでしょ」

　鏡の前でハイエナは、メアリの顔をつけた自分の姿にうっとり見とれてい

❾ admiring <admire: ～に見とれる。なぜか辞書にはまず「賞賛する」という訳語が出てくるが、この語が当てはまることはあまりない。基本的には何かを・誰かを素晴らしいと思う、ということ。

Mary's face. She had ❶nibbled very ❷neatly all around the face so that what was left was exactly what was needed.

"You've certainly done that very well," I said.

Towards evening, when the hyena was all dressed up, she
5 declared, "I really feel ❸in tip-top form. I have a feeling that I shall be a great success this evening."

When we had heard the music from downstairs for quite some time, I said to her, "Go on down now, and remember, don't stand next to my mother. ❹She's bound to realise that it isn't me. ❺Apart
10 from her I don't know anybody. ❻Best of luck." I kissed her ❼as I left her, but she did smell very strong.

Night fell. Tired by the day's emotions, I took a book and sat down by the open window, ❽giving myself up to peace and quiet. I remember that I was reading *Gulliver's Travels* by Jonathan Swift.
15 About an hour later, I noticed the first signs of trouble. ❾A bat flew in at the window, ❿uttering little cries. I am terribly afraid of bats. I

---

❶ nibble(d): ちびちびかじる
❷ neatly: きちんと、小綺麗に
❸ in tip-top form: tip-top は「最高の」。form はこの場合「形」ではなく「状態、コンディション」。shape でも同じような意味になる。*in tip-top condition [shape]*（申し分のない状態で。『コンパスローズ英和辞典』）
❹ She's bound to ...: 彼女はきっと～するはずだ
❺ Apart from ...: ～は別として、～を除いて
❻ Best of luck: Good luck とほぼ同じ。
❼ as I left her: 彼女を置いて出ていくときに
❽ giving myself up to ...: give oneself up to ... で「～に身を委ねる」。
❾ A bat: コウモリ
❿ utter(ing): ～を発する

た。顔のまわりをすごくていねいにかじり取ってあって、ちょうど必要な分だけきれいに残っていた。

「うまくやったねえ、ほんとに」とあたしは言った。

　夜も近くなって、すっかり着飾ったハイエナはこう言い放った。「もう最高の気分。あたし、今夜はぜったい大受けだと思う」

　一階から音楽が聞こえてきてしばらく経ったところで、あたしはハイエナに言った。「さあ、もう行きなさい。忘れないでね、ママのそばに行っちゃ駄目よ。あたしじゃないってわかっちゃうからね。ママ以外には知ってる人は一人もいないから大丈夫。じゃがんばって」。あたしは部屋を出ていく彼女にキスをしたが、たしかに臭いはきつかった。

　日が暮れた。昼間すっかり興奮したせいで疲れてしまって、あたしは本を手にとり、開いた窓の前に座って、のんびり静かにくつろいだ。たしかジョナサン・スウィフトの『ガリバー旅行記』を読んでいたと思う。一時間くらい経って、トラブルの最初の兆候が現われた。一羽のコウモリが、キイキイ叫びながら窓から飛び込んできたのだ。あたしはコウモリが大の苦手だ。歯

hid behind a chair, my teeth ❶chattering. ❷I had hardly gone down on my knees when the sound of ❸beating wings ❹was overcome by a great noise at my door. My mother entered, ❺pale with rage.

"We'd just sat down at table," she said, "when that thing sitting
5 in your place got up and shouted, 'So I smell a bit strong, what? Well, I don't eat cakes!' ❻Whereupon it tore off its face and ate it. And with one great ❼bound, disappeared through the window."

❶ chatter(ing): (寒さや恐怖で歯が) かたかた鳴る
❷ I had hardly gone down on my knees when ...: A had hardly done B when C did D で「AがBするかしないうちにCがD した」。
❸ beat(ing): (羽が) ばたばた動く
❹ was overcome by ...: 〜に圧倒された
❺ pale with rage: 激しい怒りに顔が白くなって
❻ Whereupon: そのすぐあとで
❼ bound: 跳躍

をがたがた震わせながら、椅子の陰に隠れた。床に膝をつく間もなく、ばたばた羽根の鳴る音に代わって、ドアの方から騒々しい物音が聞こえてきた。あたしのママが、青筋を立てて入ってきた。

「みんなでテーブルについたと思ったら」とママは言った。「あなたの席に座ったあれが立ち上がってどなったのよ、『ふん、ちょっとくらい臭うからどうだってんだよ？　こっちはね、毎日ケーキ食べてんじゃないんだからね！』そう言って自分の顔をむしり取って、食べちゃったのよ。そうしてぴょんと大きく一跳びして、窓から出ていっちゃったわ」

●

ちなみに

　裕福な家庭に生まれ、イングランドのランカシャーの大邸宅で育ったキャリントンは、幼いころから反抗的な性格で、二つの学校で放校処分になっているが、デビュタントの年齢に達したときは宮廷でしかるべくお目見えし、新聞にも記事が載った。ドレスを着た美しい姿の写真が残っている。

Casual Labour

Ken Smith

イモ掘りの日々

ケン・スミス

難易度 3
★ ★ ★

ケン・スミス
(Ken Smith, 1938-2003)

　イギリスの詩人。農場労働者の息子として各地を転々として子供時代を過ごす。20世紀末にイギリス詩の状況を大きく変えた詩専門出版社 Bloodaxe Books から多くの詩集を刊行。ここに収めた 'Casual Labour' は、1987年刊の散文詩集 *A Book of Chinese Whispers* から。

❶ Ancient history

❷ Before the potato, men ❸ scratched the earth with sticks or
❹ crouched under rocks waiting for the weather to improve.
5 But ❺ the introduction of the potato changed history ❻ when Lord
Rally came over the ocean. Since then, thousands of years ago,
our people have picked potatoes on ❼ the estates of Lord Clifton.
We have known nothing else, ❽ nor wish to, for we are pickers
❾ first and last. Five days a week, all year around, ❿ for a full five
10 shillings, there are potatoes to pick ⓫ from sea to shining sea.

⓬ The preface

⓭ In an eight hour day a good picker can fill 100 paper sacks with
potatoes, each sack containing 56 ⓮ lbs. I prefer to work with two
15 baskets, myself. It ⓯ saves walking, and two good baskets fill a sack.
I've found the quickest method is to ⓰ work two rows together,

---

Casual Labour: 臨時雇い、日雇い労働

❶ **Ancient**: 古代の

❷ Before the potato: 'before the Flood'（ノアの洪水以前＝大昔）や 'before the Fall'（アダムとイブの堕落以前）を連想させる聖書的な書き出し。

❸ scratch(ed): 〜を引っかく

❹ crouch(ed): うずくまる

❺ the introduction of the potato: ジャガイモの導入

❻ when Lord Rally came over the ocean: ジャガイモは南米原産で 15 〜 16 世紀にヨーロッパ大陸に伝えられたが、長いあいだ、伝えたのは探検家の Walter Raleigh /rɔ́:li/（1554?–1618）だとされてきた。現在ではこの説は否定されているが、ここで Rally はあきらかに Raleigh を踏まえている。

❼ the estates: 地所

❽ nor wish to: know anything else が省かれている。

❾ first and last: 何にも増して、徹頭徹尾

古代史

　ジャガイモ以前、人間は地面を棒で引っかいたり、もしくは天気がよくなるのを待って岩の下にしゃがみ込んだりしていた。だがラリー卿が海の向こうからジャガイモを導入したことで、歴史は変わった。それ以来何千年にわたって、われらが人民はクリフトン卿の地所でイモを掘ってきた。イモ以外何ひとつ我々は知らずにきたし、知りたいとも思わない。我々は根っから、骨の髄までイモ掘り人なのだ。週五日、一年じゅう、日々5シリングの給料で、輝ける海原から海原まで、掘るべきジャガイモがどこまでも広がっている。

序文

　一日8時間働けば、すぐれたイモ掘り人は、一袋25キロ入る紙袋を100袋、イモで一杯にすることができる。私自身は二つの籠を使って仕事をすることを好む。歩く手間が減らせるし、いい籠なら、二籠で一袋分入る。もっとも速い方法は、二列一度に作業を進める方法であることを経験から学んだ。脚

⑩ for a full five shillings: たっぷり5シリングで。shilling は1971年まで用いられた英国の通貨単位で、1ポンドの20分の1。

⑪ from sea to shining sea: アメリカの愛国歌 'America the Beautiful' の中で「太平洋から大西洋まで」の意味で用いられているフレーズ。このフレーズにせよ l. 8 の first and last にせよ陳腐な決まり文句であり、この一節のパロディ的性格を強めている。

⑫ **The preface**: 序文

⑬ In an eight hour day: 8時間（労働）の1日に。an eight-hour day と書く方が普通。

⑭ lb(s): pound(s). 1ポンドは約0.45kg。

⑮ save(s): ～が省ける

⑯ work two rows together: 同時に二列作業する。この work は文法的にいえば他動詞で、「～を耕作する」。

❶standing legs apart between them, filling each basket **❷**on either side of my feet. I **❸**pick from the furthest inwards, and use the gloves **❹**to protect my hands and give myself a bigger grasp. If **❺**by chance I pick stones instead of potatoes I **❻**chuck them in too. My one rule is: *if I pick it up it's a potato.* As I work I search for the golden potato, for it is said that **❼**through these fields Lord Clifton has **❽**distributed so many golden potatoes that **❾**entitle the finders to special privileges. But for myself, I am beginning to doubt the existence of golden potatoes. I am beginning to **❿**suspect a trick.

⓫Genesis

⓬First darkness, then light. **⓭**It rained for forty nights and days, but **⓮**the lads went on picking **⓯**just the same. **⓰**Lord Rally built a

---

❶ standing legs apart: 脚を離して（開いて）立ち

❷ on either side of my feet: この場合 either は「どちらかの」ではなく「どちらの〜も」。第2巻 p. 218, ll. 1-3 に 'Emmanuel waited for the two men sitting on either side of him to open their doors.'（イマニュエルは左右に座った男がそれぞれドアを開けるのを待った）の形で既出。

❸ pick from the furthest inwards: 一番遠いところ（the furthest）から始めて内側に（inwards）掘っていく

❹ to [...] give myself a bigger grasp: もっとたくさん摑めるよう

❺ by chance: 偶然に

❻ chuck them in: それらを投げ込む

❼ through these fields: これらの畑一帯に

❽ distribute(d): 〜を分配する

❾ entitle the finders to special privileges: 見つけた者に特別な特権を授ける

❿ suspect a trick: ペテンがあるのではないかと疑う。*suspect danger* [*a plot*]（危険〔陰謀の恐れ〕があると思う。『研究社 新英和中辞典』）

⓫ Genesis: 通例はむろん、旧約聖書の第一書『創世記』を指す。

⓬ First darkness, then light: 「本家」の創世記では、'In the beginning God

を広げて、二列の中間に立ち、左右一籠ずつ満たしていくのだ。いちばん奥から掘りはじめ、手を護るために、また、いっそう多量につかめるよう、手袋をはめる。もしたまたまイモではなく石を掘ってしまったら、それも同じように籠に放り込む。私の唯一のルールは——私が掘ればそれはイモなのだ。仕事をしながら私は黄金のイモを探し求める。というのも、これらの畑のあちこちにクリフトン卿は黄金のイモを植えたと言われているからだ。それを見つけた者は大きな特権を与えられる。しかし私自身は、黄金のイモの実在を疑いはじめている。これはわなではないか、と疑いはじめている。

創世記

　はじめに闇、それから光。40昼夜にわたって雨が降ったが、連中はそれでも掘りつづけた。ラリー卿は小さな舟を造って洪水を旅し、ポテト・マザー

created the heaven and the earth. / And the earth was without form, and void; and darkness was upon the face of the deep. And the Spirit of God moved upon the face of the waters. / And God said, Let there be light: and there was light.'（元始に神天地を創造たまへり　／地は定形なく曠空くして黒暗淵の面にあり神の靈水の面を覆たりき／神光あれと言たまひければ光ありき。英訳は King James Version、和訳は日本聖書協会文語訳）となっている。

⓭ It rained for forty nights and days: 創世記第7章で、堕落した人間を滅ぼそうと神が40日昼夜雨を降らせたことを踏まえている。

⓮ the lads went on ...: 聖書的なトーンから the lads（the boys とだいたい同じ）というイギリス口語に変わるのは大きな落差。

⓯ just the same: それでも

⓰ Lord Rally built a little boat to sail upon the flood [...] the dove came back with a tuber in its mouth: 創世記第8章でノアが方舟をつくって洪水を生き延び、水が引いたかどうかを確認するために放った鳩がオリーブの葉をくわえて戻ってきたことに基づく。tuber: ジャガイモなどの「塊茎」。

little boat to sail upon the flood, and came to the shores of Potato
Mother's Land. Lord Rally sent out a dove, the dove came back
with a tuber in its mouth, and from the tuber sprang the potato
plant. Lord Rally ❶ rolled up some of its leaves, and ❷ from this
5 came tobacco. He ❸ picked off some of the fruits and ate them.
❹From this came the tomato. Last he came to the roots, and found
there the potatoes, which he boiled and ate. Then Lord Rally had ❺a
vision, or — as some call it — ❻a mystical experience, or as he says
in *Lord Rally's* ❼*Logbook,* he experienced '❽a state of non-ordinary
10 reality. ❾ Terrific!' Lord Rally returned to ❿ Yetterton in Devon to
find the flood had gone and there he planted, ⓫in these very fields
we pick my brothers, ⓬the original potato plant from whose issue
this our harvest springs. That's how we got the potato, children.
And that's why, every year in spring on the anniversary of Lord
15 Rally's return, Lord Clifton walks to the centre of his estates and

❶ rolled up some of its leaves: 葉を何枚か巻いた

❷ from this came tobacco: Tobacco came from this.

❸ picked off: もぎ取った

❹ From this came the tomato: ジャガイモもトマトも南米原産でありどちらも
ナス科なので、ここでトマトが登場するのは十分理由があるが、それに加えて、
tobacco, potato との音のつながりもある。

❺ a vision: 第 2 巻に収めた Rebecca Brown, 'A Vision' という作品全体が体現
していたように、vision はそこにはないけれど「見えるもの」「見えてくるもの」
すべてを指しうるが、ここのように、何か宗教的・超自然的な「啓示」の意味
で使われることも多い（特にここのように 'have/had a vision' という使い方
の場合は）。

❻ a mystical experience: 神秘的な経験

❼ *Logbook*: 航海日誌、業務日誌

❽ a state: 状態

❾ Terrific: サイコー。第 2 巻の Paul Bowles, 'You Are Not I' (1948) では p.

の国の岸辺にたどり着いた。そして一羽の鳩を送り出し、鳩は口に塊茎をくわえて帰ってきて、その塊茎からジャガイモの茎と葉が生えた。ラリー卿はその葉を何枚か巻いて、そこからタバコが生まれた。さらに卿は実をいくつか摘みとって、食べた。そこからトマトが生まれた。最後に卿は根を掘り出し、そこにイモを見出して、茹でて、食べた。やがてラリー卿は啓示を、もしくは人によっては神秘体験と呼ぶものを、『ラリー卿の業務日誌』で卿自身言うところの「非日常的現実状態。ヤバいぜ！」を経験した。ラリー卿がデヴォン州イェタトンに戻ると洪水はすでに引いていて、卿はそこの、まさに今日我々が、兄弟よ、掘る畑に、始源のジャガイモ苗を植えた。そのひとつのイモから、今日の我々の収穫が発しているのである。子供たちよ、このようにして私たちはジャガイモを得たのだ。それゆえ毎年春、ラリー卿の帰還を記念する日に、クリフトン卿は地所の中心まで歩いていって、そこから

58, ll. 8-9 に 'she was putting up a terrific struggle'（姉はすさまじい勢いで抵抗していた）と「すさまじい」「恐ろしい」の意味で出てきたが、現代ではもっぱらこのように very good の意。

❿ Yetterton in Devon: イェタトンはおそらく（少なくともデヴォンでは）架空の地名、デヴォンはイングランド南西部の州。

⓫ in these very fields we pick my brothers: この my brothers は l. 13 の That's how we got the potato, children の children と同じく、センテンスの中に挿入された呼びかけ。

⓬ the original potato plant from whose issue this our harvest springs: the original potato plant / from whose issue / this our harvest / springs と切って考える。plant は「苗」、issue は「子孫」、this our harvest は古風な言い方で現代なら this harvest of ours。「原初のジャガイモ苗／その子孫から／この私たちの収穫が／生まれ出ている」。

there **❶**releases a white dove.

Potato olympics

❷Early morning hangover handicap. Missing the bus and trying
5 to catch up. **❸**Three-legged picking. **❹**Putt the basket. **❺**Tossing
❻the King Edward. **❼**Fighting thistles. **❽**Hurling spuds about.
Stopping others work. **❾**Sore Knee **❿**Shuffle, 300 metres. **⓫**Work
till you drop. Filling someone else's bag by mistake. Picking blind.
⓬Staggering home. Forgetting how many bags you've picked.
10 Sitting in the trailer. Waiting for **⓭** the foreman. **⓮**Spending it as
quickly as you can.

⓯The commentary

⓰Well Roger this is an interesting field we have here and we have
15 seen some very fine picking till now but **⓱**as to who will come out
with most bags this week well it is **⓲** piece-work and **⓳**just about

---

❶ release(s): 〜を解き放つ

❷ Early morning hangover handicap ...: 以下、イモ掘りの日常をオリンピック競技になぞらえている。hangover: 二日酔い。handicap: ハンディキャップ付きのレース

❸ Three-legged picking: three-legged はしばしば卑猥な意味を帯びる。「勃起掘り」？

❹ Putt the basket: putt はゴルフで、軽打してボールを転がすこと。

❺ Toss(ing): 〜を軽く投げる

❻ the King Edward: イギリス産のジャガイモの品種。

❼ Fighting thistles: アザミにはトゲがあり、繁殖力も強いことから、農作業や園芸では歓迎されない。

❽ Hurling spuds about: hurl は日本語の「放る」よりも強い投げ方。spud(s) はジャガイモを意味する口語。

❾ Sore: (傷、炎症などで) 痛む、ひりひりする

一羽の白い鳩を放つのである。

ポテト・オリンピック

　早朝二日酔いハンディキャップ・レース。バス乗り遅れ追いかけ競争。三つ足掘り。籠パット。キングエドワード・トス。アザミ障害走。ポテト投げ。仕事妨害戦。すりむけ膝シャッフル、三〇〇メートル。死ぬまで働こうレース。他人の袋に間違えて入れちゃった競争。目隠し掘り。よたよた帰還。何袋分掘ったか忘れて。トレーラーで座って。職長を待って。宵越しの金は持たねえレース。

実況中継

　なあロジャーこいつぁけっこう面白い畑だぜこれまでだってずいぶん見事なイモ掘り俺たち見てきたけど今週は誰の袋がいちばん多いかなうーんそうだな何しろ出来高払いだから何が起きたって不思議はないんだけどでもさロ

---

❿ Shuffle: 本来は足をひきずって歩くことだが、すり足で踊るダンスの名でもある。Duke Ellington, 'Showboat Shuffle' や Bruce Springsteen, 'The E Street Shuffle' など、曲名にもよくなっている。

⓫ Work till you drop: 「ぶっ倒れるまで働く＝精いっぱい頑張る」の意の成句。

⓬ Stagger(ing): よろめく、千鳥足で歩く

⓭ the foreman: （労働者の）監督

⓮ Spending it as quickly as you can: it は給料。

⓯ The commentary: commentary には「実況放送」の意もある。

⓰ Well Roger this is an interesting field we have here: ここでひとまず意味が切れる。

⓱ as to who will come out with most bags this week: ここでまた切れる。as to は「〜に関しては」。

⓲ piece-work: 出来高払いの仕事

⓳ just about: nearly, almost

anything could happen but Roger **❶**if you ask me **❷**Stagehand has **❸**the showing. **❹**He's pretty well placed there on the outside by **❺**the hedge, **❻** the slope is with him, **❼**he's sheltered from the drizzle, and **❽**there's the double planting of the headland in his favour. As

5 you know he's been pacing himself well the last couple of weeks, he's **❾** at the top of his form and he has **❿** the will to **⓫** come out ahead. **⓬**Mind you Roger if you'd asked me a couple of days ago **⓭**I would have tipped Dancer. **⓮**He's big that lad and very strong and those long arms of his give him a tremendous reach, and he does

10 have the advantage of **⓯** years of ballet training **⓰** that equip him very well now for the potato picking. As he himself said the other day **⓱** *there's nae tae mony vacancies fra mael dauncers in Glasgae.* But he's been slowing down, and I suspect the amount of beer he's

---

❶ if you ask me: 私の考えでは、言わせてもらえば。*"He is too pushy, if you ask me." "Oh, you think so too?"*（「私としては、彼は強引すぎると思います」「ああ。あなたもそう思いますか」『コンパスローズ英和辞典』）

❷ Stagehand: 舞台係、裏方

❸ the showing: 勝機、有望さ

❹ He's pretty well placed: かなりいい位置にいる。具体的にどういう位置にいるかがこのあと語られる。

❺ the hedge: 生垣、垣根

❻ the slope is with him: 坂（の傾斜）が彼に味方している

❼ he's sheltered from the drizzle: 小雨から保護されている

❽ there's the double planting of the headland in his favour: 枕地（the headland）の二本植え（the double planting）も彼の有利に働いている。枕地は本来、畝の端のトラクターなどが旋回するためのスペースで、the double planting は一か所に二つの種や苗を植えること。それがどう有利に働くのかは不明。

❾ at the top of his form: 絶好調である

124

ジャー俺に言わせてもらえば〈舞台係〉がいっとう有望だと思うね。外っ側の垣根のそばで場所もいいし坂の傾き具合も有利だし小雨からも護られて枕地（まくらち）の二本植えでも得してる。ほらあいつこの二週間ばかりいい具合に飛ばして目下絶好調やる気まんまんって感じだろ。でもさロジャーもし二日ばかり前に訊かれてたら俺きっと〈ダンサー〉推してたね。なかなかの大男でさすごく頑丈で腕が長くてリーチは抜群だし何年もバレエで鍛えてたのがイモ掘りにもすごく役立ってるんだよな。こないだ自分でも言ってたけどグラスゴーじゃ男のダンスの仕事なんてそうめったにありゃしない。ところが〈ダンサー〉の奴ここんとこペースが落ちてきてて俺が睨むところたぶんシドマスでビール飲みすぎてんじゃないかと思うんだ。さあロジャーみんな畑に出

⓾ the will: やる気

⓫ come out ahead: 勝つ（come out on top）

⓬ Mind you: いいかい君、よく聞いてくれ

⓭ I would have tipped Dancer: ダンサーを有力候補に挙げただろう。tip(ped): （人、作品、馬を勝者・有力候補などに）挙げる。*She is widely tipped as Mr. Lee's successor* [*to succeed Mr. Lee*].（彼女はリー氏の後継者と広く目されている。『コンパスローズ英和辞典』）

⓮ He's big that lad: *'He's a good man, John.'*（いい奴だよ、ジョンは）と同じように、that lad は He を言い換えている。

⓯ years of ballet training: 何年もバレエの研鑽を積んだこと

⓰ that equip him very well now for ...: equip A for B で「A が B をする能力を与える」。*training that will equip you for the job*（その仕事に必要なスキルを学べるトレーニング。*Longman Dictionary of Contemporary English*）

⓱ *there's nae tae mony vacancies fra mael dauncers in Glasgae*: グラスゴー訛りを模している。標準的な英語に直すと 'there're not too many vacancies for male dancers in Glasgow.' vacancies: 空き、勤め口

been ❶putting away in ❷Sidmouth. Well Roger ❸they're off and ❹as they go into the curve it's Stagehand then Dancer. Dancer's ❺morale seems to be ❻slipping already as he pauses to spit and ❼curse ❽the paper sack that's just split on him. Then it's Zen Buddhist, picking

5 very well today, followed by ❾Androgyny and the ❿Macrobiotic Twins. Then Poet. Then Irishman. Then comes Actor, who'll probably ⓫knock off at lunch to ⓬go collect his social security again, ⓭then comes the pack hanging about by the trailer, and lastly ⓮off to a late start ⓯The Bloke With The Black Dog. ⓰It's still

10 Stagehand's field, but there's a long day ahead of us and anything could happen yet. ⓱The unknown, The Bloke With The Black Dog, picks like ⓲a maniac ⓳at times. ⓴Just between the two of us Roger he's a very ㉑dirty picker and only takes the big ones but ㉒there we

❶ put(ting) away:（大量の飲食物を）平らげる

❷ Sidmouth: デヴォン州の、英国海峡に面したリゾート地。

❸ they're off: 彼らがスタートしたぞ

❹ as they go into the curve: 競馬中継を模している。

❺ morale: 士気

❻ slip(ping): 低下する、衰える

❼ curse: 〜を罵る

❽ the paper sack that's just split on him: たったいま（忌々しくも）破れた。on ... は「〜の不利になるように」の意。*The canary died on me this morning.*（《飼っていた》カナリヤにけさ死なれた。『リーダーズ英和辞典』）*It rained on us.*（雨に降られ〔て困っ〕た。『コンパスローズ英和辞典』）

❾ Androgyny: 普通名詞としての意味は「両性具有」。

❿ Macrobiotic: 日本ではマクロビオティックと発音されるが、英語では通常 /mæ̀kroʊbaɪɑ́tɪk /。

⓫ knock off:（仕事を）切り上げる

⓬ go collect his social security again: collect はこのように集金・支払い受け取りなどの意味で使われる。social security: 生活保護手当

⓭ then comes the pack hanging about by the trailer: come はこのように、

ていくぜまずカーブに入ってくのが〈舞台係〉で次が〈ダンサー〉だ。〈ダンサー〉ときたら何だかもうやる気なくしちまってるみたいな立ちどまっててツバ吐いたり紙袋が破けて悪態ついたりしてら。お次は〈禅僧〉だ今日は快調な掘り具合だなそれから〈両性具有〉と〈マクロバイオティック双子〉。それから〈詩人〉。それから〈アイルランド人〉。その次が〈役者〉こいつはきっと昼メシどきに抜け出して失業保険もらいに行くねそれからトレーラーのあたりにうろうろしてる連中が来てしんがりの出遅れスタートは〈黒い犬を連れた男〉だ。まだまだ〈舞台係〉有利だけどとにかくまる一日あるわけだし何が起きたって不思議ないよな。〈黒い犬を連れた男〉ありゃ大穴だぜときどき狂ったみたいに掘るんだ。ここだけの話だけどなロジャーあいつ掘り方はけっこうセコくてさでっかいやつしか掘らないんだでもまあしょうが

Here comes ..., Now comes ..., Along comes ... といった形でよく使われる。the pack: 徒党、群れ。hang(ing) about by ...: 〜あたりにたむろしている

⓮ off to a late start: 出遅れてスタートして

⓯ The Bloke with the Black Dog: チェーホフの「犬を連れた奥さん」（英題 'The Lady with the Dog'）を思わせる。bloke はいかにもイギリス的な響きの「男」「奴」。

⓰ It's still Stagehand's field: たとえば lead the field といえば「トップに立つ」。

⓱ The unknown: 未知数

⓲ a maniac: 狂人。日本語の「マニアック」とはだいぶ意味が違い、発音も /méɪniæk/。

⓳ at times: sometimes

⓴ Just between the two of us: ここだけの話

㉑ dirty: 卑劣な

㉒ there we are: まあ仕方ない。*Problems which I have been trying to solve for the last four months, without any success; for they are, so far as I can see, insoluble. So there we are. One lives and learns.*（この4か月ずっと解こうとして解けなかった問題。何しろ私が見る限り、解きえない問題なんだ。まあ仕方ない。生きていればいろいろ学ぶこともある。Aldous Huxley1957 年の書簡より。*Oxford English Dictionary* に引用）

are **❶**Nigel, filling sacks is **❷**the name of the game.

Some ❸inventions that failed

As I worked I considered methods of **❹**simplifying the potato

5 picking. **❺**I proposed planting seed in baskets so that collecting the

crop later in the year became **❻**a matter of picking up the baskets and

shaking out the soil. Then, in the laboratory of my skull, I developed

potatoes with **❼**a thin metal strip at one end, so **❽**all the pickers had

to do was walk along the field with powerful magnets. **❾**All this of

10 course done **❿**without the knowledge of Lord Clifton or the foreman

or the tractor driver, who though he wears earmuffs isn't blind.

⓫ My mate, Duncan, wondered might it not be possible to develop

a potato with a small pocket under its **⓬**jacket like **⓭**the air space in

an egg. Within the space the potato would **⓮**accumulate hydrogen

15 to lift itself out of the ground **⓯**when ripe, **⓰**hovering there waiting

---

❶ Nigel: 最後でなぜか聞き手の名前が Roger から Nigel に。

❷ the name of the game:「肝腎の点、主たる目的」という意味で広く使われるが、ここではもっと文字どおりに「まさにそういう名前のゲームをやっているんだから」という含み。

❸ invention(s): 創意

❹ simplify(ing): 〜を簡単にする

❺ I proposed planting seed in baskets so that ...: 本シリーズで頻出しているとおり、so that ... can/may ... で「〜が〜するように」の意になるフレーズだが、ここではやや変則に動詞部分が became で、can や may が使われていない。いずれにせよ、全体の意味としては、「so that 以下の事態が生じるよう」「種を籠の中に蒔くことを提案した」。

❻ a matter of ...: 〜の問題。*It's simply a matter of telling him to do it.*（それはただ彼にそうしろと言えばすむ事だ。『コンパスローズ英和辞典』）

❼ a thin metal strip: 薄い金属片

ないよなナイジェルこれって要するに袋を一杯にする競争だもんな。

挫折に終わった革新

　仕事をしながら、イモ掘りを単純化する方法を私はあれこれ考えた。種イモを植えるときに籠に入れて植え、収穫時には籠を持ち上げて土をふるい落とすだけでいいようにするのはどうだろう。それから私は、頭蓋骨の実験室のなかで、一方の端に薄い金属片がついたイモを開発した。これなら掘り手は、強力磁石を使って畑を歩くだけでいい。もちろんそれはクリフトン卿や職長やトラクター運転手には内緒でやらなくちゃいけない、運転手だってイヤマフはしてるけど目は見えてるわけだから。仲間のダンカンが考えたのは、皮の内側に小さなポケットのついたイモを開発できないか、という案だった。卵のなかのエアスペースみたいにイモがそこに水素をため込んで、熟したら自然に地面から浮かび上がり、籠に入れられるのを待ってふわふわ漂ってるってわけだ。私たちは休憩時間を利用して可能性調査の実施をしばし検討

❽ all the pickers had to do was: all A has to do is … で「A がやらなければならないことは〜だけだ＝ A は〜しさえすればいい」。

❾ All this … done: All this … would have to be done

❿ without the knowledge of …: 〜には知られずに

⓫ My mate, Duncan, wondered might it not be possible …: May/Might it not be possible … という直接話法を時制だけ間接話法的に書いている。My mate, Duncan, wondered if it might not be possible … と書くよりだいぶくだけた感じ。

⓬ jacket: イモの皮

⓭ the air space in an egg: 卵の中の気室

⓮ accumulate hydrogen: 水素を蓄積する

⓯ when ripe: 熟したら

⓰ hover(ing): （宙に）漂う

to ❶be basketed. We considered briefly ❷a feasibility study during ❸a smoke break, hired a market research team and ❹computer time and ❺canvassed investment in the project ❻before stooping to pick another ❼umpteen sacks. At lunch, eating ❽marrow jam
5 sandwiches in the trailer, ❾I proposed to the Great Potato Mother Convention in Minneapolis ❿a scheme for the self-picking potato, the SPP. ⓫The SPP grew little arms and legs. When ready, all Lord Clifton need do would be to walk through the fields playing ⓬Rose of Tralee on ⓭a little pipe, and all the potatoes would ⓮climb out of
10 the ground and into the paper sacks, shaking themselves clean ⓯as they did so. And might they not peel themselves too? ⓰Aye, they might, Duncan ⓱affirmed, his mouth full of sandwich, ⓲his thermos

---

❶ be basketed: 籠に入れられる

❷ a feasibility study: 実行可能性調査。新規事業などが実現可能かを事前に調査・検証すること。

❸ a smoke break: たばこ休憩

❹ computer time: 大型コンピュータをリースして、一定期間利用できる権利

❺ canvassed investment in the project: このプロジェクトへの投資を募った

❻ before stooping to ...: A did B before doing C というパターンは「A は C をする前に B をした」よりも、語順どおりに「A は B をして（したが）やがて C をした」と訳す方が妥当なことが多く、ここはその典型。stoop(ing): 身をかがめる

❼ umpteen: 無数の

❽ marrow jam: marrow はペポカボチャ、ナタウリ。ショウガを一緒に使って marrow and ginger jam にすることも多い。

❾ I proposed to the Great Potato Mother Convention ...:「提案した」(proposed) はそういう提案の手紙を書いたということか。Convention は同志・同業者などの集い。たとえばアメリカで the Democratic National Convention といえば「民主党全国大会」。

❿ a scheme: 案、アイデア

⓫ The SPP grew little arms and legs: 過去形になっているのは、あくまでこ

し、マーケットリサーチ・チームを雇い大型コンピュータをリースし、この
プロジェクトへの投資を募ったが、やがてまた腰をかがめて無数の袋にイモ
を詰める作業に戻っていった。昼食どきにトレーラーのなかでカボチャジャ
ム・サンドを食べながら、私はミネアポリスで開かれるグレート・ポテト・
マザー大会に向けてセルフ＝ピッキング・ポテト、その名もＳＰＰプランを
提案した。ＳＰＰは小さな腕や脚をみずから生やすジャガイモである。収穫
時が来たら、クリフトン卿はただ、小さな笛で〈トラリーの薔薇〉を吹きな
がら畑を歩くだけでいい。イモたちはみな地面から這い出し、体をゆすって
土を払い落としながら袋に入っていくであろう。ついでに自分で自分の皮も
むくのではないか？　そうだよなありうるよな、と長靴のあいだに魔法瓶を
しっかりはさんだダンカンも口いっぱいにサンドイッチをほおばりながら同

の一節全体が過去形で書かれているためで、セルフ＝ピッキング・ポテトが本
当に腕や脚を生やしたということではない。
❷ Rose of Tralee: 19 世紀アイルランドの歌。The Rose of Tralee と呼ばれた
美貌の女性が題材になっている。べつにジャガイモは出てこない。Tralee はア
イルランド南西部の町で、毎年 The Rose of Tralee International Festival
を開催している。
❸ a [...] pipe: 笛。バグパイプのように笛部分が何本もあれば pipes というので、
ここはもっとシンプルな笛。
❹ climb out of the ground: 土の中から這い出す。climb はこのように、「登る」
ではなく（out や in が次に来て）「這い出る・もぐり込む」の意味でも頻繁に
使われる。第 2 巻 p. 24, ll. 14-15: 'when the people started to climb out
the windows bleeding'（血を流した乗客たちが窓から這い出してくると）
❺ as they did so: そうしながら
❻ Aye:「賛成」の意で広く使われる（p. 8 の "The Eyes Have It" という作品題
名に関する註参照）以外に、特にスコットランドでは日常的に yes と同じよう
に使われる。
❼ affirm(ed): 肯定する
❽ his thermos gripped between his wellies: 魔法瓶（thermos）をゴム長
（wellies）のあいだでしっかり押さえて。wellies は wellington boots の略。

gripped between his wellies. ❶ And where would we be, ❷ tell me that? ❸ Laid off again. Painting railway stations. ❹ Shuttering on the motorway ❺ if there's any motorway left to shutter. ❻ On the Lump, or selling ❼ encyclopaedias. Or ❽ down the dole office
5 answering ❾ daft questions like ❿ who shot the turkey and how many bishops in Spain?

⓫The middle ages

In this period everyone ⓬ worked his own patch. They ate
10 sandwiches even on Sundays. And ⓭ if they spoke at all spoke in grunts and ⓮ had their heads chopped off for even that: '⓯nowt

---

❶ And where would we be: そしたら俺たちはどこにいるのか＝そしたら俺たちはどうなるのか

❷ tell me that?: will/can you tell me that?

❸ Laid off again: lay off は元々は「一時解雇する」の意だったが、今日では要するに「首にする」の意になることも多い。

❹ Shuttering: 型枠工事。鉄筋コンクリートの建造物を建てる際、所定の形状になるように枠を組み立て、コンクリートを流し込んで成型する工事。

❺ if there's any motorway left to shutter: 不景気でそんな型枠工事の仕事だってそんなにないだろうけど、という響き。

❻ On the Lump: the lump はイギリスの建設業界で、日払いで臨時労働者を雇うシステムのこと。*Hostels, digs, caravans, and with half of them on the lump, their bosses don't bother keeping records.* （住みかはホステル、下宿、トレイラー、半分は日払いときては、経営者はいちいち記録なんか取りゃしない。Patrick Ruell, *The Only Game*, 1993, *Collins Online Dictionary* に引用）

❼ encyclopaedia(s): 百科事典

❽ down the dole office: 職業安定所まで行って。前行の On the Lump と同じように、on the dole といえば「失業手当で暮らして」。

❾ daft: silly, stupid

意した。だけどそしたら俺たちどうなる？　またクビだぜ。駅のペンキ塗り
か。高速道路の型枠工事か、でもそもそもそんな工事の残ってるところがま
だあるかどうか。土方仕事か、百科事典のセールスか。職安に行って、七面
鳥を撃ったのは誰か、とかスペインに何人司教がいるか、とかアホな質問に
答えるのかよ。

中世

　この時代は誰もが自分の区画に取り組んだ。人々は日曜日にもサンドイッ
チを食べた。たまに口を開くことがあってもウーとうなるだけで、それだけ

⓾ who shot the turkey and how many bishops in Spain?: 'who shot
the turkey' は 'Bullshit might get you to the top, but it won't keep
you there.' （デタラメで頂点まで行けるかもしれないが、そこにとどまれ
はしない）という教訓で結ばれるジョーク（詳しくは以下を参照: https://
personalexcellence.co/blog/bullshit/ ）への言及ととれなくもないが、要す
るにどちらもいかにも無意味な質問、ということ。

⓫ **The middle ages**: middle age は中年、the middle ages （m は大文字が普
通）は中世。

⓬ worked his own patch: work が他動詞として「〜を耕作する」の意になる
のは、p. 116, l. 15 に 'I've found the quickest method is to work two
rows together'（もっとも速い方法は、二列一度に作業を進める方法であるこ
とを経験から学んだ）の形で既出。(a) patch は耕作した「一区画」の意。

⓭ if they spoke at all spoke in grunts: 少しでも（at all）話すことがあったと
しても、ウーウーうなり声（grunts）を出すだけで

⓮ had their heads chopped off for ...: 〜のせいで首を斬られた（解雇される
という意味ではなく、文字どおりに）

⓯ nowt: /náʊt/ と発音し、nothing に同じ。'used especially in the north of
England' （*Longman Dictionary of Contemporary English*）

but mice, ❶lice and bad advice'. ❷It was like South Africa for three million years. The potatoes were very small, and you heard the continual music of ❸the first three bars of the Harry Lime Theme, over and over. Fortunately things improved. The Ice Age, the Iron
5 Age, the Romans, ❹the Beaker People came and went ❺in swift succession, followed by the signing of ❻the Magna Carta, that put an end to ❼tyrannies so absolute we are ❽forbidden even now to mention them.

10 **The scene that day**

The scene that day was of a sloping field in ❾intermittent sunlight. A dozen or so pickers picked the potatoes up and down the slope, each his own patch. Later a woman came with a boy, ❿finding it difficult to establish her own space. The trailer was moved
15 at midday closer to the pickers. The foreman ⓫drove up in his

---

❶ lice: louse（虱）の複数形。

❷ It was like South Africa for three million years: この作品が収められた *A Book of Chinese Whispers* が刊行されたのは 1987 年で、南アフリカはまだアパルトヘイト（人種隔離政策）が続いていた。アパルトヘイトが撤廃されネルソン・マンデラが大統領に就任するのは 1994 年。

❸ the first three bars of the Harry Lime Theme: 映画『第三の男』のテーマ曲『ハリー・ライムのテーマ』出だしの、アントン・カラスのチターで知られる有名なメロディ。

bar(s) は「小節」。Theme の発音は /θíːm/。

❹ the Beaker People: 氷河時代、鉄器時代、古代ローマ人、と続いたあとジョークが挿入されたかと思えるがそうではない。ただし鐘形土器（beaker）を使用

でも首を斬り落とされた。「鼠、虱(マイス ライス)、悪しき忠告(アドバイス)以外は何もなし」。南アフリカが三百万年つづいた、みたいな。イモはきわめて小さく、『第三の男』のテーマの最初の三小節が何度も何度もくり返し聞こえていた。幸い、事態は好転した。氷河時代、鉄器時代、ローマ人、ビーカー族が矢継ぎ早に訪れては去り、大憲章(マグナ・カルタ)の調印がこれにつづいて、専制は終わりを告げた。かつて存在した、そのあまりに絶対的な圧政は、今日口にすることさえ禁じられている。

その日の情景

　その日の情景は、切れぎれに顔を出す陽光の下、坂になった畑のそれであった。十人あまりの掘り手が坂を上り下りし、それぞれおのれの区画のイモを掘った。やがて一人の女が男の子を一人連れてやって来たものの、自身のスペースを確保するのは困難であった。正午になって、トレーラーがイモ掘り人たちのそばに寄ってきた。職長もランドローバーで二度ばかり現われ、

していた民が活動したのは紀元前 2800 〜 1800 年頃で、紀元前 8 世紀から紀元 5 世紀までとされる古代ローマの時代よりずっと前。

❺ in swift succession: 相次いで

❻ the Magna Carta: the Great Charter を意味するラテン語。「1215 年 John 王に対して貴族が勝ち取った約束；これで英国の立憲政治の基礎ができ、国民の権利と自由が確保された」（『コンパスローズ英和辞典』）

❼ tyrannies so absolute ..: so absolute のあとに that を補うとわかりやすい。「〜するほど絶対的な暴虐」

❽ forbid(den): 〜を禁じる

❾ intermittent: 断続的な

❿ finding it difficult to establish her own space: 自分の場所を確保する（establish）のに苦労して

⓫ drove up:（車を運転して）寄ってきた

landrover a couple of times, consulted with the tractor driver, went away again. He did his business, yet **❶**seemed permanently abstracted, **❷**as if he lived within his own body and profession by accident, his life being somewhere else perhaps. Likewise the
5 tractor driver, **❸**keeping a general though not lofty distance from the pickers, with whom he occasionally conversed. **❹**Otherwise he lived in his glass-cabbed tractor, moving up and down the field, his earmuffs shutting out the sound he made. From time to time, we noticed, he placed a little white pill from **❺**a phial on his
10 tongue, and **❻**took a swig from his water bottle. **❼**Asked, he spoke of them as *his pills*, and smiled vaguely from somewhere in **❽**the interior of himself.

The coming of the Potato Mother
15 Potato Mother came, and blessed **❾**the barren fields. And the Lord Clifton **❿**went in unto the Potato Mother **⓫**back at the big house.

---

❶ seemed permanently abstracted: ずっとぼんやりした様子だった。*She was thinner, abstracted and often seemed unaware of her surroundings.* (彼女は前より痩せていて、ぼんやりした様子で、周囲が目に入っていないように見えることもしばしばだった。*Longman Dictionary of Contemporary English, Corpus*)

❷ as if he lived within his own body and profession by accident: この体の範囲内、この仕事の範囲内で生きているのはただの偶然 (accident) であるかのように

❸ keeping a general though not lofty distance: though not lofty が挿入的に入っている。「全体として距離を保っていたが、高慢 (lofty) な距離の取り方ではなかった」

❹ Otherwise he lived in his glass-cabbed tractor: cabbed は cab (運転室)

136

トラクターの運転手と何やら相談し、また帰っていった。職長として仕事はしていても、どうも心ここにあらずといった風情で、まるでこの肉体でこの仕事に就いているのは単なる偶然であって本当の人生はどこかよそにあるといった感じだった。同様にトラクターの運転手も、決してお高くとまるわけではないにせよイモ掘り人たちとはある程度の距離を保っていた。時おり彼らと言葉を交わす以外は、ガラス張りの運転室にこもって、自分の立てる音をイヤマフでシャットアウトして畑を行ったり来たりしていた。運転手は時おり、薬瓶から小さな白い錠剤を出して舌に載せ、水筒からぐいっと水を飲んだ。訊かれると彼は、それらの錠剤を俺の薬と呼んで、心のなかのどこかから発する漠然とした笑みを浮かべるのだった。

ポテト・マザーの到来

　ポテト・マザーが到来し、不毛な畑を祝福した。そしてクリフトン卿は広大な屋敷の裏手でポテト・マザーのなかに入っていった。ポテト・マザーは

から。「それ以外は（Otherwise）、ガラスの運転室がついたトラクターの中で生きていた」＝トラクターから出なかった

❺ a phial: 小瓶、薬瓶
❻ took a swig from ...: 〜からぐいとひと飲みした
❼ Asked: If/When he was asked
❽ the interior of himself: 自分自身の内部
❾ barren: 実が結ばない、子が産まれないという響き。
❿ went in unto the Potato Mother: 前行の 'Potato Mother came, and blessed ...' からすでにそうだが、ここでトーンは完全に聖書的になる。
⓫ back at the big house: 大きな家の裏で

Potato Mother **❶**conceived and **❷**brought forth the primal potato, and there was wide **❸**rejoicing. Men gathered in **❹**groves of the forest to **❺**sing her praises. **❻**No more need they plant stones and weep over thistles. Thus ended centuries when potatoes had to **❼**be
5 carved from pine cones and boiled for years before they became **❽**succulent. Oh Potato Mother, **❾**Our Soft Lady Willendorf, Little Sister **❿**of the First Water, **⓫**may we lie in thy fields forever, **⓬**thou who hast given us the potato, from which we make boots, and clothes, and books, and tractors, and which we eat and **⓭**dry for
10 fuel. **⓮**Without thee Potato Mother **⓯**would we not be crouching under rocks to this day, eating **⓰**snails?

The picker's prayer
Potato Mother, **⓱**may thy potatoes be fat and **⓲**plentiful **⓳**with

---

❶ conceive(d): 受胎する、妊娠する

❷ brought forth the primal potato: 元始のイモを産んだ

❸ rejoicing: 歓喜

❹ grove(s): 木立

❺ sing her praises: sing one's praises は普通、比喩的に「〜を褒めたたえる」の意になるが、ここは文字どおり歌ったと考えてよい。

❻ No more need they plant stones and weep over thistles: no more need A do B で「もはや A が B する必要はない」というパターン。*No more need they worry about someone coming to take him away.* (誰かがやって来て彼を連れ去るのではという心配ももはや要らない。Alice Warkentin, *Heartstrings in Haiti*, 2014)

❼ be carved from pine cones: マツボックリから彫られる

❽ succulent: 汁気が多くて美味しい ('juicy and good to eat' *Longman Dictionary of Contemporary English*)

❾ Our Soft Lady Willendorf: オーストリアのウィレンドルフで出土した旧石器時代の小像 Venus of Willendorf を踏まえている。

受胎し、原初のイモを産んだ。皆は歓喜した。男たちは森の木立ちに集まってポテト・マザーをたたえる歌を歌った。もうこれからは、石を植えたりアザミに涙したりする必要もない。こうして、何世紀もつづいた、マツボックリを彫ってイモにして柔らかくなるまで何年も茹でねばならぬ時代は終わりを告げた。おおポテト・マザーよ、我らが柔らかなる旧石器ヴィーナスよ、誰よりも栄えある女神よ、私たちが永遠にあなたの畑に横たわりますよう、私たちにイモを下さったあなたの畑に――私たちはイモからブーツを作り、服を作り、本を作り、トラクターを作り、イモを食べ、乾かして燃料にするのです。ポテト・マザーなかりせば、我々は今日もなお、岩の下にうずくまってカタツムリを喰らっているのではないだろうか？

イモ掘り人の祈り

ポテト・マザーよ、あなたのイモが肥えて豊かに育ちますように、雑草や

⑩ of the First Water: ダイヤモンドなどについて「最良質の」。

⑪ may we …: 私たちが〜しますように。いわゆる「祈願文」で、「私たちは〜してよいでしょうか」ではない。

⑫ thou who hast …: 〜して下さった汝よ。may we … といい thou といい、聖書的な言葉遣いが依然続いている。

⑬ dry for fuel: 乾燥させて燃料にする

⑭ Without thee: 汝がいなければ

⑮ would we not …?: 我々は〜しているのではあるまいか。wouldn't we …? より改まった響き。

⑯ snail(s): カタツムリ

⑰ may thy potatoes be …: l. 7 の may we lie … と同じく祈願文。thy は「汝の」。

⑱ plentiful: 豊饒な

⑲ with weeds and stones few: 雑草や石はわずかで。*with your mouth full*（食べ物を口いっぱいに頬張って）などと同じく、「付帯状況」を表わす with。

weeds and stones few and may they leap into my baskets, **❶** yea may they leap into my sacks, **❷** that my weariness at day's end **❸** be rewarded amply, amen.

5 **The picker's heaven**

No more potatoes, Sunday forever, no rain, no **❹** mucky boots, **❺** cracked nails, dust in my eyes, stones in my shoe. But the pay envelopes still come, it's best **❻** piece-work, **❼** it's 1976, and there's a pub at the corner of the field **❽** selling cider at 1958 prices. So 10 here I am in **❾** the public, waiting to be reborn to spend the next few million lifetimes as **❿** a Colorado beetle. **⓫** *Zix mower points yer scrumpie yer lanlord, yer be afercrown, Gorbless yer.*

The potato wars

15 We are **⓬** potatory says Davie. And this, says he of his 11th pint of

---

❶ yea: yeah /jéə/ は現代的だが yea/jéɪ/ は古風。

❷ that my weariness at day's end be ...: ここも古風。現代式にいえば so my weariness at day's end will be ...(私の疲れが一日の終わりに〜であるように)

❸ be rewarded amply: 十分に報われる

❹ mucky: 単に泥だけでなく汚物も混じっていそうな汚さをいう。

❺ cracked: 割れた

❻ piece-work: p. 122, l. 16 - p. 124, l. 1 に 'well it is piece-work and just about anything could happen'（何しろ出来高払いだから何が起きたって不思議はないんだけど）の形で既出。

❼ it's 1976: 1976 年といえばイギリスの経済が最悪だった時期。なのに……という含み。

❽ selling cider at 1958 prices: 1958 年から 1976 年のあいだに進んだインフレにより、物価は 3 倍以上になった。物価変動の度合いを知るには、ウェブ上に出回っている種々の inflation calculator が便利。イギリスであればたとえば Bank of England が提供している：https://www.bankofengland.co.uk/

石はわずかでありますように、イモたちがわが籠に飛び込んできますように、そう、彼らがわが袋に飛び込み、一日の終わりにわが疲れが存分に報われますように、アーメン。

イモ掘り人の天国

　イモはもうなし、永遠に日曜、雨もなし、泥だらけのブーツもなし、ひび割れた爪も、目に入る埃も、靴に入る石もなし。しかし給料袋は相変わらずやって来る、歩合は最高、時は 1976 年、畑の角にはリンゴ酒を 1958 年値段で売るパブがある。かくして私はパブに在って、次の数百万の生涯をコロラドハムシとして送るべく生まれ変わるのを待っている。よおおやじこっちにリンゴ酒もう六パイントだそら半クラウンだあんたに神のご加護がありますように。

イモ戦争

　わしらは飲み助なんだよとデイヴィーは言う。そしてこれが、とデイヴィー

---

monetary-policy/inflation/inflation-calculator。cider は p. 40, l. 12 の 'rum-and-cider hot as flame'（炎みたいに熱いラム酒のリンゴ酒割り）で触れたとおり、アメリカの cider のようにノンアルコールではなく、それなりに強い酒。

❾ the public: パブ（the public house）

❿ a Colorado beetle: コロラドハムシ。ジャガイモの大害虫で、Colorado potato beetle ともいう。イギリスでは 1877 年に見つかって以降、大量発生を繰り返している。

⓫ *Zix mower points yer scrumpie* ...: 酔っぱらって呂律の回っていない口調。標準語に直せば Six more pints (of) your scrumpy here landlord, here's half-a-crown, God bless you となる。scrumpie <scrumpy: イングランド南西部特産のリンゴ酒。afercrown <half-a-crown（旧通貨単位で 2 シリング 6 ペンス＝ 8 分の 1 ポンド）

⓬ potatory: いかにも「ポテト的」に見えるが、そうではなく「飲酒にふける」の意味で、発音も /pə́ʊtətəri/。

❶ hard cider, is our ❷ potation. From his pocket he takes a potato.
This is our ❸Roundhead potato. ❹The Royalists, the King Edwards,
❺have been disallowed under Common Market rules. He puts the
potato beside his drink, and takes from his other pocket another
5 potato. Now this, ❻this is your smoothie, your bureaucrat potato,
your Common Market spud. Oh the wars were terrible while
they lasted. ❼Some were for putting ❽razor blades in the soup
and going over with ❾spikes and broken bottles to the next field
to ❿fight it out. But Lord Clifton ⓫in his merciful temperance and
10 justice ⓬persuaded us against it. Instead, ⓭suggested he, ⓮why
not pack the potatoes full of ⓯high explosive and old chain, ⓰roll
them down the enemy's rabbit holes, and ⓱blow them out of their
beds? So we did, and ⓲disabled their tractors and ⓳kicked hell out
of their baskets. But now the wars are over, and ⓴we're not sorry,

---

❶ hard cider: 強いリンゴ酒。hard はアルコール度数が高いことを意味する。

❷ potation: p. 140, l. 15 の potatory と同根で「酒、飲み物」。

❸ Roundhead: 円頭派、円頂党（ピューリタン革命で議会を支持）

❹ The Royalists, the King Edwards: 円頭派ポテトも王党派ポテトもフィクショ
ンだが、the King Edward(s) は p. 122, l. 6 に既出のとおり事実ジャガイモ
の品種。

❺ have been disallowed under Common Market rules: 欧州共同体（EC）
はイギリスでは the Common Market と呼ばれた。「EC の取り決めにより禁
じられた」

❻ this is your smoothie, your bureaucrat potato: your は「みんなのよく口
にする、いわゆる、例の」という軽蔑的なニュアンス。(a) smoothie: 口の上手
い奴

❼ Some were for ...: 〜を推した者もいた

❽ razor blade(s): カミソリの刃

❾ spike(s): 大釘

は十一パイント目のリンゴ酒を持ち上げて言う。わしらの酒さ。ポケットからデイヴィーはイモを一個取り出す。これがわしらの円頭派ポテト。王党派すなわちキングエドワードはＥＣに締め出された。デイヴィーはイモを酒のかたわらに置いて、もうひとつのポケットから別のイモを取り出す。さてこちら、これがいわゆる口先三寸の輩、官僚ポテトだ、ＥＣおジャガだ。いやあとにかくひどい戦争だったよ。スープにカミソリの刃を入れろ、大釘や割れたガラス瓶持って隣の畑に行ってとことん戦うんだ、なんて息巻く奴もいた。でもクリフトン卿が持ち前の人柄と公正ぶりでわしらを説き伏せてやめさせたのさ。そんなことをするより、と卿は言った、イモに高性能爆薬と古チェーンを詰め込んで敵のウサギの巣穴に放り込んで、寝てるところをぶっ飛ばしてやったらどうかね？　で、わしらは言われたとおりに、奴らのトラクターを破壊して、籠をめちゃくちゃにしてやったのさ。だけどもう戦争も

⓾ fight it out: 戦い抜く
⑪ in his merciful temperance and justice: 彼の慈悲深い節度と公正さにおいて＝慈悲深い節度と公正さを発揮して
⑫ persuaded us against it: it は前文で言っている「徹底抗戦」。
⑬ suggested he: he suggested と言うよりやや古風。
⑭ why not ...: 〜したらどうか
⑮ high explosive: 高性能爆薬
⑯ roll them down the enemy's rabbit holes: 敵のウサギの巣穴の中に転がす
⑰ blow them out of their beds: 寝床にいる敵を吹き飛ばす
⑱ disable(d): 〜を運転不能にする、無力にする
⑲ kicked hell out of their baskets: kick (the) hell out of ... で 'to beat up thoroughly, to defeat or destroy'（叩きのめす、打ち負かす、破壊する）の意（Green's Dictionary of Slang）
⑳ we're not sorry: 我々は後悔していない

even though we lost.

From the picker songbook

Potatoes out of Idaho,

5 Potatoes out of France,

Grow big and fat and plentiful

And ❶in my basket dance.

Two by two, two by two,

10 Potatoes in their jackets,

Fill the baskets,

Fill the bags,

❷Fill up my paypackets.

15 Lord Rally, Lord Rally,

went riding one day,

---

❶ in my basket dance: France と韻を踏むよう、dance in my basket の語順を入れ替えている。

❷ Fill up my paypackets: 給料袋を一杯に満たす。paypacket は p. 140, ll. 7-8 の pay envelopes と同じ。jackets, baskets と韻を踏むために使われている。

終わった。わしら悔いはないよ、戦いには負けたけれどもさ。

イモ掘り唱歌集より

　　アイダホのポテト、
　　フランスのポテト、
　　大きく丸くたっぷり育ち
　　おいらの籠でぴょんぴょん踊る。

　　二つまた二つ、二つまた二つ、
　　皮をかぶったポテトたち、
　　籠一杯に、
　　袋一杯に、
　　おいらの給料袋一杯に。

　　ラリー卿、ラリー卿、
　　ある日馬に乗って出かけ、

And met an old picker
Along **❶**the highway.

His clothes were **❷**in tatters,
5   His boots were **❸**in bits,
❹For **❺**with stooping and picking
He'd **❻**picked through his wits.

Old picker, old picker
10   Says Rally to him,
❼Your rows be all pickered,
Your sacks be all in.

Lord Rally, Lord Rally,
15   The picker he said,
❽I may be picked over

---

❶ the highway: 高速道路ではなく「公道」。ちなみに高速道路はイギリス英語では現代でも motorway（p. 132, l. 3 に既出）という。

❷ in tatters: ずたずたで

❸ in bits: ばらばらで

❹ For: この for は「というのも〜」。

❺ with stooping and picking: さんざん屈んだり掘ったりで

❻ picked through his wits: 掘って掘って分別（wits）を通り抜けてしまった＝分別がなくなるほど掘った

❼ Your rows be all pickered: Your rows are all picked. row(s) はジャガイモを植えた「畝」。韻を踏ませるために名詞の picker を動詞として pick の意味で使っている。

❽ I may be picked over / But: 私はもう掘り尽くされているかもしれないが

146

老いぼれイモ掘りに
街道で出会った。

爺さん服はぼろぼろ、
ブーツはばらばら、
腰をかがめて掘りまくり
気がふれるまで掘ったから。

爺さんイモ掘りよ、爺さんイモ掘り、
ラリー卿が翁に言う、
お前の畑は掘りつくされた、
お前の袋は満たされた。

ラリー卿、ラリー卿、
爺さんイモ掘りは言った、
わしは掘り尽くされちまうかもしれんが

But they'll pick off your head.

And that was what happened —
❶Lord Rally got chopped.
5   So **❷**don't count your potatoes
Before they're all cropped.

And that is my **❸**moral,
The theme of my song,
10   **❹**As I pick the potatoes
❺The green fields among.

---

❶ Lord Rally got chopped: chopped は p. 132, l. 11 に 'had their heads chopped off'（首を斬り落とされた）の形で既出。歴史上のウォルター・ローリーも最後は斬首刑となった。

❷ don't count your potatoes / Before they're all cropped: 'Don't count your chickens before they are hatched.'（ひなが孵（かえ）る前ににわとりを数えるな＝取らぬ狸の皮算用は禁物）のもじり。

❸ moral:「道徳」ではなく「教訓」。

❹ As I pick the potatoes: この as は「～するときに」「～しながら」。

❺ The green fields among: Among the green fields

あんたは首をもぎ取られちまうだろうよ。

そして果たせるかな──
ラリー卿は断頭台の露と消えた。
だから皆の衆、収穫もせんうちから
イモを数えちゃいかんぞな。

それがおいらの教訓、
おいらの歌の題目、
今日もおいらはイモを掘る
緑の畑に埋もれて。

❶The triumph of Lord Rally

❷Oh ar er lived down yer a bit. Roit ❸bugger ee as ❹put eez coat in road fer Queen an ey do zay ❺ee ad eez wicked way of er an er a virgin all er dayz.   ❻Zounz mazed er. Ztill talk about ee round
5 yer. Zome zay az ❼Drake carn't ❽ztomach ee, bit of ❾a fancy bloke Oi reckon, ❿carn't old ez zoider. But ee were roit good ⓫elmsman,

---

❶ The triumph: 輝かしい勝利

❷ Oh ar er lived down yer a bit ...: 以下、訛りに訛った英語が続く。いちおう「翻訳」を試みると：'Oh I have lived down here a bit. Right bugger he was, put his coat on the road for Queen, and they do say he had his wicked way of her, and her a virgin all her days. It sounds like he amazed her. [They] still talk about him around here. Some say that Drake couldn't stomach him, [he thought Rally was] a bit of a fancy bloke I reckon, [Rally] couldn't hold his cider. But he was a right good helmsman, landed gentry or not, better than Drake. Drake was a good steersman, oh yes, and an engineer, built Plymouth Leat up Dartmoor, I have seen it. Runs for miles, John. Of course Rally was a squire here, here's the potatoes which he brought from the New World. They were Red Indian crop, grew in little heaps, before Rally had them. 'Yes', said he when he was in America and he saw a few of them, 'I'll try a few of them back there in Collerton Rally.' And he shipped home a tonne or two. They grew all right, they bloody grew, John. But those were no good, they were too small, these, get away with you. Then it was drought. It was drought. And now I was picking them it was bloody raining like pigs' bladders. And then it was Common Market. It wasn't just drought forcing prices up, it was those buggers drinking tea in bloody Brussels, bureaucrats, bloody Brussels sprouts more like. Scrumpie disappearing. Now it's the same price as beer, you spend a bloody fortune here, we do, eh John? You could have a good laugh for a sixpence once, a night out on half-a-crown, council houses were six for a shilling and even little lambs had underpants on. Here. Funny lot that, there. Casual labourers. Usual crew of layabouts, labour

ラリー卿の勝利

　うんそうじゃなわしがここに住むようになってもうだいぶ経つな。奴もよくやるわい女王のためにコートを地面に投げ出したりしての二人でしっぽりやっとったって話じゃそれで女王様は一生処女であられましたとか言っとるんだからな呆れたもんじゃこのへんじゃまだみんな噂しとる。ドレイクの奴ラリーのことが我慢ならなかったって話での何せ気取り屋だからなリンゴ酒

exchange and social security scruffs, hippies and all. When I was a lad they were mostly kids and women, they had a week off school for them, potato picking and larking about. Blokes squeezing worms and that, John, women that would take you in the bushes, in those days. Now it's your hairy hippies and they are here from Sidmouth smoking their funny cigarettes.'

❸ bugger: man, fellow などと同じ意味で、文脈によっていろんなニュアンスを帯びるが、総じてかなり下品・卑猥。

❹ put eez coat in road fer Queen: 道に水たまりがあったので、エリザベス女王が歩けるようにウォルター・ローリーが外套を脱いでそこに広げたという有名な逸話（たぶん神話）に基づく。

❺ ee ad eez wicked way of er: He had his wicked way of her.（邪に彼女と交わった）たしかにローリーは長年エリザベス女王の寵愛を得ていたが、いわゆる関係があったと考える根拠はないようである。エリザベス女王は生涯独身を通したので the Virgin Queen と呼ばれた。

❻ Zounz mazed er: 断言不能だが 'It sounds like he amazed her' もしくは 'Zounds! he amazed her' あたりか（Zounds! は軽い罵り・驚きを表わす言葉）。

❼ Drake: Sir Francis Drake (1540? – 1596)。ローリーと同じくエリザベス女王に仕えた提督・私掠船長。

❽ ztomach <stomach: 〜に耐える。cannot stomach ... の形で使うことが多い。

❾ a fancy bloke: 洒落者

❿ carn't old ez zoider <can't hold his cider: can hold ... は酒などが「飲める」。 *She can hold her drink [liquor]*.（彼女は酒を少々飲んでもなんともない、酒がいける。『リーダーズ英和辞典』）

⓫ elmsman <helmsman: 舵手、操舵手

❶landed genry or nor, bettern Drake. Drake a good ❷steerzman, oh ar, an engineer, built ❸Plymouth Leat up Dartmoor, Oi zeen er. Go for miles Jahn. Courz Rally were ❹squoir yer, eerz yer ❺taterz whor ee bror from New World. Er were ❻Red Indian crorp, grew in little

5 heaps, fore Rally ad er. 'Ar,' zayz ee when eez in Armericer an ee zeez a few of ey, 'Troy a few back yer in ❼Collerton Rally.' An ee shipz ome a ton er two. Ey growz or right, ey ❽bloddy growz Jahn. But eze yer no good, ey too zmall ey, ❾geddyorf. Tiz ❿drought tiz. Tiz drought. An now eyz pickin ey erz bloddy ⓫rainin pigz

10 bladderz. An tiz Common Market. Tizn juss drought forcin prizez up, tiz ey ⓬boggerz drinkin tea in bloddy Bruzzelz, bureaucratz, bloddy ⓭Bruzzelz sproutz more loike. ⓮Zcrumpie dizappearin. Now erz zame proiz as beer, ⓯zpend a bloddy fortune in yer uz doz eh Jahn? Could ⓰have a good laugh fer ⓱a tanner onze, night

---

❶ landed genry or nor: gentry（紳士階級）であろうとなかろうと。土地持ちの紳士階級ともなれば船の操縦などには無縁と思うかもしれないが、という含み。

❷ steerzman <steersman: p. 150, l. 6 の (h)elmsman と同じ。

❸ Plymouth Leat up Dartmoor: 16 世紀後半に造られたプリマス水路は、建設に関わったフランシス・ドレイク卿にちなんで Drake's Leat とも呼ばれる。イングランド南西部の水源ダートムアから約 28 キロ先の港湾都市プリマスまで水を運んだ。

❹ (a) squoir <squire: 地主

❺ taterz <tater: ジャガイモを意味する口語。

❻ Red Indian: West Indian（西インド諸島の住民）と区別してアメリカ先住民を呼んだ言い方。いまでは不快に響くとされ、使われない。

❼ Collerton Rally <Colaton Raleigh: イングランド南西部デヴォン州にある村。元は単に Colaton という村名だったが、13 世紀に Raleigh 家の所有となって Colaton Raleigh になった。ウォルター・ローリーもここで洗礼を受けたといわれる。

❽ bloddy <bloody: p. 100, l. 14 に "What a bloody nuisance," I said to

一口飲めんかったんじゃ。でも船の舵とりはうまかった、地主のくせしてド
レイクなんかよりよっぽどうまかった。ドレイクだってそう下手じゃあない
技師としての腕も確かでのプリマス水路を造ったのも奴さそうそうダート
ムアまで延びてるやつだわしも見たことあるよ。何マイルも延びておったよ
ジョン。むろんラリーはここの地主での、ほれこいつが新世界から奴が持っ
てきたイモじゃ。インディアンが細々と作っておったのをラリーが大々的に
広めたんじゃ。アメリカでイモを見てラリーは言った、「これだよこれ、こ
いつをコラトン・ラリーで試してみようじゃないの」。で、一トンか二トン
持ち帰って植えてみたらこれがまあ一応育っての。だけどこいつはいかん、
やたら小っちゃい、日照りのせいじゃ何せ日照りが悪い。ようよう収穫と
思ったら今度はブタの膀胱みたいに雨が降りよる。で、おつぎはＥＣ。値上
がりは日照りのせいだけじゃない。ブリュッセルで乙に澄まして紅茶飲んで
る奴らがいかんのじゃ官僚どもめなあにがブリュッセルだ芽キャベツみたい
な面しよって。リンゴ酒もめっきり少なくなってきたな。いまじゃビールと

her.'（「嫌んなっちゃうわよ」とあたしは彼女に言った）の形で既出。
⑨ geddyorf: Get away with you（冗談じゃねえよ）か。
⑩ drought: 干ばつ
⑪ rainin pigz bladderz <raining like pigs' bladders:「豚の膀胱のように降る」
といえば、少なくともしとしと降る雨でないことは明白だろう。
⑫ boggerz <bogger: *Green's Dictionary of Slang* には 'a derogatory term
for an Irish person; thus ext. as any stupid country person'（アイルラ
ンド人を示す軽蔑語。広く、愚かな田舎者誰でも）とあるが、ここではブリュッ
セル（EC の本部がある）でお上品にお茶を飲んでいる人々を指すので、「田舎者」
の含みは抜けて軽蔑の念のみが残っている。
⑬ Bruzzelz sproutz <Brussels sprout: 芽キャベツ（ブリュッセル原産）
⑭ Zcrumpie <scrumpie: p. 140, l. 2 に既出。
⑮ zpend a bloody fortune <spend a bloody fortune: a fortune は spend
や cost とつながると「一財産」。
⑯ have a good laugh: 楽しく過ごす
⑰ a tanner: 6 ペンス貨

out on **❶**afercrown, **❷**counzil houzez zix fer a shillin an even little lambs ad underpantz on. Ere. **❸**Funny lot that thar. Cazul labour. **❹**Uzul crew er layaboutz, **❺**labour egzchange an zochial zecurity zcruffz, **❻**ippiez an a. When Oi were a lad er were moztly kidz
5 an women, ad a week off zchool fer er, potato pickin an **❼**larkin about. Blokez squeezin wormz an at Jahn, women az ad takee in a bushez, in em dayz. Now itz yer airy ippiez an eez yer from **❽**Zidmouth zmokin **❾**er funny zigarettez.

10 **A new phase: we meet ❿the running dogs and fascist ⓫lackeys of capitalism and imperialism. ⓬The east wind no longer prevails and ⓭the black gang seizes ⓮the means of production.**

First **⓯**drive off the smallholders, promising new land in the
15 middle of the Atlantic. Our banks **⓰**foreclose on their mortgages.

---

❶ afercrown <half-a-crown: p. 140, l. 2 に既出。

❷ counzil houzez <council house: 公営住宅

❸ Funny lot: おかしな奴ら。lot がこのように「グループ」「群れ」の意になるときはしばしば軽蔑的。

❹ Uzul crew er layaboutz <Usual crew of layabouts: crew は本来、船員や乗組員を言うが、広く group の意味で使われる。layabout(s): 浮浪者、のらくら者 (lay about= のらくらする から)

❺ labour egzchange an zochial zecurity zcruffz <labour exchange and social security scruffs: 公共職業安定所 (labour exchange) と生活保護 (social security) の世話になっている薄汚い奴ら (scruffs)

❻ ippiez an a <hippies and all: ヒッピーだの何だの

❼ larkin about <lark about: ふざけまわる

❽ Zidmouth <Sidmouth: p. 126, l. 1 に既出のリゾート地。

❾ er funny zigarettez <their funny cigarettes: マリワナ煙草のこと。

同じ値段でうかうかしてりゃ一財産飲んじまうよなあジョン。昔は六ペンス
でたっぷり楽しめたもんじゃ一晩遊んだって半クラウン、公営住宅の家賃な
んざほんとに二束三文子羊だってちゃんとパンツはいてたもんだ。ほれあそ
こ、ったくおかしな奴らじゃわい。臨時雇い。よくいる浮浪者どもさ職安だ
か生活保護だか知らんが、ヒッピーだの何だの。わしが若かったころはだい
たいみんな女子供だったよ学校一週間休んでイモ掘って遊び呆けたもんだ。
ガキどもはイモ虫つぶしたり女たちは草むらでやらせてくれたりそういう時
代だったんじゃよ。それがいまじゃヒッピーだの何だの、シドマスあたりか
らやって来ておかしなタバコ喫いよって。

新段階――資本主義と帝国主義の走狗、
ファシズムの追従者登場。
東風はもはや力を失い、黒帮が生産手段を掌握。

　まず小自作農を追い払う、大西洋の真ん中に新しい土地を約束して。我々

❿ **the running dog(s)**: 追従者。共産主義者・社会主義者が反革命的な人物を非
　難するときに使う。そもそも語源も中国語の「走狗」。

⓫ **lackey(s)**: 従僕、お先棒担ぎ。直前の running dogs とほぼ同義。

⓬ **The east wind no longer prevails**: 東風はもはや優勢ではない。毛沢東の
　言葉「東風圧倒西風」（The East wind prevails over the West wind: 社会
　主義が資本主義を圧倒している）を踏まえた表現。

⓭ **the black gang**: 文化大革命で弾圧の標的にされた勢力「黒帮」が英語圏では
　こう呼ばれた。毛沢東の「東風」によって駆逐された勢力が、ここでは権力掌
　握に成功している。

⓮ **the means of production**: 生産の手段

⓯ **drive off the smallholders**: 小自作農を追い払え

⓰ **foreclose on their mortgages**: 抵当に入れた彼らの資産（mortgages）を
　抵当流れにする(foreclose)。mortgage は t を読まず、/mɔ́:gɪdʒ/ と発音する。

Bulldozers and ❶rentacops knock down hedges and villages, and we plant the land with potatoes from horizon to horizon. A man may walk ❷from dawn to dusk seeing nothing but potatoes ❸yet not leave one field of our domains. The people live in pickers'
5 barracks and ❹work for nothing save a little meat, cheap beer, and as many potatoes as they can steal. We export ❺the surplus, ❻underselling everyone else and ❼crippling the economies of ❽emergent nations, ❾bringing on world famine which we ❿cure by exchanging potatoes for complete economic and political control.
10 Then we ⓫take over the world, live ⓬lives of responsible and spartan luxury, ⓭organise everything down to the last teaspoon, and grow potatoes on every available inch. As for ⓮this Marx fellow, he gets to pick a hundred sacks a day, and peel them too, for the rest of ⓯his rotten life.

❶ rentacop(s): 警備員、雇われ保安要員（軽蔑的）
❷ from dawn to dusk: 夜明けから夕暮れまで
❸ yet not …: それでもまだ〜しない
❹ work for nothing save …: 働いても〜以外報酬はない。「〜を除いて」を意味する save は、第5巻 p. 36, l. 12 - p. 38, l. 1 に 'all is silent save the voice of the clock'（時計の声以外いっさいが沈黙する）の形で既出。
❺ the surplus: 余剰
❻ undersell(ing): 〜よりも安値で売る
❼ crippling <cripple: 〜を無力にする、駄目にする
❽ emergent nation(s): 新興国
❾ bringing on world famine: 世界的飢饉（famine）をもたらし
❿ cure by exchanging potatoes for complete economic and political control: イモと完全な経済的・政治的支配権とを交換することによって（飢饉を）解決する

Ken Smith

の銀行が彼らの抵当物を抵当流れ処分にする。ブルドーザーと雇われ保安要員が生け垣や村を押しつぶし、その土地に我々は地平線から地平線までイモを植える。夜明けから日没まで歩きつづけてもイモ以外何も見えず、いまだ我々の領土の中のひとつの畑を出てもいない、なんてこともありうる。人々はイモ掘り人用のバラックに住み、わずかな肉と安ビールのみを報酬に働く、あとはイモをくすねられるだけくすねる。我々は余剰のイモをほかのどの国よりも安く輸出し、発展途上国の経済に壊滅的打撃を与え、世界規模の飢餓を生じさせて、イモを与えてそれを解決し、見返りとして経済的・政治的支配権を完全に掌握する。こうして我々は世界を支配し、責任ある禁欲的贅沢に貫かれた生活を送り、スプーン一杯に至るまですべてを組織化して、利用できる最後の一インチまでイモを植える。マルクスとかいう野郎には、腐りきった人生終わるまで一日百袋イモを掘らせ、ついでに皮もむかせる。

⓫ take over ...: 〜を引き継ぐ、支配する
⓬ lives of responsible and spartan luxury: 責任ある、質実剛健の贅沢な生活。spartan は日本語の「スパルタ式」とは違い「質素」が基調。spartan luxury はほとんど論理的矛盾に思えるが、「黒帮」の新体制がもたらす「真に」豊かな生活、ということ。
⓭ organise: 〜を組織化する
⓮ this Marx fellow, he gets to pick a hundred sacks a day ...: このマルクスとかいう奴が、一日百袋イモを掘らされて……。共産主義が敗北し、その生みの親はなかなか散々な扱いである。get to ...: 辞書には「〜する機会を得る」とあるが、ここを見ればわかるとおり、かならずしも有難い機会とは限らない。*John, who usually has a cleaner, gets to scrub the toilet in the show.*（ふだんは掃除人を雇うジョンだが、番組では自分でトイレ掃除をする羽目になる）
⓯ his rotten life: 腐った、ろくでもない人生

❶The totalitarian potato

Anyone who isn't a potato picker, ❷ a chargehand, tractor driver or foreman is ❸ scum, and will be sent to pick in ❹ the Antarctic. Anyone who doesn't volunteer for ❺double shifts will ❻be poked in
5 both eyes. Anyone who doesn't ❼sing aloud all 27 verses of *Potato Pickers of* ❽*Collaton Raleigh* ❾*Rejoice in* ❿*the New Five Year Plan and Unite to Defeat the Enemy* all day as he works will ⓫have his bags tipped out and start again. Anyone who doesn't pick seven days a week all hours and weathers will be sent to live underground.
10 I, ⓬ the Little Father of the Potato Nation, have spoken. ⓭ *Edict One*: No stones, ⓮no muck, and no rotten spuds. *Edict Two*: the ⓯insidious religion of the Potato Mother ⓰banned. *Edict Three*: pickers to ⓱commence growing shorter, starting now, developing large flat feet, long arms and large hands with at least ten fingers

---

❶ **The totalitarian potato**: 社会主義の次に全体主義が現われるのは、現実の歴史をなぞっていると言うべきか。

❷ **a chargehand**: 次行に出てくる foreman の次に位置する職人。「職工主任」

❸ **scum**: かす、くず

❹ **the Antarctic**: 南極

❺ **double shift(s)**: 二シフト勤務（要するに倍働く）。

❻ **be poked**: つつかれる

❼ **sing aloud**: （はっきりと）声を出して歌う。このように aloud は、「大声で」ではなく「声に出して」の意。第 1 巻 p. 26, l. 3 などに既出：'"Hold it up in your right hand and wish aloud," said the sergeant-major.' (「右手で持ってかざして、願いごとを口にするのです」と特務曹長は言った)

❽ *Collaton Raleigh*: p. 152, l. 6 では Collerton Rally と訛っていたローリー卿ゆかりの地名がここではほぼ現実（Colaton Raleigh）どおりに。

❾ *Rejoice*: 歓喜せよ

❿ *the New Five Year Plan*: 旧ソ連時代によく聞いた言い方。

全体主義ポテト

　イモ掘り人でないすべての者——親方、トラクターの運転手、職長——は人間のクズであり、南極に送られるであろう。二倍勤務に志願せぬ者は両目をつぶされるであろう。『コラトン・ローリーのイモ掘り人、新五ヶ年計画に歓喜し敵を倒さんと団結す』の歌詩二十七番までを仕事しながら一日じゅう歌わぬ者は袋の中味を空けられ一からやり直しを命じられるであろう。一週間七日、朝から晩まであらゆる天候の下でイモを掘らぬ者はみな地下生活を余儀なくされるであろう。朕ジャガイモ国家皇帝、ここに勅令を宣す。勅令一。石は不可、堆肥は不可、腐ったイモは不可。勅令二。ポテト・マザーの邪教を禁ず。勅令三。今日よりイモ掘り人は背丈を縮めはじめるべし、かつ、大きな扁平足、長い腕、大きな手を育て、手にはそれぞれ最低十本の指

❶ have his bags tipped out: 籠をひっくり返されて空にされる。have A + 過去分詞 の形が、p. 34, ll. 4-5 では 'the Squire's mother had Andrey turned out of the house as a vile impostor'（下劣なペテン師、と地主様の御母堂はアンドリーを罵って屋敷から叩き出し）と「A を～させる」の意になっていたのに対し、ここでは「A を～される」。

❷ the Little Father of the Potato Nation: 'the Little Father' はロシア皇帝の伝統的呼称。

❸ *Edict*: 布告

❹ no muck: muck は p. 140, l. 6 に 'no mucky boots'（泥だらけのブーツもなし）の形で既出。

❺ insidious: 狡猾な、陰険な

❻ ban(ned): ～を禁止する

❼ commence growing shorter: 身長を小さくしはじめる。commence は begin と意味は同じだがやや改まった響きなので、こういう Edict にはぴったり。

on each hand. *Edict Four*: secret. *Edict Five*: use of language spoken or written ❶hereby reserved solely for government use; pickers read this and the next three edicts, then nothing else: no one teach it, write it, speak or sing it without licence from the nearest post
5 office. *Edict Six*: ❷suspension of postal services; all post offices to be ❸demolished immediately; anyone who can still read and write better forget it ❹or else, this is ❺punk potato power speaking; we want nothing but ❻grunts and snarls from ❼you lot — ❽snaps and whimpers, ❾male chauvinist guffaws, ❿groans, ⓫pleas for mercy,
10 ⓬snoring, that's O.K. Anything else is ⓭treason, mutiny, sabotage, ⓮piracy, ⓯interference with interstate commerce, ⓰rebellion, and makes you ⓱go blind. *Edict Seven*: all the women come and live in the big house with us. *Edict Eight*: ⓲watch it that's all.

---

❶ hereby reserved solely for ...: これより (hereby) 専ら〜にのみ与えられ

❷ suspension of postal services: 郵便サービスの中止

❸ demolish(ed): 〜を取り壊す

❹ or else: さもないと。そのあとの「ひどい目に遭う」等はこのようにしばしば省かれる。

❺ punk potato power: それまでは単に「チンピラ」「クズ」程度の意味だったpunk という語だが、1970 年代半ばの punk rock の登場でその意味は一気に広がった。むろんここではその現代的な意味でのパンク・スピリットもパロディのネタにされているわけだが。

❻ grunts and snarls: 同じうなり声でも grunt は豚が出しそうな、snarl は犬が出しそうな声。

❼ you lot: 軽蔑的に「お前ら」。この意味の lot は p. 154, l. 2 に 'Funny lot that thar.'（ったくおかしな奴らじゃわい）の形で既出。

❽ snaps and whimpers: すぐ前の grunts and snarls はある程度同義だったが、こちらは対照的で、snap(s) はぴしゃっという声、whimper(s) はメソメソ声。

❾ male chauvinist guffaws: 1960-70 年代のフェミニズムにあっては、この

を生やすべし。勅令四。極秘。勅令五。今後話し言葉・書き言葉はすべて、専ら政府が使用するものとす。イモ掘り人はここまでの勅令とこの後三つの勅令を読み、以後ほかは何も読むべからず。何人も最寄りの郵便局より許可を得ずして言葉を教えたり書いたり話したり歌ったりしてはならない。勅令六。郵便事業の停止。すべての郵便局は即刻取り壊されるものとす、いまなお読み書きできる者はさっさと忘れた方が身のためである、こちらパンク・ポテト・パワー、我々はお前たち人民にうなり声やののしり声以外何も望まぬ、ガミガミ声、泣き声、男性優越主義的高笑い、うめき声、慈悲を乞う哀願、いびき、これらはよろしい。ほかはすべて反逆罪であり、謀反、サボタージュ、海賊行為であり、国家間通商への干渉であり、治安妨害であり、人を盲目へと追いやる悪行である。勅令七。女は全員我々とともに大屋敷（ザ・ビッグ・ハウス）に住むものとする。勅令八。以上を心して遵守すべし。

male chauvinist（男性優越主義の）というフレーズのあとにしばしば pig の一語が続いた。guffaw(s): 馬鹿笑い

❿ groans: 前行の grunts が「うなり声」なら、こちらは「うめき声」。grunt がしばしば、まともに答える気もない人間の返答ならざる返答であるのに対し、groan は落胆・不満・苦痛の念から絞り出される声。

⓫ pleas for mercy: 慈悲を求める嘆願

⓬ snoring: いびき

⓭ treason, mutiny, sabotage: 謀反、反乱、サボタージュ。treason はたとえばシェークスピアに、mutiny は海洋小説に、sabotage はプロレタリア小説などにいかにも出てきそうな語。

⓮ piracy: 海賊行為

⓯ interference with interstate commerce: 国家間商取引に対する妨害

⓰ rebellion: 反乱

⓱ go blind: 盲目になる。go mad, go bald などと同じ発想。

⓲ watch it: 気をつけろ

❶The peasant revolt

Funny, the foreman says. It happens every year. They pick for a
month and then ❷ walk off. Nick's asleep under the tractor. It's
raining again. Charley ❸ tips out his half-filled sack and ❹ rips it
5 up. ❺He kicks over more sacks. ❻*They bags cost nine pence each,* the
foreman says, *and we pay you ten pence ❼per bag to fill 'em.* Charley
begins kicking baskets. ❽ *Profiteering* ❾ *mother-robbing* ❿ *sweated
labour* ⓫*slave-driving* ⓬*black hearted* ⓭*sons of fatherless bitches.* ⓮*The*
Jesus Freaks ⓯ move to cut him off, but the revolt spreads down
10 the rows: one by one the pickers look up to see Mick wearing the
tractor driver's earmuffs, and Nick and Charley tipping everyone's
bags unless they'll ⓰ pack up and go down the pub. The whole
field walks off and stays off all day while the foreman sits in the

---

❶ **The peasant revolt**: 農民の蜂起。peasant は farmer（農場経営者）より
もはるかに「持たざる者」の響きが強い。revolt は p.160, l. 11 の rebellion
とほぼ同じだが、rebellion より突発的な反乱という響き。

❷ **walk off**: 立ち去る。「ストライキを打つ」の意味もある。先回りすれば、この
あと ll. 12-13 でも 'The whole field walks off'（畑にいた全員が持ち場を離れ
る）の形で出てくる。

❸ **tips out his half-filled sack**: tip out は p. 158, ll. 7-8 に have his bags
tipped out（袋の中味を空けられて）の形で既出。このあと ll. 11-12 では
out 抜きで 'Nick and Charley tipping everyone's bags'（ニックとチャーリー
が全員の袋の中身をぶちまけて）の形で出てくる。

❹ **rips it up**: びりびり破く

❺ **He kicks over more sacks**: この over は *He knocked the chair over.*（彼
はいすを倒した。『コンパスローズ英和辞典』）の over と同じ。

❻ *They bags*: Those bags

❼ *per bag*: 一袋ごとに

❽ *Profiteer(ing)*: 暴利を貪る

❾ *mother-robbing*: 母親から盗むような。作家ウィリアム・フォークナー

農民の反乱

　変だな、と職長は言う。毎年こうなるんだ。奴らは一ヵ月イモを掘って、それからいなくなっちまう。ニックはトラックの下で眠っている。また雨が降っている。チャーリーは半分入った袋の口を下にして、袋をびりびりに破く。そしてさらにいくつも袋を蹴飛ばす。一袋九ペンスするんだぞ、と職長は言う。その上お前らに払う賃金が一袋十ペンスだ。チャーリーが今度は籠を蹴りはじめる。強欲ずくの、母親からだってかっぱらう、搾取労働のお先棒かつぎの奴隷酷使の根性真っ黒の父なし子の雌犬の息子どもめ。熱狂的キリスト教信者たちが割って入ろうとするが反乱は畝を下ってどんどん広がってゆく。一人一人、イモ掘り人たちは顔を上げ、ミックがトラクター運転手のイヤマフをつけるのを目にし、ニックとチャーリーが、大人しく仕事をやめてパブへ行かぬ奴らの袋の中身を片っ端からぶちまけるのを見る。畑にいた全員が持ち場を離れ、一日じゅう帰ってこない。職長はその間ランドロー

1956 年のインタビューの、'If a writer has to rob his mother, he will not hesitate'（作家は母親から盗まねばならないとなっても躊躇しない）という発言が思い出される。

❿ *sweated labour*: 搾取労働。sweatshop といえば低賃金・長時間の搾取工場のこと。

⓫ *slave-driving*: 奴隷を酷使する

⓬ *black hearted*: ハイフンがあいだに入る方が普通。

⓭ *sons of fatherless bitches*: a son of a bitch（クソッタレ）のバリエーション。

⓮ The Jesus Freaks: 1960 年代後半から 70 年代前半、アメリカ西海岸のヒッピーのあいだに現われた the Jesus movement の参加者を軽蔑して呼んだ名。... freak は一般に「〜狂」の意で、特に軽蔑的ではない。*a jazz freak*（ジャズマニア）

⓯ move to cut him off: 彼（チャーリー）をさえぎろうと出てくる

⓰ pack up and go down the pub: 荷物をまとめて（＝仕事を終わりにして）パブに行く。go down the road, go down the river などの down は「〜を」に当たるが、この場合は「〜に」「〜へ」。ほかに the shops, the park でも同じように使う。

landrover cursing Lord Clifton's potatoes. ❶Who would have thought the final ❷death agonies of capitalism would ❸turn out to be so few and simple?

5 **Potatoism**

Now we have the Revolution. Terrific. The land, the potatoes, the baskets, bags, tractors, machinery, barns, landrovers, telephones, all belong to the people. The women come back. Sometimes we go north along ❹the shores of the big water, ❺the picking's good
10 there, ❻once I saw a blue heron that had stood for an hour without moving rise in the great smokey wingspread of himself and fly all ease and grace across the estuary. Oh ❼we like working now it's the Revolution. This year we're once more hoping ❽for yet another bumper harvest yet again. Next year we will ❾greet a delegation of
15 carrot pickers from ❿the New Surbiton Collectives. Everything's fine now: schools, hospitals, ⓫main drainage and TV. There's

---

❶ Who would have thought ...?: 誰が〜などと思ったことだろう（常套句）
❷ death agonies: 最期の悶え
❸ turn out to be ...: 結局（いざ起きてみれば）〜になる
❹ the shores of the big water: 現実の大河か大きな湖への言及のようにも読めるが、アメリカで the Big River といえばミシシッピ河を指すのと同じような the big water はイギリスにはない。
❺ the picking's: the picking is
❻ once I saw a blue heron ...: once I saw a blue heron / that had stood for an hour without moving / rise in the great smokey wingspread of himself / and fly all ease and grace / across the estuary と切って読む。
a blue heron: アオサギ。in the great smokey wingspread of himself: 大いなる、煙に包まれた、自らの身を翼一杯広げた姿で。all ease and grace:

バーに座ってクリフトン卿のジャガイモを呪っている。誰が予想したであろう、資本主義最後の断末魔の叫びが、かくもあっけないものになろうとは？

ジャガイモ主義

いまや我々は革命を成し遂げた。やったぜ。土地、イモ、籠、袋、トラクター、機械、納屋、ランドローバー、電話、すべて人民のものだ。女たちも帰ってくる。ときおり私たちは大いなる水の岸辺を北へ行く、向こうではイモがたくさん掘れるのだ、あるとき私は一時間じっと身動きしていなかったアオサギがその翼を煙のごとく一杯に広げて悠然と舞い上がり入江の向こうへ飛んでいくのを見た。ああ、革命が訪れたいま私たちは喜んで労働に励む。今年もまた豊作になるのを私たちは楽しみにしている。来年にはニュー・サービトン集団農場の人参掘り人の代表団を迎える予定だ。何もかもがうまく行っている――学校、病院、上下水道、テレビ。最低労働時間が定められ、老齢

いかにも気楽に、優雅に。the estuary: 入江

❼ we like working now it's the Revolution: 革命となったいま（now [that] it's the Revolution）働くのは楽しい

❽ for yet another bumper harvest: さらにもう一度豊作（bumper harvest）になるのを。このあとの yet again は文法的には余分で、「さらに感」がさらに強調される。

❾ greet a delegation: 派遣団を迎える

❿ the New Surbiton Collectives: サービトンはロンドン南西部の郊外。Collective(s) は「集産組織」「集団農場」の意で、いかにも革命っぽい響き。

⓫ main drainage: 主要排水組織

❶ minimum hours and old-age pensions, ❷ the state has withered away and ❸it's the end of history. We don't mind the extra effort, not when it's for the Revolution. Some days ❹a pheasant breaks from cover close by and ❺goes whirring and rushing across
5 the tops, men trying to ❻down him for dinner, ❼it's like ❽the planet paused in its spin, ❾the world *there* again, childhood and summer, ❿all history a babble through the mind and ⓫we speak again, love, in no one else's language.

10 **A picker's humble question**

What was it ⓬St Francis preached to the birds about?

The end of all history

That all ⓭came out jumbled ⓮in all the different heads, ⓯Napoleon

---

❶ minimum hours and old-age pensions: 最低労働時間と老齢年金

❷ the state has withered away: 国家は衰亡した

❸ it's the end of history: 自由主義の最終的勝利を謳った Francis Fukuyama, *The End of History and the Last Man* がベストセラーになったのは 1992 年なので、これはその先を行っている。

❹ a pheasant breaks from cover close by: キジ (a pheasant) がそばの (close by) 隠れ場所 (cover) から飛び出し

❺ goes whirring and rushing across the tops: whirr (または whir) も rush も速い動きを伝える動詞。whirr は動きだけでなく音も伝える。鳥が羽音を立てながら一目散に飛んでいく感じ。across the tops: 山の頂が並ぶ上を

❻ down him for dinner: down は動詞で「～を撃墜する」。

❼ it's like ...: より改まった英語であれば it is as if ...

❽ the planet paused in its spin: 惑星が自転を一時停止した

❾ the world *there* again: 世界がたしかに戻ってきた、しっかり「そこ」にあるという手応えをイタリクスが伝えている。

年金もある。国家は衰退し、歴史は終焉した。革命のためとあれば、余分な
努力を強いられることも私たちはいとわない。ときおりキジがそばの隠れ場
所から飛び出して、ひゅうっと山の上を飛んでいき、男たちは夕食のおかず
にとそいつを撃ち落とそうとする。まるで惑星が自転をしばし停止したかの
ような、世界がふたたび戻ってきたような感覚。子供の年月が、夏の日々が
帰ってくる。すべての歴史は心を流れゆく泡と化し、私たちは、愛する人よ、
ふたたび語るのだ、ほかの誰のものでもない言葉で。

イモ掘り人の素朴な疑問

聖フランチェスコは鳥たちに何を説いたんですかね？

すべての歴史の終焉

それがみんな、いろんな頭のなかでごっちゃになって出てくる。ナポレオ

---

❿ all history a babble through the mind: 歴史すべてが、心を通りすぎていく
戯言となって
⓫ we speak again, love, in no one else's language: love は「愛しい人よ」と
いった呼びかけ。
⓬ St Francis: 聖フランチェスコ（1182-1226）。鳥に向かって説教したという
逸話で知られる。
⓭ came out jumbled: ぐじゃぐじゃに混ざって出てきた
⓮ in all the different heads: p. 102, l. 2 の "'There'll be a great many
different things to eat," I told her.'（「いろんな食べ物が出るのよ」とあたし
は彼女に言った）について述べたとおり、different は複数形の名詞があとに来
ると、「違う」というより「いろいろな」。
⓯ Napoleon v. Attila the Hun: ナポレオン対フン族アッティラ。アッティラは
フン族の王だった、5世紀に中欧から黒海に至る帝国を建設した人物で、ナポ
レオンとは時代が違う。これが 'came out jumbled' の第一例。

v. Attila the Hun, Marie Antoinette in bed with Nostradamus, ❶ the Romans agreeing at last to sign the human rights charter at Runnymede and ❷ grant majority rule within two years. ❸ And so forth. Words words words, example: *potato* from Spanish
5 *patata* from ❹ Carib Taino *batata*, meaning unknown; example *avocado* ❺ from Spanish *aquacate* from ❻ Nahuatl *ahuacatl*, meaning ❼ testicle. ❽ Oh ar Oi loiks er bit er specerlatin moiself Oi do, the odd ounze come in roit andy when erz tattyin to do. ❾ But yet I think there must be someone else beside me on this endless field,
10 or am I all alone, working in the rain, ❿ assuring myself my boots don't leak, asking who makes these gloves, and these shiny metal buttons stamped ARMY? Someone must ⓫ weave these blue shirts, the colour of the sky beyond these clouds, someone must have invented this language I speak to myself in. Very interesting. But

---

❶ the Romans agreeing at last to sign the human rights charter at Runnymede: Runnymede はイングランド南部のテムズ川岸にある草原で、1215 年に King John がここでマグナカルタに調印したといわれる。the Romans といえば誰もが古代ローマのことを考え、古代ローマは 5 世紀に終焉したと考えるのが通例。

❷ grant majority rule: 多数決原理を認める

❸ And so forth: などなど

❹ Carib Taino: タイノ語はカリブの先住民タイノ族が使用していた、アラワク語族の言語。

❺ from Spanish *aquacate*: 正しくは aguacate（アボカド）。

❻ Nahuatl: ナワトル語。現在もメキシコなどで使用されている。

❼ testicle: 睾丸

❽ Oh ar Oi loiks ...: これも標準語に翻訳を試みると、'Oh yeah I like a bit of speculating myself, I do, the odd ounce comes in right handy when

ン対フン王アッティラ。ノストラダムスとベッドを共にするマリー・アント
ワネット。ラニミードにおいてついに人権憲章に調印し二年以内の多数決原
理を導入することを約束するローマ人。等々。言葉言葉言葉、例——ポテト
はスペイン語のパタタから、パタタはカリブ海タイノ語のバタタから、バタ
タの意味は不明。例——アボカドはスペイン語のアクアカテから、アクアカ
テはナワトル語のアワカトル、これは睾丸の意。うんそうさなわしもああだ
こうだ考えるのは好きでの何もすることないときにゃこれがどうしてなかな
か役に立つんじゃよ。だがこのはてしなく広がる畑には私のほかにも誰かい
るのではないだろうか、それとも私は独りぼっちなのか、雨のなかで働き、
大丈夫さ俺の靴は水なんか染みないさと自分を励まし、この手袋いったい誰
が作ってるんだろう、**陸軍**と字を打ち抜いたこのピカピカの金属ボタンは誰
が、と自問しながら。誰かがこの青いシャツを縫ったにちがいない、この雲
の向こうの空と同じ青のシャツを。私がこうして独り言を喋る言語も誰かが
発明したものにちがいない。実に興味深い。だがだらだらと降りつづく雨の

there's nothing to do.' か。specerlatin (speculating) <speculate: 思 索
する。the odd ounze (ounce): ちょっとした上乗せ。*She tells her story
with the odd ounce of humour.*（彼女はちょっとしたユーモアを添えて物語
を語る）come in roit (right) andy (handy): come in handy で「役に立つ、
重宝する」の意の成句。right は強調。p. 16, ll. 4-5 に 'My knowledge of
biology came in handy, at this point.'（ここで私の生物学の知識が役に立っ
た）の形で既出。

❾ But yet: 第 2 巻 p. 110, ll. 6-7 の 'And yet he understood that wars also
provide many lessons to those who survived them.'（とはいえ、戦争が
また、それを生き抜く者たちに多くを教えていることも彼は理解していた）の
and yet について述べたとおり、yet は but とだいたい意味は同じだが、and
や but と一緒にも使えるところが違う。

❿ assuring <assure: 〜に請けあう

⓫ weave: 〜を織る

with all these spuds to pick in **❶**the piddling rain I've no more time to think about it. I've these bags to fill before dark, and potatoes don't pick themselves.

❶ the piddling rain: ちょろちょろ降る雨

なか、掘るべきイモはまだいくらでもあり、これ以上そんなことを考えている暇はない。日が暮れるまでにこれらの袋を一杯にしなくてはならないのだし、イモたちは自分で土から出てきてはくれないのだ。

ちなみに

　この 'Casual Labour' と並んでもうひとつ、ジャガイモ小説の傑作
と呼べるのが（というか、ジャガイモ小説と呼べる作品はこの二つし
か思いつかないのだが）Nicholson Baker の 'Subsoil'（下層土）であ
る。Stephen King に自作をけなされたことに腹を立てたベイカーが、
キングばりの恐怖小説を書いてやろうと思って書いた作品なのだが、
人間の体を乗っとる恐怖のジャガイモをめぐる、戦慄の恐怖小説なの
か、爆笑ユーモア小説なのか、よくわからない短篇である。*The New
Yorker*, June 27 / July 4, 1994 に掲載された。

HOME RUN
Steven Millhauser

ホーム・ラン

スティーヴン・ミルハウザー

難易度 3
★ ★ ★

スティーヴン・ミルハウザー

(Steven Millhauser, 1943-)

　アメリカの作家。緻密な想像力・幻視力に貫かれた数々の短篇小説で知られる。19 世紀ドイツ文学を思わせるヨーロッパの香りと、20 世紀アメリカの大衆文化が不思議に共存しているところも特徴。ここに収めた "Home Run" は思いきりアメリカの側に針が振れている。オンライン文芸誌 *Electric Literature*, November 6, 2013 に初出(https://electricliterature.com/home-run-steven-milhauser/)。

Bottom of the ninth, two out, ❷ game tied, ❸ runners at the corners, ❹ the count full on McCluskey, the fans ❺ on their feet, this place is ❻ going wild, ❼ outfield shaded in to guard against ❽ the blooper, ❾ pitcher looks in, shakes off the sign, ❿ a
5 big lead off first, ⓫ they're not holding him on, ⓬ only run that matters is the man ⓭ dancing off third, shakes off another sign, McCluskey ⓮ asking for time, steps out of ⓯ the box, ⓰ tugs up his batter's glove, knocks dirt from his spikes, it's ⓱ a cat 'n' mouse game, ⓲ break up his rhythm, make him wait, now ⓳ the big guy's
10 back in the box, ⓴ down in his crouch, the tall ㉑ lefty ㉒ toes the rubber, looks in, ㉓ gives the nod, ㉔ will he go with the breaking ball, ㉕ maybe thinking slider, ㉖ third baseman back a step, ㉗ catcher

---

❶ Bottom of the ninth: 9 回（the ninth inning）裏
❷ game tied: 試合（game）は同点で。*The game was tied (at) 9–9 [9 all] with one inning to play.*（試合はあと 1 回を残して 9 対 9 で同点だった。『コンパスローズ英和辞典』）
❸ runners at the corners: 両方の角に走者がいて＝ランナー 1・3 塁で
❹ the count full on ...: ～に対してフルカウント（3 ボール 2 ストライク）で
❺ on their feet: 立ち上がって
❻ go(ing) wild: 熱狂する
❼ outfield shaded in: 外野手はやや内野（in）寄りに動いた＝前進守備態勢を取った。shade は打球の来そうな方に「シフト」すること。
❽ the blooper:（内野と外野のあいだに力なく落ちる）ポテンヒット
❾ pitcher looks in, shakes off the sign: ピッチャー、（キャッチャーの）サインを見て（同意できず）首を振った
❿ a big lead off first:（ランナーが）1 塁から大きくリードを取って
⓫ they're not holding him on: 守備側はランナーを（牽制球で 1 塁に）釘付けにしようとはしない。on なしで hold だけでも「牽制球でリードを取らせない」の意になる。
⓬ only run that matters is ...: the only run that matters is ... 「唯一問題にな

九回裏ツーアウト、同点でランナー一・三塁、バッターはマクラスキー、フルカウント、ファンは総立ち、球場中が熱狂しています、外野はポテンヒットを警戒して若干前進守備、ピッチャー、サインを覗き込んで首を横に振った、一塁ランナー、大きくリードを取っています、ファーストは事実上ノーマーク、サードでいまぴょんぴょん跳ねているランナーがホームを踏めばゲームは終了、ピッチャーふたたび首を横に振る、マクラスキーがここでタイムを要求しました、バッターボックスから出て手袋を引っぱり、スパイクの泥を叩いて落とす、このあたりなかなか微妙な駆け引き、相手のリズムを崩して、じらして、いま大きな体でバッターボックスに戻って構えに入る、マウンド上では長身の左腕、ピッチャーズプレートを爪先でつついて、サインを覗き、今度はうなずきます、変化球で行くでしょうか、ひょっ

る得点は〜だけだ」。野球の「得点」はこのように run という。

⓭ dancing off third: 跳びはねるように 3 塁からリードを取って

⓮ ask(ing) for time: タイムを要求する

⓯ the box: バッターボックス

⓰ tugs up his batter's glove: バッター用の手袋を引っぱって直す

⓱ a cat 'n' mouse game: 猫と鼠の追いかけっこのような駆け引き、心理戦。'n' は and。

⓲ break up his rhythm: 彼（ピッチャー）のリズムを崩す

⓳ the big guy's: the big guy is

⓴ down in his crouch: 腰を落として（構えて）

㉑ lefty: 左投げ投手

㉒ toes the rubber: ピッチャーズプレート（the rubber; 素材がゴムなので）付近を爪先で均す

㉓ gives the nod: （サインに同意して）うなずく

㉔ will he go with the breaking ball: 変化球（the breaking ball）で行くのか

㉕ maybe thinking slider: ひょっとするとスライダーを考えているのか

㉖ third baseman back a step: 三塁手が一歩下がって

㉗ catcher sets up inside: キャッチャーは内角に構える

sets up inside, pitcher taking his time, ❶ very deliberate out there, now he's ready, ❷ the set, the kick, he deals, it's ❸ a fastball, ❹ straight down the pipe, McCluskey swings, ❺ a tremendous rip, he ❻ crushes it, the crowd is screaming, the center fielder back,

5 back, ❼ angling toward right, ❽ tons of room out there in no-man's-land, still going back, ❾ he's at the track, that ball is going, going, he's at the wall, looking up, that ball is ❿ gone, ⓫ see ya, ⓬ hasta la vista baby, McCluskey ⓭ goes yard, over ⓮ the 390-foot mark in right center, game over, he ⓯ creamed it, that baby is gone and she

10 ⓰ ain't comin back anytime soon, sayonara, the crowd yelling, the ball still ⓱ carrying, the stands going crazy, McCluskey ⓲ rounding

---

❶ very deliberate out there: マウンド上（out there）非常に慎重で

❷ the set, the kick, he deals: セットポジション（the set [position]）に入り、マウンドを蹴るように足を上げ、投げた。日本の野球中継は「投げた……打った」と過去時制が基本だが、英語ではこのように現在形が基本。

❸ a fastball:「速球」ではなく「直球」「ストレート」。

❹ straight down the pipe:（パイプの中を通るように）ど真ん中を通って。(straight) down the middle と言っても同じ。

❺ a tremendous rip: すさまじい痛打

❻ crush(es):（球を）強打する

❼ angling toward right: ライト方向へ寄って

❽ tons of room out there in no-man's-land: 外野のがら空き状態を言っている。tons of ... は「膨大な〜」、room は「部屋」ではなく「スペース」、out there は〈ここ〉ではない「外の世界」「あっちの方」(ll. 1-2 ではマウンド上のピッチャーを "very deliberate out there" と形容)、no-man's-land は「無人地帯」。tons of room は第2巻 p. 136, l. 5 に既出："the terrace had big green fields behind where cows roamed at leisure and we had tons of room to play."（裏は広い野原で、牛がのんびりうろついて、あたしたちの遊ぶ場所もたっぷりあった）out there はこの巻 p. 74, l. 13 に既出："You would die out there in China, Mr. Kosak."（あなたははるか中国で死ぬんですよ、ミスタ・コーサック）

とするとスライダーか、三塁手が一歩うしろに下がる、キャッチャー内角に構えてピッチャー、マウンド上じっくり慌てず急がず、セットポジションの構え、足が上がって、投げました、ストレートが真ん中に入る、マクラスキーバットを振る、力一杯強振、打ちました、観客の歓声が上がる、センターバック、バック、ややライト側に走る、大きく開いた右中間を走ります、なおもバック、フェンス前に達した、球はなおも伸びている、伸びている、センターフェンスに貼りついて見上げた、入った、入りました、サヨナラの一打、マクラスキー柵越えの一打、右中間フェンスの119メートルと書かれた上をボールは越えてゲームセット、サヨナラベイビーもうお別れ、観客は大歓声、ボールはまだ飛んでいて球場はいまや狂乱状態、マクラスキー

❾ he's at the track: the track は the warning track（警告帯）。ボールを追って走る外野手にフェンスが近いことを知らせるために、外野の端に沿って設けた土や石炭殻の部分。

❿ gone: フェンスを越えて。野球中継で「入るか、入るか、入った！」は "Going, going, gone!"。

⓫ see ya: see you (later) さよなら、あばよ

⓬ hasta la vista baby: hasta la vista はスペイン語で、文字どおりには Until the (next) view=See you later。最後に baby を付けたこのフレーズは、映画『ターミネーター2』（1991）でアーノルド・シュワルツェネッガーが言う科白として有名。

⓭ go(es) yard: ホームランを打つ

⓮ the 390-foot mark in right center: 右中間のフェンスに付けた、390フィート（118.9m）の飛距離を示す掲示（distance marker）。

⓯ cream(ed): （ボールを）強打する

⓰ ain't comin back anytime soon:「もう帰ってこない」の意の決まり文句。anytime soon: すぐには、当分は。否定文・疑問文で「〜しない」の含みで使われることがほとんど。

⓱ carry(ing): （ボールが）飛ぶ

⓲ rounding second: 二塁を回って

second, the ball still up there, **❶**way up there, high over the right-center-field **❷**bleachers, headed for **❸**the upper deck, **❹**talk about **❺** a tape-measure shot, **❻** another M-bomb from the Big M, **❼** been doing it all year, he's rounding third, ball still going, still going,
5 that ball was **❽**smoked, **❾**a no doubter, wait a minute wait a minute oh oh oh **❿** it's outta here, that ball is out of the park, cleared the upper deck, **⓫** up over the Budweiser sign, **⓬** Jimmy can you get me figures on that, he hammered it clean outta here, **⓭**got all of it, can you believe it, **⓮**an out-of-the-parker, **⓯**hot diggity, **⓰**slammed

---

❶ way up there: はるか上空に。way は強調で、第2巻 p. 24, ll. 1-2 に "[I] hated to see them disappear way off up the valley toward the next town"（（列車が）隣り町に向かって谷間のずっと奥のほうに消えていくのを見るのも嫌だった）の形で既出。

❷ bleachers:（屋根のない）外野席

❸ the upper deck: スタンド上段

❹ talk about ...:～とはまさにこのことだ。*Talk about rude! She slammed the door in my face!*（なんて失礼なんだ！　ぼくの鼻先でドアをぴしゃりと閉めやがった！　『動詞を使いこなすための英和活用辞典』）

❺ a tape-measure shot: 特大ホームラン。1953 年に大打者ミッキー・マントル（当時21歳）が打った大ホームランの飛距離を巻き尺（a tape-measure）で測ったことに由来すると言われるが、実際に巻き尺を使ったという部分は神話。

❻ another M-bomb from the Big M: "M-bomb" は A-bomb (atomic bomb ＝原爆) や H-bomb (hydrogen bomb ＝水爆) のもじり。the Big M は「巨漢マクラスキー」。

❼ been doing it all year: it はホームランを打つこと。

❽ smoke(d):（ボールを）強打する。以下、本作品には「（ボールを）強打する／した」を意味する表現が頻出：hammered it clean (l. 8), slammed it (ll. 9 - p. 180, l. 1), socked one out (p. 180, l. 4), scald it, drilled it (ll. 6-7), jack it (p. 182, ll. 10-11), blistered it (p. 184, l. 1), powdered it (l. 1), plastered that ball (p. 184, l. 5), paste it (p. 186, l. 6), whack it, shellacked it (p. 188, l. 8), that

二塁ベースを回ってボールは依然空中を飛んでいます、右中間外野席のはる
か上、スタンド上段に向かう、これぞまさしく特大の一発、ビッグMマク
ラスキーのM爆弾、今シーズンはずっと好調をキープ、いまサードを回っ
て、ボールはまだ飛んでいる、まだ飛んでいる、まさにフルスイングの強打
でした、おや待ってください待って、何と場外、場外に出ました。上段も越
えてバドワイザーの看板も越えた、ジミー、データ頼むよ、いやー実にす
ごい、真っ芯に当たった一打、信じられません、場外打、何メートル飛ん
だでしょうか、大柄のバッターいまホームプレートを踏んでチームメート

---

ball was spanked（l. 13）

❾ a no doubter: 文句なしのホームラン

❿ it's outta here: the ball is out of here (the ballpark)

⓫ up over the Budweiser sign:（最上段の屋根の上にある）バドワイザービー
ルの看板も越えて

⓬ Jimmy can you get me figures on that: 記録担当のスタッフ、ジミーが登場。
figures on that は「いまの一打に関する数字、データ（figures）」。

⓭ got all of it: "get all of it" で「会心の当たりを飛ばす」で、通常ホームランを
意味する。*As a hitter, there have been instances where I felt that "Oh,
I got all of it," but it ended up being caught deep in the outfield or
bounced off the wall instead.*（打者として、「うん、これは行ったな」と思っ
たのにフェンスギリギリで捕られたり、フェンスに当たったりしたこともあり
ます＝飛ばないボールが採用されてどう変わったかを問われた韓国野球リーグ
選手 Heo Kyoung-Min の返答。April 23, 2019, *Fangraphs*）

⓮ an out-of-the-parker: l. 5 の no doubter と同じ発想の造語。

⓯ hot diggity: これは野球とは関係ない普通のスラング。「こりゃーすごい！」

⓰ slammed it a country mile: a country mile は a long way のユーモラスな
言い換え。*There were no other houses within a country mile of where
we lived.*（私たちの家の周り、ほかの家なんか全然なかった。*Cambridge
Advanced Learner's Dictionary & Thesaurus*）

it a country mile, the big guy's ❶crossing the plate, ❷team's all over him, the crowd roaring, ❸what's that Jimmy, Jimmy are you sure, ❹I'm being told it's a first, ❺that's right a first, ❻no one's ever socked one out before, ❼the Clusker ❽really got around on
5 it, ❾looking fastball all the way, got ❿the sweet part of the bat on it, ⓫launched a rocket, ⓬oh baby did he scald it, I mean he drilled it, the big guy is strong but ⓭it's that smooth swing of his, ⓮the King of Swing, puts his whole body into it, ⓯hits with his legs, he smashed it, ⓰a Cooperstown clout, ⓱right on the screws, the ball
10 still going, unbelievable, up past ⓲the Goodyear blimp, ⓳see ya

❶ crossing the plate: ホームプレートを踏んでいる
❷ team's all over him: all over ... は寄ってたかって手荒く祝福している感じ
❸ what's that Jimmy: what's that はよく聞きとれなかった言葉を聞き返すときのごく一般的な言い方。
❹ I'm being told ...: まさにたったいま言われているところだというニュアンス。
❺ that's right: 「そうなんですよ」。まさかと思われるかもしれませんが……という含み。
❻ no one's ever socked one out before : out はこの場合 out (of) the ballpark の意。
❼ the Clusker: アナウンサーがその場の勢いで McCluskey のニックネームを作っている。
❽ really got around on it: The Dickson Baseball Dictionary によれば get around は "To swing the bat fast enough to hit the pitch"（振り遅れずにボールを捉える）。If he [Ichiro Suzuki] can get around on an inside pitch, he has surprising pop for a player listed at 5' 9'' and 160 pounds.（もしイチローが内角球もしっかり打てるとすれば、175cm、73kg のプレーヤーとしては驚くべきパワーだ：イチローがメジャーリーグにデビューした当時のジャーナリストの発言。The Dickson Baseball Dictionary に引用）
❾ looking fastball all the way: 直球が手元に来るまでじっくり見て
❿ the sweet part of the bat: バットの一番よく飛ぶ面。the sweet spot という言い方もある。

の手荒い祝福を受けています、観客の声はいまや怒号、え何だってジミー、ほんとかいジミー、皆さん、史上初だそうです、そうです史上初、この球場で場外弾は誰一人打ったことがなかった、その偉業をマクラスキーが成し遂げました、ストレートをじっくり待ってガツンと当ててロケットを発進、いやーすごかった、大きな大きな当たり、パワーはもとよりそのスイングの滑らかさはまさにキング・オブ・スイング、全体重をかけ腰を一杯にためて渾身の一振り、殿堂入りものの一打、見事に真芯で捉えたボールはまだ飛んでいます、信じられません、グッドイヤータイヤの飛行船も通り過ぎ、see ya later alligator、はるか青空に上がっていきます、まだ飛ん

❶ launched a rocket: ロケットを打ち上げた

❷ oh baby did he scald it, I mean he drilled it: oh baby, boy などといった感嘆の語句のあとに、倒置形が来て内容を強調する、というのはよくあるパターン。*She was told women aren't supposed to travel alone. Boy, did she prove them wrong!*（女は一人で旅しちゃいけないと言われた彼女。身をもって証明、全然そんなことない！ Jacob H. Fries, *Inlander*, March 7, 2019）I mean と言って言い換えているが、別に大きく訂正しているわけではない。

❸ it's that smooth swing of his: 大事なのはあの滑らかなスイングだ

❹ the King of Swing: 元来は 1930 〜 40 年に大人気だったスイング・ジャズバンドのリーダー Benny Goodman に使われた呼称。

❺ hits with his legs: 腰をしっかり据えて打つ

❻ a Cooperstown clout: 殿堂入りものの一発。Cooperstown はニューヨーク州中部の町で、野球発祥の地とされ、野球の殿堂（the National Baseball Hall of Fame）がある。clout はこれまた「強打」。

❼ right on the screws: バットの真芯でとらえて。元はゴルフ用語で、昔の木製クラブのねじ留め（the screws）のある箇所が打面の中心だったことから。

❽ the Goodyear blimp: （タイヤメーカーの）グッドイヤー社の宣伝用小型飛行船

❾ see ya later alligator: 冗談めかした別れの挨拶。alligator が出てくるのは単に later と韻を踏むから。

later alligator, up into ❶ the wild blue yonder, still going, ❷ ain't
nothing gonna stop that baby, ❸ they're walking McCluskey back
to the dugout, fans ❹swarming all over the field, they're pointing
up at the sky, the ball still traveling, up real high, that ball is way
5 way outta here, Jimmy what have you got, going, going, ❺hold on,
what's that Jimmy, I'm told the ball has gone all the way through
❻the troposphere, is that a fact, now ❼how about that, the big guy
❽hit it a ton, really ❾skyed it, up there now in ❿the stratosphere,
⓫good golly Miss Molly, ⓬ help me out here Jimmy, stratosphere
10 starts at six miles and goes up 170,000 feet, ⓭man did he ever jack
it outta here, ⓮ a dinger from McSwinger, ⓯a whopper from the
Big Bopper, going, going, the stands ⓰emptying out, the ball up

❶ the wild blue yonder: 荒々しき青き彼方＝大空。アメリカ空軍の歌 "The U. S.
Air Force" の別タイトルでもある。
❷ ain't nothing gonna stop ...: これでまとまったフレーズ。折り目正しい英語
に直せば There is nothing that's going to stop ... となる。「～を止めるもの
は何もない＝もうどうにも止まらない」
❸ they're walking McCluskey back to the dugout: walk ... back で「～を連
れて帰る」。
❹ swarm(ing): 群れをなしてうごめく
❺ hold on: ちょっと待ってください
❻ the troposphere: 対流圏。大気圏の最下層で、地表から約 10 ～ 15 キロ上空
付近まで。
❼ how about that: どうですかこれは、何ということでしょう
❽ hit it a ton: 途方もないやつをかっ飛ばした
❾ skyed it: ボールを天高く飛ばした
❿ the stratosphere: 成層圏。対流圏の上の層で、上空 50 キロぐらいまで。
⓫ good golly Miss Molly:「どひゃあ、すげえ」を意味する俗語。ロックンロー
ル歌手 Little Richard のヒット曲（1958）のタイトルとしても有名。

でいる、いやーもはや何ものにも止められない、バッターはチームメートに囲まれてダッグアウトへ戻ります、ファンの皆さんがグラウンド一面に群がっています、みんな空を指さしている、ボールはまだはるか上空を駆けています、本当に本当に高い、ジミー、データは、まだぐんぐん上がっている、え、ちょっと待てジミー、皆さん、ボールは対流圏を突き抜けたそうです、ほんとかいジミー、これは驚き、巨漢による超大型の一発、空高く舞い上がり目下成層圏に入っています、good golly Miss Molly、ジミー数字、おお来た来た、成層圏は地上9キロメートルの高さから始まり約50キロメートルまで続きます、いやとんでもない一打もあったものです、試合を決める一発、強打者マクラスキー、またの名をマクスインガー、怪力スイングが生んだ一撃、まだ飛んでいる、スタンドはもはや人もまばら、ボールはいま成

⓬ help me out here Jimmy:「成層圏」とは何なのか教えてくれとジミーに言っている。help ... out で「〜に手を貸す」。p. 70, ll. 14-15 に "You'd expect some member of the Aryan race to help you out a little, wouldn't you, Mr. Kosak?"（誰か白人が救いの手をさしのべてくれたらって思いますよね、そうでしょうミスタ・コーサック？）の形で既出。

⓭ man did he ever jack it outta here: man は「うわあ、すげえ」という感嘆詞。did he ever ... は p. 180, l. 5 に出てきた "oh baby did he scald it"（いやーすごかった、大きな大きな当たり）と同じく倒置を使った強調。

⓮ a dinger from McSwinger: a dinger は「ホームラン」、McSwinger は Swinger（フルスイングする強打者）と McCluskey の名をかけ、dinger と韻を踏ませている。

⓯ a whopper from the Big Bopper: a dinger from McSwinger にほぼ同じ。Bopper は「ホームラン打者」だが、the Big Bopper は the Big Dipper（北斗七星）のもじりでもある。

⓰ empty(ing) out:（客が帰って）空になる

in ❶ the mesosphere, ❷ the big guy blistered it, he powdered it, ❸the ground crew picking up bottles and paper cups and ❹peanut shells and hot dog wrappers, ❺power-washing the seats, ❻you can bet people'll be talking about this one ❼for a long time to come, he

5 plastered that ball, ❽a pitch right down Broadway, ❾tried to paint the inside corner but missed his spot, ❿you don't want to ⓫let the big guy extend those arms, up now in ⓬ the exosphere, way up there, never seen anything like it, ⓭ the ball carrying well all day but ⓮ who would've thought, wait a minute, ⓯ hold on a second,

10 ⓰holy cow it's left ⓱the earth's atmosphere, ⓲so long it's been good ta know ya, up there now in outer space, I mean that ball is outta

---

❶ the mesosphere: 中間圏。成層圏の上の層で、上空 80 キロぐらいまで。

❷ the big guy blistered it, he powdered it: blister と powder の元の意味はそれぞれ「〜を水ぶくれにする」「〜を粉にする」。

❸ the ground crew: グラウンドの係員

❹ peanut shells: ピーナツの殻

❺ power-wash(ing): 〜を高圧洗浄する

❻ you can bet ...: (賭けてもいいが) 絶対〜だ

❼ for a long time to come: 「今後長いあいだ」の意の定型句。

❽ a pitch right down Broadway: ど真ん中を通る球。Broadway は「ホームプレート中央」の意で、この right down Broadway という形でよく使う。

❾ tried to paint the inside corner: *The Dickson Baseball Dictionary* によれば paint は "To throw pitches over the inside or outside corners of home plate" (ホームプレートの内角・外角のコーナーに球を投げる)。要するに日本語の「コーナーを突く」の「突く」。

❿ you don't want to ...: 〜したくない＝〜してはまずい。*You don't want to eat too much.* (食べすぎないほうがいいよ。『コンパスローズ英和辞典』)

⓫ let the big guy extend those arms: 巨漢が (フルスイングで) あの腕をのばすのを許す

⓬ the exosphere: 外気圏。大気圏の最上層で高度 500 キロ以上の部分。

層圏を越えて中間圏に入る、とてつもない代物を打ったものです、渾身にして快心の一撃、係員が壜や紙コップ、ピーナツの殻にホットドッグの包み紙を拾い集め、高圧洗浄機で座席を洗っています、これは間違いなく長年語り草となることでしょう、真ん中の速球、内角のコーナーを狙ったが外れて真ん中に入り、巨体のマクラスキーにフルスイングを許してしまった、球はいま外気圏に達しました、いやこんなすごいのは私（わたくし）アナウンサー生活で見たことがありません、一日ずっとボールがよく飛ぶ日ではありましたが、それにしても誰がこんなものを予想、待ってくださいちょっと待ってください、これは参りました、ボールは大気圏外に出たそうです、いまや宇宙空間を飛んでいる、さらば友よいまこそ別れの云々かんぬん、本当に外も外、大気圏外

⓭ the ball carrying well all day: ボールは今日一日ずっとよく飛んでいて。carry は p. 176, ll. 10-11 でも "the ball still carrying"（ボールはまだ飛んでいる）の形で出てきたが、特にここのように風・湿度などの影響で球が「飛ぶ」「飛ばない」を言うときに使う。*Right off the bat I thought it was a routine play, honestly, because the ball wasn't carrying well all day," Campbell said. "But as I was running it kept carrying.*（「打ったときは正直言って平凡な打球かと思ったんです、一日ずっとボールがあまり飛んでいなかったから」とキャンベルは語った。「ところが走ってるとぐんぐんのびていったんです」 *The Oregonian*, oregonlive.com, June. 10, 2012）

⓮ who would've thought ...: 誰が〜などと思っただろう。*Who would have thought she'd end up dancing for a living?*（彼女が踊りで生計を立てることになるなんて、誰が思っただろう? *Longman Dictionary of Contemporary English*）

⓯ hold on a second: すぐ前の wait a minute とほぼ同じ。

⓰ holy cow: えっ、まさか。これも野球とは関係ない一般的なフレーズ。

⓱ the earth's atmosphere: 地球の大気圏

⓲ so long it's been good ta know ya: さよなら (so long)、会えてよかったよ。ta know ya = to know you. フォーク歌手 Woody Guthrie の歌 "So Long, It's Been Good to Know Yuh"（1935）から。

here, **❶**bye bye birdie, still going, down here at the park the stands are empty, sun gone down, moon's up, nearly full, it's a beautiful night, **❷** temperature seventy-three, another day game tomorrow then out to the West Coast for **❸**a tough three-game series, the ball
5 still going, looks like she's headed for the moon, **❹** talk about a moon shot, **❺** man did he ever paste it outta here, higher, deeper, going, going, it's gone past the moon, **❻** you can kiss that baby goodbye, **❼** good night Irene I'll see you in my dreams, the big guy **❽** got good wood on it, **❾** right on the money, **❿** swinging for
10 the downs, the ball still traveling, **⓫**sailing past Mars, up through **⓬**the asteroid belt, **⓭**you gotta love it, **⓮**past Jupiter, see ya Saturn,

---

❶ bye bye birdie: 1960 年初演のミュージカル (*Bye Bye Birdie*) の題名を踏まえている。birdie は「小鳥ちゃん」。

❷ temperature seventy-three: 華氏 (Fahrenheit) 73 度は摂氏 (centigrade) 22. 8 度。

❸ a tough three-game series: 手強い（相手との）3 連戦

❹ talk about a moon shot: talk about ...（〜とはまさにこのこと）は p. 178, ll. 2-3 に "talk about a tape-measure shot"（これぞまさしく特大の一発）の形で既出。

❺ man did he ever paste it: こうした倒置による強調は、p. 182, ll. 10-11 に "man did he ever jack it outta here"（いやとんでもない一打もあったものです）の形で既出。

❻ you can kiss that baby goodbye: kiss ... goodbye で「〜をあきらめる」の意の成句。*You have to kiss the plan goodbye.*（その計画はあきらめなきゃしょうがないよ。『コンパスローズ英和辞典』）

❼ good night Irene I'll see you in my dreams: 1933 年にフォーク・ブルース歌手 Leadbelly が録音して有名になったフォークソング "Good Night, Irene" の一節。

❽ got good wood on it: "put/get good wood on the ball" で「ボールを（バットの）芯で捉える」。good wood は p. 180, l. 5 の the sweet part of the

をまだ飛んでいる、バイバイバーディ、こちらスタジアムは観客席ももう空っぽ、陽は沈み月はのぼってほぼ満月、美しい夜です、気温は23度、明日もデーゲームを戦い次は西海岸で手ごわい三連戦、ボールはまだ飛んでいる、月に向かう勢いです、ムーンショットとはまさにこのこと、よくぞ飛ばしたものです、どんどん高く、遠くへ、飛んで、飛んで、とうとう月も越えました、グッバイベイビー、サヨナラ三角また来て四角、グッナイアイリーン、夢で逢いましょう、ガツンと芯で捉えた狙いどおりの一打、ボールはまだ飛んでいる、火星を過ぎて小惑星帯も抜けた、これはもう脱帽するしかありません、木星を越えた、さらば土星、アデュー天王星、アリヴェデ

---

bat と同じくバットの一番よく飛ぶ部分のこと。

❾ right on the money: まさにぴったり、的を射て。*You were right on the money when you said that he would have to resign.*（彼には辞任してもらうしかない、と君が言ったのはまさにそのとおりだったよ。*Longman Dictionary of Contemporary English*）

❿ swinging for the downs: go for the downs で「ホームランを狙う」。go for the fences, go for the pump といった言い方もある。*Distant fences discourage home-run cuts; no wonder National batters are less inclined to go for the downs.*（フェンスが遠ければバッターはホームラン狙いをしなくなる。〔フェンスが概して遠い〕ナショナル・リーグのバッターたちが一発狙いをあまりしないのも不思議はない。*Sports Illustrated*, April 4, 1983）

⓫ sailing past Mars: sail はこのように飛行物体が「滑るように飛ぶ」の意でも使う。

⓬ the asteroid belt:（火星と木星のあいだの）小惑星帯

⓭ you gotta love …: gotta = have got to だがこの形で決まり文句で、「誰でも〜を好きにならずにいられない＝〜は絶対いい」。

⓮ past Jupiter, see ya Saturn, so long Uranus, arrivederci Neptune: 順に木星、土星、天王星、海王星に別れを告げている。arrivederci はイタリア語で「さよなら」。

so long Uranus, arrivederci Neptune, up there now in ❶the Milky
Way, ❷a round-tripper to the Big Dipper, ❸a galaxy shot, a black-
hole blast, how many stars are we talking about Jimmy, Jimmy
says two hundred billion, that's two hundred billion stars in the
5 Milky Way, ❹a nickel for every star and you can stop worrying
about your ❺401(k), the ball still traveling, out past the Milky
Way and headed on into ❻intergalactic space, hooo ❼did he ever
whack it, he shellacked it, ❽a good season but came up short in
the playoffs, McCluskey'll be back next year, the ball out past
10 the Andromeda galaxy, going, going, the big guy mashed it, ❾he
clob-bobbered it, wham-bam-a-rammed it, he's looking good in
spring training, ❿back with that sweet swing, out past ⓫the Virgo
supercluster with its thousands of galaxies, ⓬that ball was spanked,
a Big Bang for the record book, ⓭a four-bagger with swagger, out

❶ the Milky Way: 天の川、銀河
❷ a round-tripper to the Big Dipper: round-tripper は「本塁から出発して
元の本塁まで往復（round trip）すること」つまり「ホームラン」。the Big
Dipper は p. 182, ll. 11-12 の the Big Bopper の註で触れたように「北斗七
星」。
❸ a galaxy shot, a black-hole blast: 銀河（galaxy）に届く一発、ブラックホー
ルへ飛び込む一撃。さすがにこのあたりまでホラがエスカレートしてくると、
既成のベースボールスラングではなくミルハウザーの造語。
❹ a nickel for every star: 星一つにつき5セント貨が1枚（あれば）
❺ 401(k): 米国の積み立て退職金制度。four-oh-one k と読む。
❻ intergalactic space:（銀河系を越えた）銀河間の宇宙空間
❼ did he ever whack it: ふたたび強調の倒置。
❽ a good season but came up short in the playoffs:（マクラスキーは）活
躍のシーズンだったがプレーオフではいまーつだった。ここで時間の流れが一
気に早くなっている（球はまだ飛んでいるのにシーズンはもう終わりポストシー

Steven Millhauser

ルチ海王星、いまや天の川に浮かんでいます、ビッグディッパー（北斗七星）めがけたラウンドトリッパー（本塁打）、銀河に放たれたショット、ブラックホールも破裂かという勢い、ジミーあのへん星っていくつあるのかね、ほぉ、ジミーが言うには二千億あるそうです、天の川には星が二千億、星ひとつが五セントだったら年金の心配も要りませんねぇ、失礼しました、ボールまだ飛んでいる、天の川を過ぎて銀河系間空間に突入、いやまったくよくぞここまで飛ばしたもの、天晴れ（あっぱれ）と言うほかありません、大活躍のシーズンでしたがポストシーズンではいまひとつだったマクラスキー、来年もまたプレーが楽しみ、ボールはアンドロメダ星雲を過ぎてなおも飛んでいる、飛んでいる、よくぞ飛ばした、満身の力を込めた一打、何という怪力、今年は春のトレーニングから好調でした、美しいスイング見事復活、球はすでに数千の銀河群を有する乙女座超銀河団も越えた、空前絶後の飛距離、ギネスブックもののビッグバ

ズンも終わっている）ことに注意。

❾ he clob-bobbered it, wham-bam-a-rammed it: "clob-bobber(ed)" は clobber（ぶっ叩く）に「上乗せ」し、"wham-bam-a-ram(med)" も wham, bam, ram（いずれも「ぶっ叩く」）を合体させて、これまで以上の「強打感」を出している。

❿ back with that sweet swing: あの滑らかなスイングが戻って

⓫ the Virgo supercluster:（天の川、アンドロメダ銀河などいくつもの銀河を含む）乙女座超銀河団

⓬ that ball was spanked: これも「強打した」のもうひとつの言い方だが、spank は本来は「子供の尻を叩く」というような文脈で使われる。

⓭ a four-bagger with swagger: 堂々たるホームラン。a four-bagger は１塁から本塁まで４つの塁（bag）を踏むということ。swagger はいばって歩く感じをいうが、意味よりも bagger と韻を踏むところがポイント。

189

past ❶the Hydra-Centaurus supercluster, still going, out past ❷the
Aquarius supercluster, thousands and millions of superclusters
out there, McCluskey still remembers it, he's ❸coaching down
in Triple A, the big man a sensation ❹in his day, the ball still out
there, still climbing, sailing out toward the edge of ❺the observable
universe, ❻the edge receding faster than the speed of light, the ball
still going, still going, he remembers the feel of ❼the wood in his
hands, the good sound of it as he swung, smell of ❽pine tar, ❾bottom
of the ninth, two on, two out, a summer day.

❶ the Hydra-Centaurus supercluster: 海蛇座 = ケンタウルス座超銀河団
❷ the Aquarius supercluster: 水瓶座超銀河団
❸ coaching down in Triple A: (現役引退して) トリプルA (マイナーリーグの
トップクラス) でコーチをやって
❹ in his day: 全盛期は、若いころは
❺ the observable universe: 観測可能な宇宙。直径約930億光年とされる。
❻ the edge receding: (膨張しつづけるので) 宇宙の果てが後退してゆく
❼ the wood: (木製の) バット
❽ pine tar: (滑り止めにバットに塗る) 松材のタール、松やに
❾ bottom of the ninth, two on, two out: 無限に拡がっていく話なのに、語り
の最後は一番最初の言葉に戻って円環を閉じることの妙。two on は「塁上に
二人」。

ン、勝負を決めた超特大の打球、海蛇座・ケンタウルス座超銀河団も抜けてなお飛んでいる、水瓶座超銀河団をいま過ぎた、このあたりは超銀河団が何千、何万、何百万と群がっています、マクラスキー自身この一発はいまも忘れておりません、目下３Ａのコーチを務める元巨漢スラッガー、往年の一大センセーション、ボールはいまだ彼方にあり、いまだ上昇し、観察可能な宇宙の果てに向かってなお邁進中、宇宙の果ては光速より速く後退していてボールはなおも飛んでいる、なおも飛んでいる、両手に握ったバットの感触をマクラスキーはいまも覚えています、スイングしたときのあの快音を、滑り止めパインタールの匂いを、九回裏、ランナー二人、ツーアウト、夏の日。

●

ちなみに

　1986年に発表した長篇 *From the Realm of Morpheus* の冒頭でも、ミルハウザーは野球を印象的な形で使っている。気だるい午後の、ピッチャーの球を待つバッターでさえ "slowly, dreamily, like a boy underwater"（ゆっくり、夢見るように、水中にもぐった少年のよう）にバットを振る公園で、主人公の少年はファウルボールを探しに藪の中に入っていって、地下への通路を発見する……兎を追って穴に落ちるアリスの、これ以上正しいアメリカ的「意訳」があるだろうか？

Sugar and Spice and Everything Lice: The Spitdog's Set Free
Jack Napes

スピットドッグを解放せよ——英国道中膝栗毛

ジャック・ネイプス

難易度 2
★ ★ ☆

ジャック・ネイプス
（Jack Napes, 1950- ）

「猿」もしくは「猿のように悪辣な人間」を意味する語 jackanapes
と妙に似た名を持つこの著者の正体は謎に包まれている。日本在住
と信じられており、国際レプラコーン結社と河童同盟との提携成立
を画策中といわれる。

*M*ost fairy tales begin with something like "in a land far away" or "once upon a time," **❶**whatever that means. **❷**Forget it kids, this is not one of those tales. This story is about **❸**here and now and then and there and characters that may live in your very neighborhood, maybe even

5 in the basement of your building. If you haven't seen them, it is because you haven't been looking hard enough. This story will open your eyes.

Chapter 1 **❹**The Tribe Transported

10

❺Squatsy found it first. Being short and having very good eyesight made it easier for her to do so. It **❻**was green and hard and beautiful and stuck in a crack in the pavement. But it was a bit of a mystery to her. "What's this?" she asked as she **❼**yanked it up.

15   **❽**Brownsnout Spookfish was **❾**uniquely qualified to answer her question. **❿**After all, **⓫**he had mirrors in the vicinity of his eyes,

---

Sugar and Spice and Everything Lice: マザーグースの一節 "What are little girls made of？/ Sugar and spice / And everything nice"（女の子って何でできてる？ 砂糖にスパイス、すてきなもの全部）のもじり。nice がここでは lice（louse＝ シラミ の複数形）に替わっている。

❶ *whatever that means*: いま挙げた二つの決まり文句に、あまり意味がないと思っているらしき口調。

❷ *Forget it*: 同じく「そんなの意味ないからね」という感じ。

❸ *here and now and then and there*: here and now, then and there でそれぞれまとまっている。

❹ **The Tribe Transported**: 直訳は「移動させられた一団」だが、別世界に拉致されたような響き。

❺ Squatsy: squat（動詞で「うずくまる、しゃがむ」、形容詞で「ずんぐりした」）

たいていのおとぎばなしは「どこか遠い国で」とか「むかしむかし」とか、なんだかよくわかんない言葉からはじまる。けどいいかい、よい子のみんな、これはそういう話とは違うからね。これは＜いま・ここ＞と＜そのとき・そこ＞の物語。登場するキャラクターたちも、まさに君の暮らす界隈に——下手すりゃ君の住んでる建物の地下室に——住んでるかもしれない。こんな奴ら見たことないとしたら、それは君がちゃんと見てないからかもよ。この物語を読めば目が開くはず。

第1章　有象無象団、拉致される

　真っ先に見つけたのはスクワッツィだった。背が低く、視力はすごくいいので、彼女には訳ないことだったのだ。それは緑色で、硬くて、美しく、舗道のひびにはさまっていた。けれどそれは、彼女にとってちょっとした神秘だった。「何かな、これ？」と、ぐいっと引き抜きながらスクワッツィは言った。
　ブラウンスナウト・スプークフィッシュは彼女のこの問いに答える上で誰

を連想させる名前。
❻ was [...] stuck in a crack: ひび・裂け目にはさまっていた
❼ yanked it up: 力いっぱい引っぱって抜いた
❽ Brownsnout Spookfish: デメニギス（出目似鱚、barreleye）科の深海魚の一種。文字どおりに訳すと「茶色い鼻面のお化け魚」。
❾ uniquely qualified to ...: 特に〜する資格があって、〜するのにうってつけで
❿ After all: 何しろ
⓫ he had mirrors in the vicinity of his eyes: 眼のそば（the vicinity）に鏡を持っていた。この魚は実際に目の一部に鏡のように光を反射する構造を持ち、網膜に光を集中させることができる。

which gave him exceptional ❶hindsight. "That's an emerald," he answered. "It's a precious stone, ❷a gem."

Spookfish took the emerald from Squatsy and wiped it with a clean handkerchief, as other members of the Tribe gathered round.
5 The stone ❸had a cool, calming effect on the group. Its green was the green of relaxation, ❹a green-room green, ❺if you will.

"It must be from ❻the Emerald Isle," observed ❼the Odd Duck, who was frequently wrong but very ❽conventional, always willing to say or think whatever most people happen to be saying or
10 thinking at the moment.

But ❾Suctrocious, the suckerfish, who liked to emphasize words beginning in "s," said, "❿Simply not so. Such stones are from Colombia, not Ireland."

To which the Odd Duck replied, "I see," but ⓫he didn't really.

15   ⓬Squeezle approached the stone slowly and said in her sweet voice, nearly a whisper, "There's something in there."

---

❶ hindsight: 普通は時間的な意味での「あと知恵」だが、ここでは字面どおりに、バックミラーのような後ろの (hind) 視界 (sight) の意。

❷ a gem: 宝石

❸ had a cool, calming effect on ...: 〜に対して、頭を冷静にし、静める効果があった

❹ a green-room green: a green room で「楽屋、休憩室」。

❺ if you will: そう言いたければ、何なら〜と言ってもいいが

❻ the Emerald Isle: アイルランド島の詩的な呼び名でもある。

❼ the Odd Duck: odd fish, oddball などと同じく「変人、変わり者」の意。

❽ conventional: 「ごく普通の」というニュートラルな意味になることも多いが、この場合のように、「〈普通〉に合わせたがる」という否定的な意味を帯びることも多い。

よりも適役だった。何と言っても、目の近くに鏡がついていて、うしろを見る視力が異様に高いのだ。「エメラルドだね。宝石だよ」

スプークフィッシュがスクワッツィからエメラルドを受け取り、きれいなハンカチで拭いていると、有象無象団の仲間が集まってきた。宝石は彼らの気持ちを冷静に、穏やかにする効果をもたらした。その緑はリラックスの緑、言うなれば休憩室（グリーン・ルーム）の緑だったのである。

「きっとエメラルドの島で獲れたんだな」とオッド・ダックが言った。オッド・ダックの言うことはたいてい間違っていた。とにかくいつもありきたりなことばかり言って、その時その時にたいていの人が言ったり考えたりしていることをそのまま言ったり考えたりしていた。

一方、小判鮫（サカーフィッシュ）のサクトローシャスは、sから始まる言葉を強調することを好み、このときも「それは、錯誤だ。そういう、珠玉は、アイルランドではなくコロンビアから来たものだ」と言った。

オッド・ダックはそれに応えて「なるほど」と言ったが、全然なるほどとは思っていなかった。

スクイーズルがそっと石に近づいていき、優しい、ほとんどささやくような声で「中に何かいるわ」と言った。

---

❾ Suctrocious, the suckerfish: Suctrocious は atrocious（極悪の）を連想させる。suckerfish は「コバンザメ」。

❿ Simply not so: それは全然違う

⓫ he didn't really: he didn't really see.「わかった」(I see) と答えたもののわかっていなかったということ。

⓬ Squeezle: squeeze（ぎゅっと抱きしめる）を連想させる名。

"It must be an ant or plant or something," the Odd Duck said.

"Simply not so. You're thinking of ❶amber. Experts, people who ❷know what they're talking about — and *you* don't — call that ❸an 'inclusion.' It is something that was there before the gem

5 was formed," said Suctrocious, who ❹figured the Odd Duck was, ❺as was often the case, in need of a head cleaning. So he waved his ❻suctorial disks over his conversation partner and chanted:

❼Octopus, octopi, ❽a misinformed person I descry

10   ❾Suctorial power, remove ❿the clutter

That ⓫has turned his brain into butter.

Squeezle continued staring into the inclusion. After a few minutes, she thought she saw things moving inside, people or animals

15 perhaps. It was ⓬hazy, blurry ⓭like some of those famous French paintings they show you in art class. ⓮The images gradually

---

❶ amber: 琥珀

❷ know what they're talking about: 自分が何を言っているかわかっている ＝物事をちゃんと理解して言っている。第 1 巻 p. 52, l. 10 では "You don't know what you are saying."（馬鹿を言うんじゃない）という形で出てきた。

❸ an 'inclusion': 包有物。鉱物結晶内部に含有された各種の異物。

❹ figure(d): 〜と思う

❺ as was often the case: しばしばあることだったが、例によって例のごとく

❻ suctorial disks: 吸盤

❼ Octopus, octopi: octopi は複数形。

❽ a misinformed person I descry: I descry a misinformed person. misinformed は「思い違いをした」、descry は「見つける、見える」。

❾ Suctorial power: 吸引力

「きっとアリか、植物とかだな」とオッド・ダックが言った。

「それは、**錯誤**だ。君が考えているのは琥珀だ。専門家は、ちゃんと物がわかっている人たちは——そして君はそうじゃない——これを『**包有物**』と呼ぶ。宝石が形成される前からあったものを、**総称して**、その言葉で、**指し示**すのだ」とサクトローシャスが言った。オッド・ダックが頭の清掃を必要としていると、サクトローシャスは考えたのである（実際、必要なことも多かった）。かくして彼は、己の吸盤を話し相手の頭上で振り、こう唱えた。

　　　蛸よ、蛸たちよ、思い違いの人間がいたぞ
　　　吸引力よ、取り除け混乱を
　　　脳味噌をバターに変えた錯乱を。

　スクイーズルはなおも包有物の中をじっと覗いていた。数分後、中で何かが動くのが見えた気がした。人間か、動物か。ぼんやりもわっとしていて、美術の授業で見せられる有名なフランスの絵画みたいだった。でも像はだんだん、朝早くの霧が晴れるみたいにはっきりしてきた。「中に人間たちがい

❿ the clutter: 散らかり、乱雑。a clutterer といえば「片付けられない人」。
⓫ has turned his brain into butter: 脳みそをバターにしてしまった。
⓬ hazy, blurry: 霞みがかった、ぼやけた
⓭ like some of those famous French paintings they show you in art class: モネなどの印象派絵画を思い浮かべればよい。
⓮ The images: このように image は、基本的な意味としては「イメージ」よりも「像」。

199

became clearer, though, like the ❶lifting of early morning fog.
"There are people, old-time people in there," she said.

　　The stone was passed among the Tribe and all saw the vision,
but no one could explain it.

5

Chapter 2 18th-Century ❷Leprechaun

As often happens in stories but less often in reality, at that precise
moment a number of things occurred, ❸none of which were
10 especially good for the Tribe. ❹A superstorm struck suddenly, and
❺it started to rain, not cats and dogs but elephants and hippos.
❻As might be expected ❼lightning flashed from and across the
darkened sky, and tornado-like ❽conditions ❾took hold. ❿A
vortex — a kind of ⓫swirling and twirling of the air — was created
15 and like a terrible toilet sucked the unlucky group ⓬like so much
poop into the emerald's inclusion.

---

❶ lift(ing): (霧などが) 晴れる
❷ **Leprechaun**: アイルランドの伝説に登場する、小さな老人の姿をした妖精。
❸ none of which were ...: そのうちのどれも〜ではなかった
❹ A superstorm: 超特大の嵐
❺ it started to rain, not cats and dogs but elephants and hippos: rain
　 cats and dogs (土砂降りの雨が降る) という慣用句を踏まえている。
　 hippo(s) は「カバ」。
❻ As might be expected: よくあるように、案の定
❼ lightning flashed from and across the darkened sky: 稲妻が暗い空から
　 (from) 落ち、と同時に空一面に (across) 走った
❽ conditions: 気象状況、天候
❾ took hold: take hold で「定着する、本格化する」。*Grass-roots democracy*

るわ、昔の人間たちが」とスクイーズルは言った。

　宝石が団員たちの手から手に渡り、誰もが中の情景を見たが、それを説明
できる者は一人もいなかった。

第2章　18世紀のレプラコーン

　現実にはそれほどないけれど物語ではよくあるように、まさにこの瞬間い
ろんなことが同時に起き、そのどれひとつ、有象無象団にとって格別いいこ
とではなかった。超特大の嵐がいきなり襲ってきて、雨が降り出し、それも
土砂降りどころではなく大岩降りという激しさだった。となれば次は案の定、
暗くなった空から稲妻が落ちてきて、かつ空一面を覆い、トルネードのごと
き事態が広がった。空気がクルクルグルグル回って渦巻きが生じ、ウンチを
吸い込む恐怖のトイレという感じに哀れ一同をエメラルドの包有物の中に吸
い込んでしまった。

has not taken hold in this country.（この国では草の根的民主主義は定着し
ていない。『研究社 新英和中辞典』）
⓾ A vortex: 渦
⓫ swirl(ing) and twirl(ing): 渦巻き、ぐるぐる回る
⓬ like so much poop: この so much は「すごくたくさんの」ではなく（もちろん、
たくさんという含みはあるが）「同量の」。つまり「まるで同量のウンチ（poop）
のように」。第5巻p. 162, ll. 8-9ではso muchの代わりにso many（「同数の」）
を使った類似の例が出てきた：“so many Lazaruses out of their graves
they spring again in time for the next performance”（墓から出てくるラ
ザロの群れさながらに、次の公演時間が来ればふたたびパッと飛び上がり）

A few seconds later, the Tribe found itself in ❶a green pasture
❷populated by cows, ❸mooing and munching in cow-like fashion.
The unlucky Odd Duck discovered that he had been ❹plopped
onto ❺an under-baked cow pie. Squeezle ❻actually landed on the
5 back of ❼a bovine and, as was her custom, immediately ❽gave the
big cow a cuddle. The others were spread out among the cows, the
grass, and ❾the droppings.

Almost immediately everyone's attention was turned to a little
man dressed in green who greeted them in, ❿considering his size,
10 a ⓫booming voice. "Hello, my name is ⓬Ver Dure, your leprechaun
guide. Welcome to 18th-century England."

⓭The Cold Duck, who until now had not uttered a word, spoke:
" ⓮In the name of all things wee and weird, ⓯what is a leprechaun
doing with a French name? And ⓰while you're at it, ⓱perhaps you
15 can tell us why you speak English with an American accent."

"Let's call it international English, shall we? I understand

---

❶ a green pasture: 放牧用の草地
❷ populated by cows: 牛たちのたむろする
❸ mooing and munching: モーと鳴いたり（草を）もぐもぐやったり
❹ plop(ped): 〜をぼとっと落とす
❺ an under-baked cow pie: cow pie は「牛の糞」の意。なので、under-baked（焼き方が足りない）なのは当然。
❻ actually landed on ...: あろうことか〜の上に落下した、という感じ。
❼ a bovine: ウシ科動物（つまり牛）
❽ gave the big cow a cuddle: give ... a cuddle で「〜を抱きしめる」。
❾ the droppings: （牛の）落とし物
❿ considering his size: その体格を思えば、体格の割には
⓫ booming: 轟くような
⓬ Ver Dure: verdure（新緑、若葉）に基づく名前。
⓭ The Cold Duck: 今日では安価なスパークリングワインの名だが、起源につい

数秒後、団員たちは気がつけば緑の牧場にいた。牛たちがいかにも牛らしくモーモー鳴き、もぐもぐ草を食んでいる。オッド・ダックは不運にも生焼け「牛パイ」の上に墜落していた。スクイーズルは何と牛の背中に着陸し、いつもの習慣どおり、ただちに大きな牛をぎゅっと抱きしめた。ほかの連中は牛たちと牧草と排泄物のひしめくなかであちこちに散らばっていた。

ほぼ瞬時にして、全員の注意が、緑の服を着た小さな男に向けられ、男は小柄な体にしては桁外れの大声で彼らにあいさつした。「こんにちは、私の名まえはヴァー・ジャー、あなた方をご案内するレプラコーンのガイドです。18世紀のイングランドへようこそ」

それまで一言も発していなかったコールド・ダックが、「すべての小さきもの、奇っ怪なものの名において問う、レプラコーンがフランス系の名とはなぜ？　ついでに教えてくれ、なんだってまたアメリカ訛りの英語を喋るのかね」

「インターナショナル英語って言いましょうよ。あなた方のいらしたところ

ては p. 222, ll. 15-16 で後述される。普通名詞としての cold duck は cold fish と同じで「お高くとまった人」。

⓮ In the name of all things wee and weird: 小さく（wee）奇妙な（weird）あらゆるものの名において（訊ねるが）。レプラコーンがまさに小さくて奇妙なのでこう訊いている。

⓯ what is a leprechaun doing with a French name?:（アイルランドの）レプラコーンが、フランス語の名前なんか使って何をしているのか＝なんでフランス人みたいな名前を名のってるんだ。verdure は元来フランス語で、vert（緑）から来ている。

⓰ while you're at it:「ついでに」の意の成句。*I'm contributing to the economy and enjoying myself while I'm at it.*（家計に貢献していてついでに自分も楽しんでいる。*Cambridge Advanced Learner's Dictionary and Thesaurus*）

⓱ perhaps you can ...: よかったら〜してくれないか

that it's a big business ❶where you come from. As for my name, perhaps you can tell me why ❷Sean McBride had an Irish one but spoke with a French accent."

"Oh, never mind all that," ❸squawked Squatsy. "❹What was that stuff about the 18th century and England?"

"I don't want to shock you, my friends, but that is where you are. ❺That nasty little vortex that sucked you into the inclusion has brought you here, fortunately to me," answered Ver Dure, with a ❻sly smile.

"How do we get back?" asked Squatsy.

"We'll ❼work that out later. ❽Why the rush?" ❾the lep replied. "Enjoy your stay here. ❿Speaking of which, I think we should ⓫hit the road, but before doing so, I believe, like any good tour guide, that I should ⓬take a headcount. Well, how many are here? ⓭Um, I see five. Is that correct?"

It was then that a sixth member of the Tribe rose slowly

---

❶ where you come from: あなた方がいたところでは

❷ Sean McBride had an Irish one but spoke with a French accent: ショーン・マクブライド（1904-88）はアイルランドの政治家でノーベル平和賞を受賞した（1974）が、フランスで生まれ育ったため生涯フランス語訛りが抜けなかった。

❸ squawk(ed): ガーガー声で言う。元来は鳥がやかましく鳴く声を意味する。

❹ What was that stuff about ...?: （さっきの）〜ってのは何の話なの？

❺ That nasty little vortex: little は大小を言っているのではなく、「けちな」「嫌な」の意。「しばしば nasty, cheeky, stupid などの形容詞の後に用いる」（『リーダーズ英和辞典』）

❻ sly: ずるそうな。smile, glance, wink などと一緒によく使われる。

❼ work ... out: （問題を）解決する

じゃビッグビジネスなんですよね。私の名まえにしてもですね、ショーン・マクブライドがなぜアイルランド系の名でフランス訛りなのか、教えていただきたいですね」

「わかったわかった、それはもういい」とスクワッツィがキーキー声を上げた。「18世紀のイングランドがどうこうってのは？」

「ショックを与えたくはないんですが、いまみなさんはそこにいらっしゃるんです。あなた方を包有物に吸い込んだあのいけすかない渦巻き、あれにここへ連れてこられたんです。まあ私のところにいらしたのは不幸中の幸いでしたが」とヴァー・ジャーは悪戯っぽくニヤッと笑った。

「どうやって帰れるの？」とスクワッツィが訊いた。

「まあそれはあとで考えましょう。急ぐこと、ないでしょ？」とレプ。「ここでの滞在をお楽しみください。そうそう、そろそろ出かけないといけませんが、まずは良きガイドらしく、人数を数えておかないとね。で、何人いらっしゃいます？　えーと、見たところ5名かな。合ってますか？」

　そのとき、団の第6のメンバーが、盛り上がった土のうしろからゆっくり

---

❽ Why the rush?: なぜそんなに急ぐんですか、まあのんびり行きましょうよ

❾ the lep: the leprechaun の短縮形。

❿ Speaking of which: 話を本題に戻しているような響き。「で、その滞在ですけど……」

⓫ hit the road: begin a journey

⓬ take a headcount: 人数確認をする

⓭ Um, I see five: えーと、全部で5名ですね

from behind a mound in the pasture. Much older than the other members of ❶the bunch, ❷Uncle Rebus differed from them in one other respect, as well. He was mute; in other words, he didn't speak. But that did not mean that he couldn't communicate.

5   "And who are you?" inquired Ver Dure.

At which point, Uncle Rebus ❸whipped out a tablet and quickly ❹prepared ❺the following response.

"Oh, I can see this is going to be ❻a fun group. And, ❼that
15 wasn't me in the movie, okay," responded the lep, who ❽was slightly disturbed by being associated with such ❾a horrible film.

---

❶ the bunch: 一団、一行
❷ Uncle Rebus: 黒人民話に基づいた物語Joel. C. Harris, *Uncle Remus*(1880) のもじり。rebus はこのページにあるような絵や文字を組み合わせた判じ物のこと。
❸ whipped out a tablet: さっとタブレットを取り出した
❹ prepared: 「用意した」というよりは「作成した」。
❺ the following response: 解読すれば Hello I am Uncle Rebus I saw ...
❻ a fun group: fun は "It's fun!" のように名詞となることが多いが、このように形容詞にもなる。*She's a really fun person to be with.*（彼女はいっしょにいてとても楽しい人だ。『コンパスローズ英和辞典』）
❼ that wasn't me in the movie, okay: okayは「いいですね」と念を押していて、いささか感情を害している響き。

と現われたのだった。ほかのメンバーたちよりだいぶ歳を食ったこの人物、名をアンクル・リーバスといい、もうひとつの点でも仲間たちと違っていた。すなわち彼は唖者、物を言わぬ身であった。かといって、意思疎通ができないわけではない。

「で、あなたはどなたです？」とヴァー・ジャーが訊ねた。

　するとアンクル・リーバスはタブレットをさっと取り出し、すばやく次の返答を作成した。

　こんにちは。私はアンクル・リーバス。レプラコーンという映画であなたを見ました。

「いやあ、なかなか楽しいツアーになりそうですね。だけど、あの映画に出てたのは私じゃありませんよ」とレプは、あんなひどい映画と結びつけられたことにいささか動揺しながら答えた。

❽ was slightly disturbed: わずかに心乱された
❾ a horrible film: *Leprechaun* (1993) は邪悪なレプラコーンが人間を襲うアメリカのホラー映画（邦題『レプリコーン』）。

Chapter 3 ❶What's Cooking in the 18th Century?

The Odd Duck was curious. "So, Mr. Ver Dure, what's cooking in
5 the 18th century?"

"Well, politically speaking these are ❷ hot times. You see, the
American colonies are ❸ getting a bit uppity. Money seems to be
the…" but the lep stopped speaking, as he was interrupted by the
Odd Duck.

10 "❹ Actually, I meant that literally. I'm quite hungry. ❺ Haven't
eaten in about 300 years."

Everyone laughed at this, though it ❻wasn't all that funny.

"Oh, I see," said Ver Dure. "Well, let me take you into town for
❼a roast. I know of a great place. It's called ❽the 'Stumble Inn.' I
15 hope there are no vegetarians here."

Uncle Rebus replied ❾by way of his tablet:

---

❶ **What's Cooking**: 「何が起きてるの、どんな様子なの」を意味する成句。

❷ hot times: 動きの激しい時代、激動の時代

❸ getting a bit uppity: ちょいとばかり生意気になって。18 世紀には北米大陸
のイギリス植民地が本国の支配に反抗して独立戦争を起こし、1776 年にアメ
リカ合衆国独立を宣言。

❹ Actually, I meant that literally: ll. 4-5 の what's cooking in the 18th
century について言っている。

❺ Haven't eaten in about 300 years: 21 世紀から 18 世紀まで 300 年さかの
ぼって来たのでその間食べていないということ。

❻ wasn't all that …: それほど〜ではなかった。*He isn't all that rich.* (そんな
に金持ではない。『リーダーズ英和辞典』)

❼ a roast: (しばしば骨付きの) 焼いた肉のかたまり。

第3章　18世紀って何があるわけ？

　オッド・ダックは興味津々だった。「で、ミスタ・ヴァー・ジャー、18世紀って何があるわけ？」

「そうですねえ、政治的には熱い時代ですよ。アメリカの植民地がですね、いささか生意気を言い出してるんです。どうやら金が……」だがそこでオッド・ダックにさえぎられて、レプは話すのをやめた。

「いや、食べ物は何があるか訊いたんだ。私、お腹がペコペコで。もう300年くらい食べてないんだ」

　何がそんなに可笑しいのか、これを聞いてみんなが笑った。

「あ、なるほど」とヴァー・ジャーは言った。「じゃあ町へお連れしましょう、ローストを食べられるところに。いい店知ってるんです。『千鳥足亭^{スタンブル・イン}』って言うんです。ここにベジタリアンの方、いらっしゃらないですよね」

　アンクル・リーバスがタブレットを使って答えた。

❽ the 'Stumble Inn': inn はパブの名などによく付く語だが、stumble in（フラフラ入る）の洒落でもある。

❾ by way of ...: 〜を使って

 F

"Okay, let's go," shouted Ver Dure. And they all left the pasture
5 for ❶ the dirt road that would take them into town. Before doing
so, Squeezle kissed the cow she had been sitting on, and the Odd
Duck tried as best he could to ❷scrape the cow pie off his butt.

Roads in those days were not what they are today. For one
thing, they were not paved, which, when it rained, made them
10 as ❸ messy as a finger-painting session among two-year-olds. But
more importantly, there was a danger that does not exist today in
many lands—the presence of ❹the highwayman. This person was
somewhat similar to the men and women who work at present-
day ❺tollbooths. He collected money, was unpleasant, and could
15 punish the poor traveler for not ❻paying up. The highwayman
differed from them in two ways. First, he collected money for

---

❶ the dirt road: 舗装していない田舎道
❷ scrape the cow pie off his butt: 「牛のパイ」を尻 (butt) からそぎ落とす
❸ messy: 取り散らかった、ぐじゃぐじゃの
❹ the highwayman: (街道で待ち伏せしている) 強盗
❺ tollbooth(s): 高速道路の料金所
❻ paying up: pay up はその人が払いたがっていない、支払が遅れている、と
　 いうニュアンスを帯びることが多い。*If they don't pay up we will take legal
　 action.* (もし彼らが支払わなければ法的手段に訴える。*Longman Dictionary
　 of Contemporary English, Corpus*)

私、牛肉大好きです。

「オーケー、行きましょう」とヴァー・ジャーが叫んだ。そしてみんな牧草地を出て、町へ続く田舎道へ向かった。その前にスクイーズルは座っていた牛にキスし、オッド・ダックは尻から精いっぱい牛のパイをこそげ落とそうと努めた。

当時の道路は今日の道路とは違っていた。まず、舗装されていないので、雨が降ると、二歳児たちのフィンガーペインティング教室みたいにぐじゃぐじゃになる。が、より重要なことに、今日多くの土地では存在しない危険がひとつあった。追い剥ぎである。この人物は、今日高速道路の料金所で働く人々に近い。金を取り立てるし、感じが悪いし、金を払わない哀れな旅人を罰することができるからである。だが二つの点で追い剥ぎは違っている。まず、金は自分のために集め、好きなように使うことができる。現代の料金所

himself and could spend it **❶**how he pleased, whereas the tollbooth guys collect money for politicians, who can spend it as *they* please. Second, he could kill the traveler who **❷** failed to cooperate with him. This, of course, was a very big difference. The highwayman
5 was, like many citizens of the United States, a country the Tribe **❸** had yet to visit, usually armed and willing to use his weapon. "**❹** Stand and deliver," he would shout to the passengers in **❺** the coaches he would meet, and if the unlucky travelers had any common sense, they would get out and hand over their purses.

10 Spookfish, who **❻**knew his history, **❼**was, well, spooked by the prospect of meeting a highwayman. As the Tribe approached the road they would take, he addressed the lep as follows: "Mr. Ver Dure, **❽**what steps have you taken to protect us from highwaymen? We don't have any weapons on us, and, quite frankly, **❾**I've got the
15 jitters."

"**❿** Keep your pants on, or should I say scales on?, **⓫** Spooky.

---

❶ how he pleased: この how は however（どうにでも〜ように）の意。*Do it how (＝as best) you can.*（どうにでもやってごらん。『リーダーズ英和辞典』）

❷ failed to cooperate with ...: fail to ... は「〜するのに失敗する」というよりは、このようにほとんど「〜しない」程度の意であることが多い。第2巻 p. 22, ll. 14-15 に "But how everyone could get so excited I still fail to understand."（でもどうしてみんなあんなに興奮できるのか、あたしにはいまだにわからない）の形で既出。cooperate with ...: 〜の要求に応じる、言うことをきく

❸ had yet to visit: have yet to ... は「まだ〜しないといけない」というよりは「まだ〜したことがない」の意になることが多い。*Smith has yet to score a point.*（スミスはまだ得点していない。『ロングマン英和辞典』）

❹ Stand and deliver: 日本で言う「身ぐるみ脱いで置いていけ」に相当。

にいる連中は、政治家のために金を集め、それを政治家が好きなように使うのである。第二に、追い剥ぎは協力的でない旅人を殺すことができる。言うまでもなくこれは実に大きな違いである。追い剥ぎは、団員たちがまだ行ったことのないアメリカ合衆国の多くの市民と同じく、たいてい武装していて、いつでも武器を使う気でいる。「立ちて有り金出せ！」と追い剥ぎは乗合馬車の乗客たちに叫ぶ。そして不運な旅人たちに少しでも分別があれば、財布を取り出して渡すのである。

　スプークフィッシュは歴史に詳しいので、追い剥ぎに出会うんじゃないかと思ってまさしく震撼（スプーク）させられた。そしてみんなで道路に近づいていく最中、レプにこう話しかけた。「ミスタ・ヴァー・ジャー、お訊ねしますが、我々を追い剥ぎから護ってくださるためにどんな手段を取られましたか？　私たちは武器を携帯していませんし、率直に申し上げて、私、ビクビクしてるんです」

　「落ち着いてズボンはいてなさい、いやそれとも、ウロコつけてなさい、かな。大丈夫、大船に乗ったつもりでいてください。ほら、この三角帽」そ

---

❺ the coach(es): 馬車
❻ knew his history: know one's ... で「〜の知識がある、〜に詳しい」。
❼ was, well, spooked: Spookfish が spook（おどかす）されてしまう、では見え透いた駄洒落になってしまうので、ややためらっ（たふりをし）て well が入っている。
❽ what steps have you taken: take steps で「処置を取る、取り計らう」。
❾ I've got the jitters: びくついています
❿ Keep your pants on, or should I say scales on?: keep your pants [shirts] on で「落ち着け、あわてるな」の意の成句。相手が魚なので「（ズボンではなく）『鱗を』と言うべきかな」と言っている。
⓫ Spooky: Spookfish の愛称。

213

You're ❶in good hands here. You see ❷this tri-cornered hat," he said pointing to his head. "Well, this is no ordinary ❸head covering. It's ❹an isosceles triangle, with ❺steel-tipped edges and razors sticking out of its tips. I can toss it like one of your Frisbees

5 and ❻have it spin through the air in the direction of any bad guy we may meet ❼along the way. It's basically ❽an airborne salad shredder. Or, ❾I have the option of ❿launching the hat like a paper airplane, in which case it becomes an airborne ⓫dagger."

Uncle Rebus raised his tablet high, which read

10

U R OK

"Thank you," replied the lep, who was getting used to the Rebus-style ⓬rap. "But that's not all, you see. I have my ⓭*spre na skillenagh.*"

15 "What's that?" asked Spookfish.

"It's my 'shilling fortune,' my magic purse. If I spend the coin

---

❶ in good hands: しっかり守られて、安全で

❷ this tri-cornered hat: ナポレオンの絵などでしばしば見かける三角帽。

❸ (a) head covering: かぶり物、帽子

❹ an isosceles triangle: 二等辺三角形

❺ steel-tipped: 端に鋼をかぶせた

❻ have it spin through the air: have A do B で「A に B させる」。*I'll have him* (= *get him to*) *come early.* (彼に早く来てもらおう。『リーダーズ英和辞典』)

❼ along the way: 途中で

❽ an airborne salad shredder: 空を飛ぶスライサー

❾ I have the option of ...: ～という選択肢もあります

❿ launch(ing): ～を発射する、投げる

う言って自分の頭を指さす。「これはね、そんじょそこらのかぶり物とは訳が違うんですよ。二等辺三角形で、辺に鋼がかぶさっていて、そこからカミソリが突き出してるんです。あなた方のフリスビーみたいに投げれば、道中どんな悪者に出会っても、くるくる回転してそいつのいる方向に飛んでいきます。まあ空飛ぶサラダ・シュレッダーみたいなもんですね。あるいはこの帽子を、紙飛行機みたいに飛ばすこともできます。その場合は空飛ぶ短剣だね」

　アンクル・リーバスはタブレットを高く掲げた。そこには

あんた　いいね

と書いてあった。

「ありがとうございます」とレプは答えた。リーバス式の喋りに、もうだいぶ慣れてきていた。「でもそれだけじゃないんですよ。私にはね、*spre na skillenagh* があるんです」

「何だい、それ？」スプークフィッシュが訊いた。

「私の『1 シリングの幸運』、魔法の財布です。中に入っているコインを遣う

⓫ (a) dagger: 短剣
⓬ rap: お喋り
⓭ *spre na skillenagh*: アイルランドの公用語の一つであるゲール語で、「スプレー・ナ・シュキリナー」のように発音する。spre の原義は「飼い牛（cattle）」で、そこから「所有する家畜、財産」の意味になった（英語でも cattle と capital〔資本〕は同語源）。na は定冠詞 an の属格、skillenagh は "of the shilling" を意味する。

that is in there, it is magically replaced by another coin of the same value." At which point, Ver Dure demonstrated this marvel by taking out his purse, removing a coin, and tossing it to Rebus. He then showed the Tribe the inside of the purse, which was empty,

5 but ❶before you could say "A penny spent is a penny earned," the coin was immediately replaced by another.

Rebus resisted the temptation to make a joke about ❷Keynesian economics and ❸simply said:

10

And with that simple expression of ❹gratitude, the Tribe and their ❺mischievous guide hit the road that would eventually take

15 them to ❻Crapstone, ❼a village with an unforgettable name and a great roast.

---

❶ before you could say "A penny spent is a penny earned": before you could say Jack Robinson という言い方が一番一般的で、「あっという間に」の意。A penny spent ... は "A penny saved is a penny earned."（一銭の節約は一銭のもうけ）ということわざのもじり。

❷ Keynesian economics: この魔法の財布の働き方や、"A penny spent is a penny earned." という消費礼賛のフレーズは、英国の経済学者 John M. Keynes (1883–1946) が主張した経済政策（たとえば国債を無際限に発行するなど財政赤字を容認する政府主導型の積極財政）に通じるものがある。

❸ simply said ...: この tank/thank の駄洒落は the Marx Brothers の映画 Duck Soup（邦題『我輩はカモである』、1933）にも出てくる。Chico: I wouldn't go out there unless I was in one of those big iron things, go up and down like this ... What do you call-a those things?（いやーあそこには行く気しないね、あのおっきな鉄のやつに乗るんじゃないと、ほら、

と、あら不思議、同じ値の別のコインが現われるんです」。そう言うとヴァー・ジャーは、実演してみせようと、財布を取り出し、コインを一枚出して、リーバスに向けて放り投げた。それから団員たちに、財布の中身を見せた。中は空っぽだったが、「1ペニーの消費は1ペニーの得」と言う間もなく、そこにたちまち別のコインが現われた。

　リーバスはケインズ経済学についてジョークを言いたい誘惑に駆られたが、それはこらえて、単にアイルランド英語で

　　<ruby>戦車<rt>タンキュー</rt></ruby>U

と言っただけだった。

　そのシンプルな感謝の表現とともに、一同とその悪戯なガイドは、道を歩き出した。ここを行けばいずれ、<ruby>糞　石<rt>クラップストーン</rt></ruby>なる忘れがたい名の、ローストが美味い村にたどり着くのだ。

こんなふうに上下に動くやつ……あれ、なんてゆったっけ?)　相手: Tanks. Chico: You're welcome!(Chico は実際にはアメリカ生まれだが、劇中ではイタリア系で th などは苦手という設定)

❹ gratitude: 感謝

❺ mischievous: 悪戯好きな

❻ Crapstone, a village with an unforgettable name: unforgettable なのは crap が「糞」を意味するので。イングランド南西部デヴォン州には同名の村が実在し、由来は不明だが少なくとも「糞」が語源ではないようで、一説では石切場があったことから "crop of stone"(採れた石)の訛り、また一説では地元の一家の姓に由来するとされる。

❼ a village: Ver Dure は town と呼んでいた(p. 208, l. 13 と p. 210, l. 5)。town と village は「町」と「村」よりも区別がゆるやかで、時として入れ替え可能。

Chapter 4 On the Road to Crapstone

It was midafternoon, and the weather was pleasant enough. Ver
5 Dure estimated that it would take them about two or three hours
to reach the village, just in time for dinner. ❶Squatsy and the lep
determined the pace. As they had short legs, it was impossible for
them to walk quickly. This gave the others more time to ❷make
observations. Rebus and Squeezle ❸made note of the birds and
10 plants that they saw. The Odd Duck ❹peppered his conversation
with ❺inaccurate but widely believed "facts" about England,
❻claiming, for instance, that ❼the present-day British royals are
Anglo-Saxons, when, in fact, they have German roots. Suctrocious,
of course, was quick to ❽set the record straight and chanted loudly:
15

Octopus, octopi, a misinformed person I descry

❶ Squatsy and the lep determined the pace: スクワッツィとレプラコーンの
歩く速さで全体のペースが決まった
❷ make observations: （周りを）いろいろ観察する
❸ made note of …: 〜に目をとめた
❹ peppered his conversation with …: 会話の中に〜を盛んにさしはさんだ
❺ inaccurate but widely believed "facts": 不正確だが広く信じられた「事実」。
このように、その言葉の意味に疑義を呈す（「これ、間違ってるんですよね」と
いうサインを送る）ような引用符を "scare quotes" という。日本語では「　」
をつけて強調の意を示すことも多いが、英語では逆の意味に取られかねないの
で注意が必要。
❻ claiming, for instance, that …: claim は第 1 巻 p. 206, l. 5 の "But I never
claimed to have any answers." （でも、正しい答えを持っていると主張した

第4章　クラップストーンへの道中

　午後もなかば、天気はまずまず快適だった。ヴァー・ジャーの計算ではその小さな町まで2、3時間で、ちょうど夕食に間に合いそうである。スクワッツィとレプがペースを定めた。二人とも足が短いので、速く歩こうにも歩けないのである。おかげでほかの連中には、周りを観察する時間ができた。リーバスとスクイーズルは目に入る鳥や植物に注目した。オッド・ダックはイングランドをめぐる不正確な、だが広く信じられている「事実」を会話のあちこちにちりばめた。たとえば「今日のイギリス王室の人々はアングロサクソン系である」——実際はルーツはドイツ系。むろんサクトローシャスがすかさず誤りを正し、大声で唱えた。

　　蛸よ、蛸たちよ、思い違いの人間がいたぞ

ことは一度もない）で述べたように、「クレームをつける」ではなく「主張する」が基本的な意味。
❼ the present-day British royals are Anglo-Saxons, when, in fact, they have German roots: ヴィクトリア女王（1819-1901）までさかのぼるなら、その夫アルバート公はドイツの Sachsen-Coburg und Gotha 家の出身だったが、第一次世界大戦中に敵国ドイツ由来の家名を避け、居城の地にちなみウィンザー家（the House of Windsor）と改名した。
❽ set the record straight: 記録の間違いを直した、誤解を正した

Suctorial power, remove the clutter
That has turned his brain into butter.

The Cold Duck tried to kill time by starting a discussion about
tea and coffee. "Why," he asked, "do the British and the Irish
prefer tea and the French coffee?" No one could answer that, and
apparently no one seemed to care. Spookfish, ❶ being concerned
with historical matters, commented on a horrible ❷ device that
was in use at ❸ the time they were in — ❹ the scold's bridle, an
iron mask with a needle that would pierce the tongue if ❺ the
wearer tried to speak. They all agreed that the device was cruel
and inhuman. "❻ Who could possibly deserve such treatment?"
Squeezle asked. "No one that I can think of," answered the Cold
Duck, "except maybe, in some cases, ❼telemarketers."

As this discussion was coming to an end, they came to ❽a bend
in the road, and as they went around it, they were startled to see

❶ being concerned with ...: ～に関心があるので
❷ (a) device: 装置、道具
❸ the time they were in: 彼らがいま滞在している時代（つまり18世紀）
❹ the scold's bridle: ガミガミうるさい女（scold）の（口につける）轡。a witch's bridle とも言い、事実女性に対して使われることが多かった。
❺ the wearer: それを着けた者
❻ Who could possibly deserve such treatment?: deserve は日本語の「値する」と同じで、「～をもらうに値するほど立派だ」の意味にもなれば、この場合のように「～を喰らうに値するほどひどい」の意味にもなる。
❼ telemarketer(s): 電話セールスの販売人
❽ a bend: 曲がり目

吸引力よ、取り除け混乱を

脳味噌をバターに変えた錯乱を。

　コールド・ダックは時間をつぶそうと、紅茶とコーヒーをめぐる議論を試みた。「なぜイギリス人とアイルランド人は紅茶が好きで、フランス人はコーヒーが好きなのか？」。誰も答えられなかったし、どうやらみんなどうでもいいらしかった。歴史に関心のあるスプークフィッシュは、目下自分たちがいる時代に使われていた恐ろしい装置について触れた。〈ガミガミ女の轡（くつわ）〉と呼ばれる、針が付いている鉄の仮面で、着けている人間が喋ろうとすると針が舌に突き刺さる。残酷で非人間的な装置だ、と全員の意見が一致した。「そんな扱いに値する人、どこにいるっていうの？」とスクイーズルが訴えた。「一人も思いつかないね」とコールド・ダックが答えた。「ま、一部の電話セールスの人間くらいかな」

　この議論が終わるころ、一同は道の曲がり目に来て、そこを抜けると馬に

a man on horseback. "Stand and deliver, ❶flatterers," was his
❷puzzling greeting.

   "❸What on earth do you mean by that?" asked Ver Dure.

   "Sorry, I meant 'travelers.'"

5   "❹I'll say you did, ❺and, by the way, we *are standing*. Do you
see a coach around here? We're walking!" the lep said angrily.

   "Okay, well, just deliver," the man said hastily.

   "Not so fast," Ver Dure replied. "Who are you, anyway?"

   "I am the notorious highwayman Richard Turpentine, and this
10 is my horse, Black Mess."

   The leprechaun couldn't believe his ears. "Don't you mean
❻'Richard Turpin' and 'Black Bess'?"

   "No, that's another guy," Turpentine answered. "❼And let's see
some deliveries here. ❽I don't have all day."

15   The Cold Duck, who was named after ❾a hodgepodge drink
created by a thrifty German prince and was ❿a bit of a skinflint

---

❶ flatterer(s): お世辞を言う連中、おべっか使いたち

❷ puzzling: 意味不明の

❸ What on earth do you mean by that?: それ（flatterer という呼びかけ）は
いったいどういう意味だ

❹ I'll say you did: そりゃそうだろうよ（I'll say you meant "travelers"）

❺ and, by the way, we are standing: Stand and deliver とお前は言うが、と
いうこと。

❻ 'Richard Turpin' and 'Black Bess': リチャード・タービン (1706-39) は通
例 Dick Turpin と呼ばれるイングランドの有名な追い剝ぎで、Black Bess は
彼の愛馬。彼を題材にした多くの伝説や俗謡がある。Turpin が Turpentine（テ
レビン油）、Bess が Mess（ぐじゃぐじゃ）になることで野暮ったさ、滑稽さ
が生じている。

乗った男が現われたので驚いてしまった。「立ちて有り金出せ、媚する者ども」というのがその奇妙な挨拶だった。

「それいったい、どういう意味だ？」ヴァー・ジャーが訊いた。

「失礼、『旅する者ども』だった」

「そうだろうよ。ところで、私らもう立ってるんだぜ。ここらに馬車とか見えるか？　私ら、歩いてるんだぞ！」レプが怒って言った。

「わかったよ、じゃとにかく、有り金出せ」と男はせわしなく言った。

「まあそうあわてるな」ヴァー・ジャーは答えた。「だいたいあんた、何者だ？」

「我こそは悪名高き追い剥ぎリチャード・ターペンタイン、そしてこいつはわが愛馬、『黒いゴチャゴチャ』だ」

レプラコーンは自分の耳が信じられなかった。「それって『リチャード・ターピン』と『ブラック・ベス』じゃないのか？」

「いいや、それは別の奴だ」ターペンタインは答えた。「さ、皆さん、出してもらおうか。こっちも暇じゃないんだぜ」

コールド・ダックという名は、倹約家ドイツ人君主の発案になるゴタマゼ飲料にちなむ名で、本人もなかなかのケチンボであり、21 世紀にいたとき

❼ And let's see some deliveries here: そろそろ出すべき物を見せて（出して）もらおうじゃないか

❽ I don't have all day:「俺だって忙しいんだ」と言うときの決まり文句。夜なら当然 day は night になる。

❾ a hodgepodge drink created by a thrifty German prince: a hodgepodge は「ごた混ぜ」で、the Cold Duck は一説によれば、Prince Clemens Wenceslaus of Saxony（1739-1812）がシャンペンの残りにあれこれのワインを混ぜるよう命じて作ったのが始まり。thrifty: 倹約家の。prince は第 5 巻所収 Edgar Allan Poe, "The Masque of the Red Death" の主人公 the Prince Prospero について述べたとおり（p. 21 の註❿）「王子」ではなく「君主」。

❿ a bit of a skinflint himself: 本人も（その名のとおり）ちょっとしみったれ

himself, offered Turpentine some coupons he had clipped from a newspaper when he was back in the 21st century.

"What are *these*?" he asked with **❶**a frown, looking at pictures ranging from **❷**Lucky Charms to **❸**Pop-Tarts and other things
5 impossible to eat. "Let's see some silver."

"Do you accept bitcoin?" the Cold Duck asked **❹**sarcastically.

"**❺**Bits of coin? **❻**Now, why would I accept pieces of coins, **❼**you grey-bearded loon."

The Cold Duck stroked his beard **❽**self-consciously and
10 considered offering one of his many credit cards. But not wanting to anger the highwayman further, he didn't.

At that point the lep stepped forward and offered his *spre na skillenagh*.

"That's all you have, **❾***one measly coin*?" the highwayman
15 **❿**exclaimed in great pain as he looked into the purse. He then jumped from his horse and **⓫**launched into a monologue about **⓬**how

---

❶ a frown: しかめ面

❷ Lucky Charms: General Mills 社製のシリアルで、マスコットキャラクターは他ならぬレプラコーン。

❸ Pop-Tarts: Kellogg 社製の薄く四角い菓子パンの一種。

❹ sarcastically: 嫌みったらしく

❺ Bits of coin?: むろんビットコインなど聞いたこともないので bits of coin（コインのかけら）と聞き間違えている。

❻ Now:「おい」に近い。

❼ you grey-bearded loon: 白髪まじりのひげの（いい年こいた）アホが。loon は「馬鹿な奴」のほかに「アビ」（水鳥の一種）も意味し、crazy as a loon（ひどく狂気じみて）という表現もある。相手が duck なのでこう呼んだ。

❽ self-consciously: 自意識過剰になって

に新聞から切りとったクーポンを何枚かターペンタインに差し出した。

「何なんだ、これ？」とターペンタインは眉をひそめ、ラッキー・チャームやらポップ＝タートやら、およそ食に適さないものの写真を見ながら言った。

「金(かね)出せよ、金」

「ビットコインは受けとってもらえるかね？」とコールド・ダックが嫌みたっぷりに訊いた。

「コインのかけら(ビッツ・オブ・コイン)？　俺がなんでそんなもの受けとるんだ、この白髪ひげの阿呆が」

コールド・ダックはひげを気にして撫で、何枚も持っているクレジットカードの一枚を出そうかと考えた。だがこれ以上追い剝ぎを怒らせても、と思ってやめにした。

ここでレプがあいだに入り、自分の *spre na skillenagh* を差し出した。

「これしかねえのか、しけたコイン一枚だけか？」財布の中を覗き込みながら追い剝ぎはさも苦々しげに叫んだ。そして馬から飛び降り、ああ俺はこんな商売に向いてねえんだ云々の長話をやり出した。話し終えると、地面にばっ

---

❾ *one measly coin*: たった1枚のケチなコイン、コイン1枚ぽっち

❿ exclaimed in great pain: さも辛そうに叫んだ

⓫ launched into a monologue: くどくど独白を始めた

⓬ how bad he was at ...: 〜がいかに不得手か

bad he was at what he did for a living. He ended his speech by
falling to the ground, pounding the road with his fist, and crying like
a baby.

❶ This display of emotion had an immediate impact on
5 Squeezle, who patted the highwayman on the back and ❷told him
that he was among friends.

"You're my *friends*? But I tried to rob you!"

"❸Never you mind about that," Squeezle reassured him.

"Who are you people? You're not from around here, are you?"

10 The Cold Duck ❹laid it on the line for him: "I'll say we're not.
We're from the 21st century."

Surprisingly, this news did not surprise Turpentine, who ❺held
all things to be possible.

"You shouldn't be worried about money matters, my friend.
15 Where we come from there are people who buy things with
no money whatsoever! ❻ Even the governments of our greatest

---

❶ This display of emotion: このように感情をあらわにしたこと

❷ told him that he was among friends: （ここにいる）みんながあなたの味方
だと言った

❸ Never you mind about that: このように命令文に you が入ることはしばしば
あり（"Hey, don't you do it!"〔おい、やめろ！〕）、これが威嚇・親愛などど
ういう響きを帯びるかは言い方次第。ここはもちろん親愛。

❹ laid it on the line: はっきり言った、率直に伝えた

❺ held all things to be possible: hold A to be B で「A を B だと考える、主
張する」。We hold these truths to be self-evident, that ...（「我々は以下の
ことを自明とする」アメリカ独立宣言の書き出し）

❻ Even the governments of our greatest countries do this. They
accumulate great debt, but they keep spending: ふたたびケインズ経済学

たり倒れて、げんこつで道をボカボカ叩き、赤ん坊みたいに泣き出した。

　こうした感情の吐露が、たちまちスクイーズルの心を動かした。彼女は追い剝ぎの背中を撫でてやり、大丈夫よ、みんなあなたの味方よ、と慰めた。
「あんたらが味方？　だって俺はあんたらから金を奪おうとしたんだぜ！」
「そんなこと、気にしなくていいのよ」スクイーズルが請けあった。
「あんたら、何者なんだ？　ここらの人間じゃないだろ？」

　コールド・ダックがきっぱり言った。「違うとも。私ら、21世紀から来たんだ」

　驚いたことに、この知らせにターペンタインは驚かなかった。どんなことも可能だと彼は信じていたのである。
「いいかい君、金のことなんかで心配するな。私たちがいたところじゃ、金なんか全然持ってないのに物を買う人間がいるんだぜ！　大国の政府だってそれをやってる。負債をどっさり作って、なのに相変わらず遣って、遣って、

的姿勢を揶揄。

countries do this. They accumulate great debt, but they keep spending, spending, spending — on silly games, crazy projects, ❶enough arms to destroy the Earth thousands of times over, ❷you name it. It's a great thing: we never have to pay," the Odd Duck
5 said.

"❸My god," Turpentine shouted, "we have ❹debtors' prisons for that: they throw us in jail if we can't pay our bills, but you have debtors running your governments! But, but, really someone must pay. Who is it?"

10 "Future generations," Squeezle said sadly, "their children and their children's children."

"Oh, they ruin their children's futures for silly games? I can't believe it. What are these games?" the highwayman asked.

"Basically, the games started as some rich guy's hobby, ❺a Baron
15 Pierre somebody. He managed to convince some governments to pay for this hobby of his, and people have been suffering ❻ever

---

❶ enough arms to destroy the Earth thousands of times over: 地球を何千回も破壊するに十分な武器（arms）

❷ you name it: ほかにも何だってある。*You name it, we've got it.*（《何でも言ってみて》うちにはすべてある〔そろっている〕から。『リーダーズ英和辞典』）

❸ My god: なんてこった、信じられん

❹ debtors' prison(s): 債務者監獄。欧米では返済できない債務者を投獄し強制労働をさせる制度が 19 世紀まで存続した。ロンドンにあった the Marshalsea Prison（1373–1842）が有名で、ディケンズの小説によく登場する。

❺ a Baron Pierre somebody: フランスの教育家ピエール・ド・クーベルタン男爵（Pierre de Coubertin, 1863–1937）のこと。古代ギリシャのオリュンピア競技祭をモデルに国際オリンピック大会の開催を提言し、1896 年にアテネで第 1 回大会を開催。

遣って——阿呆なゲームだの、狂ったプロジェクトだの、地球を何千回と滅
ぼせるだけの武器だの、何にでも遣う。すごいもんだよ。私ら、全然払わな
くていいんだ」とオッド・ダックが言った。

「そりゃたまげた」とターペンタインは叫んだ。「ここじゃそういうのには
債務者監獄ってのがあるんだぞ。勘定が払えなかったら、牢屋に入れられる
んだ。なのにあんたらは負債者に政府をやらせてる！　だけど、だけど、誰
かが払わなくちゃならんだろうが。誰なんだ？」

「未来の世代よ」スクイーズルが悲しそうに言った。「子供たちと、子供た
ちの子供たち」

「じゃあ、阿呆なゲームのために子供たちの未来をメチャメチャにするの
か？　信じられん。そのゲームって、何なんだ？」追い剥ぎは訊ねた。

「ざっくり言うと、どっかの金持ちの趣味で始まったんだよ、ピエール・何
とか男爵の。こいつがあちこちの政府を言いくるめて、自分の趣味に遣う金
を出させたのさ、それ以来みんなずうっと苦しんでるんだ。とにかくおそろ
しく金がかかる、無駄の多いゲームなんだよ。あんたにもわかる例で言えば

❻ ever since: 以来ずっと。第 5 巻 p. 96, ll. 10-11 に "The spectre came
back a week ago. Ever since, it has been there, now and again, by fits
and starts."（亡霊が一週間前に戻ってきたのです。以来ずっと、切れぎれに
何度もあそこに現われているのです）の形で既出。

since. These games are very expensive and ❶wasteful. I'll give you an example you will be able to understand. Imagine if the Roman Empire had constructed ❷ the Colosseum for ❸ a two-week event and then almost immediately after the show ❹tore it down. That's
5 the kind of thing that they do. They call these games the modern Olympics," the Cold Duck said.

"❺And they call highwaymen thieves," Turpentine replied.

The Odd Duck ❻piped in at this point, claiming that countries make money from the games. "Ah, but in the long run everyone
10 ❼benefits," he ❽falsely claimed.

Suctrocious was about to give many examples that would easily ❾ disprove this, including the fact that it took the city of Montreal thirty years to pay off ❿ the debt they took on from the 1976 Olympics, but he decided that it would take too much time to
15 explain these things to a man from the 18th century, so he chanted in an ⓫exceedingly loud voice:

---

❶ wasteful: 無駄が多い

❷ the Colosseum: 西暦 80 年にローマに作られた大円形闘技場。

❸ a two-week event: 第 5 巻 p. 218, l. 10 の "a six-foot baby"（大人の背丈 の赤ん坊）について述べたとおり、こういう場合 week は複数形にならない。

❹ tore it down: tear ... down で「〜を取り壊す」。

❺ And they call highwaymen thieves:（そんなぼったくりをしておきながら） 追い剝ぎのことを盗っ人呼ばわりするんだからな

❻ piped in:（甲高い声で）口をはさんだ

❼ benefit(s): 利を得る

❽ falsely claimed: 間違った主張をした

❾ disprove: 〜の誤りを証明する、反証する

❿ the debt they took on: 彼ら（モントリオール市民）が抱え込んだ借金

だ、ローマ帝国が、二週間のイベントのためにコロセウムを建てて、お祭り
が終わったらほぼすぐにそれを取り壊したと考えてみろよ。そういうことを
やるわけさ。このゲームを称して、近代オリンピックという」とコールド・ダッ
クが言った。

「で、追い剝ぎを泥棒呼ばわりするわけか」とターペンタインが答えた。

　オッド・ダックがここで話に割り込み、各国がこのゲームで金を儲けるの
だと主張した。そして「ま、最終的には誰もが利益を得るのさ」と例によっ
て誤りを唱えた。

　サクトローシャスは、これをあっさり論駁（ろんばく）する例をいくつも挙げようかと
思ったが（たとえばモントリオール市が 1976 年のオリンピックの負債を返
済するには 30 年かかった）、こういうことを 18 世紀の人間に説明するのは
時間がかかりすぎると踏んで、代わりにものすごい大声で唱えた。

❶ exceedingly loud: おそろしく大きな

Octopus, octopi, a misinformed person I descry

Suctorial power, remove the clutter

That has turned his brain into butter.

5

The lep felt that enough time had been wasted on ❶ this stuff and was eager to get to Crapstone at supper time, so he ❷came up with a solution. "Mr. Turpentine, I'm taking these visitors from the future to Crapstone for a roast. It seems to me that ❸you could use a little

10 cheering up. Why don't you join us for dinner? ❹It's on me."

Turpentine rose from the road and simply said, "Thank you."

❺Journeys tend to loosen the lips, especially in a world without Smartphones, and as the Tribe and their guide once again ❻ set off for Crapstone — this time ❼ with guest in tow — ❽ the chin-

15 wagging never stopped.

The Cold Duck was curious about the name "Crapstone." "How

---

❶ this stuff: この件。stuff という語は「件」が大したものだと思っていないことを示唆。

❷ came up with a solution: 解決策を思いついた。*We need to come up with some good ideas.*（何かよいアイデアをひねり出す必要がある。『動詞を使いこなすための英和活用辞典』）

❸ you could use a little cheering up: この use はたとえば *I could use a drink.* で「一杯やりたいなあ」というふうに使う。a little cheering up: ちょっとした元気づけ

❹ It's on me: 私のおごりです

❺ Journeys tend to loosen the lips: 旅は人の口を緩ませるものだ

❻ set off for ...: 〜に向かって出発した

❼ with ... in tow: 〜を引き連れて。*Hannah arrived with her four kids in*

蛸よ、蛸たちよ、思い違いの人間がいたぞ

吸引力よ、取り除け混乱を

脳味噌をバターに変えた錯乱を。

　もうこの一件には十分時間を無駄にしたとレプは判断し、とにかく夕食時間にクラップストーンに着きたいと思って、解決策を出した。「ミスタ・ターペンタイン、いまですね、この未来からのお客さま方を、ローストのディナーにお連れしようとしているんです。あなたもどうやら気晴らしを必要とされているご様子。よかったら一緒に召し上がりませんか？　私のおごりです」

　ターペンタインは道路から立ち上がり、あっさりひとこと「ありがとう」と言った。

　旅は人の唇を緩めるもの。特にスマートフォンのない世界であればなおさらである。一同とそのガイドが、ゲスト一名も加わってクラップストーン行きを再開するなか、あごの上下運動はいっこうに止まらなかった。

　コールド・ダックは「クラップストーン」という名に好奇心を抱いていた。

tow.（ハンナは子供 4 人を引き連れてやって来た。*Longman Dictionary of Contemporary English*）

❽ the chin-wagging: あごをしきりに動かす（wag）こと、つまりお喋り。

did this stone of crap ❶come about, anyway? Was it some kind of ❷ritual, people doing it for good luck or something?"

Turpentine was about to answer the questions when the lep interrupted. "Come on, come on, this ❸ is supposed to be a story
5 for kids. Please don't ❹get into that, will you?"

"❺He who spends the cash determines what is labeled ❻'trash,'" the Cold Duck ❼quipped, displaying his knowledge of marketing, after which he avoided the topic.

As they ❽neared their destination, Turpentine started to ask
10 his ❾new-found friends about ❿future developments. He ⓫was astounded by what he learned about ⓬the centuries to come. ⓭It gradually dawned on him that, ⓮armed with this knowledge, this ⓯bungling 18th-century highwayman could easily become the most powerful man in his world. Soon it would be time for him to
15 ⓰put down his pistol in favor of a new weapon, ⓱a crystal ball.

---

❶ come about: 生じる。物よりも出来事について使う方が多い。*A great change has come about since the war.* (戦後大きな変化が生じた。『コンパスローズ英和辞典』)

❷ ritual: 儀式

❸ is supposed to be ...: 一応〜ということになっている

❹ get into ...: (話・口論などを) 持ち出す。*Let's not get into that subject. I don't wish to discuss it.* (その話題に入るのはやめよう。それについて話したくないんだ。『動詞を使いこなすための英和活用辞典』)

❺ He who spends the cash determines ...: 金を出す奴が〜を決める。He who ... はいかにも格言調。

❻ trash: クズ

❼ quip(ped): 皮肉を言う、気の利いた科白を吐く

❽ near(ed): 〜に近づく

234

「その糞の石<ruby>クラップストーン</ruby>、どうやって生まれたんです？　それってなんかの儀式だったんですか、幸運か何かを呼ぼうとしてやったわけ？」

　ターペンタインがその問いに答えようとしたところで、レプがさえぎった。「よしなさいよ、これって子供向けの物語ってことになってるんですよ。そんな話はやめてくださいよ」

「何が『クズ』のレッテルを貼られるかは、キャッシュを出す奴が決める」とコールド・ダックは軽口を叩いてマーケティングの知識をひけらかし、あとはもうこの話題に触れなかった。

　目的地が近づいてくると、ターペンタインは未来の展開について、新たに得た友らにあれこれ訊きはじめた。来たるべき諸世紀に何が起きるか聞かされて、はじめはひたすら仰天していたが、やがてだんだん、ヘマな18世紀の追い剝ぎにも見えてきた——この知識で武装すれば、簡単にこの世界で誰より権力ある人間になれるではないか。もうじき短銃を捨てて、新しい武器を手に取る時が来るのだ——水晶玉を。

❾ new-found friends: できたばかりの友
❿ future developments: 世界が今後どうなって行くかということ。
⓫ was astounded by ...: 〜にびっくりした
⓬ the centuries to come: これから来る数世紀。to come は p. 92, l. 12 に "for some days to come" の形で既出。
⓭ It gradually dawned on him that ...: It dawned on A that ... で「〜だということが A にわかった」。gradually: 徐々に
⓮ armed with this knowledge: この知識を武器にすれば
⓯ bungling: 間抜けな、どじな
⓰ put down his pistol in favor of ...: ピストルを捨てて、代わりに〜を手にする。 *The city abandoned streetcars in favor of buses.* (市は路面電車を廃止してバスにした。『コンパスローズ英和辞典』)
⓱ a crystal ball: 占い用の水晶玉。追い剝ぎをやめて占い師になるということ。

Chapter 5 Entry of the Tribe into Crapstone

As **❶**the brown gates of Crapstone came into view, a few members
5 of the Tribe became **❷**visibly excited, **❸**some owning to curiosity,
others to hunger. "**❹**There it is," shouted Squatsy." "Simply
splendid," **❺**hissed Suctrocious. "!!!" tapped Rebus.

❻Captain Crapstone, the gatekeeper, **❼**eyed **❽**the motley crew
with suspicion as they approached the **❾**rusted gates **❿**bearing the
10 symbol of the city, a **⓫**nearly circular brown stone partially covered
by **⓬**some kind of crust. "**⓭**Identify yourselves," he **⓮**bellowed.

"We are travelers in search of a meal in your fine town,"
answered Ver Dure. "I understand that you have an excellent place
that offers a fine roast. It is called 'Stumble Inn,' I believe."

15   "**⓯**You heard right, little man. It is indeed a good place for a
fine meal. But I must say that all of you **⓰**with the exception of him

❶ the brown gates of Crapstone came into view: 昔の町や村の外れには門
  があるのが普通だった。
❷ visibly: 目に見えて、明らかに
❸ some owning to ..., others to ...: ある者は〜のため、またある者は〜のため
  に
❹ There it is: ほらあそこだ
❺ hiss(ed): 普通は「シーッと言う」の意だが、ここは「s の音を強調して喋る」。
❻ Captain Crapstone, the gatekeeper: なぜか町と同じ Crapstone という名
  の門番。
❼ eye(d): 〜をじろじろ見る
❽ the motley crew: （格好が）バラバラの一行
❾ rusted: 錆びついた

第５章　有象無象団、クラップストーンの町に入る

　クラップストーンの茶色い門が見えてくると、有象無象団の何人かが見るからに興奮した様子になった。ある者は好奇心ゆえに、ある者は空腹ゆえに。「あれだわ」スクワッツィが叫んだ。「真_{しん}に、壮観だ」とサクトローシャスがｓ音をきわだたせた。「‼」とリーバスがタップした。

　錆びた門に種々雑多な一団がやって来るのを、門番のキャプテン・クラップストーンは訝_{いぶか}しげな目で見た。門には町のシンボルがついていて、ほぼ円形の茶色い石の一部がある種の殻に覆われている。「貴様ら、名を名のれ」とクラップストーンは胴間声を上げた。

「わたくしどもは、この立派な町に、食事を求めてやって参った旅人です」とヴァー・ジャーが答えた。「美味しいローストを出す素晴らしい店があると伺っております。『スタンブル・イン』という名だと思います」

「そのとおりだ、小さな男よ。美味しい食事をするにはもってこいの店である。だがお前たちみな、まあこいつ（ターペンタインを指さす）は別として、

---

❿ bearing the symbol of the city: 町の紋章をつけた

⓫ nearly circular: ほぼ円形の

⓬ some kind of crust: crust はパンの皮、カニの甲殻などをいうが、ここはどうやら町名どおり crap が描いてある模様。

⓭ Identify yourselves: 身分を明らかにせよ、何者か名のれ

⓮ bellow(ed): どなる

⓯ You heard right: おまえが（人から）聞いたことは正しい、いかにもおまえの言うとおりだ

⓰ with the exception of ...: 〜を除いて、〜以外は

(pointing to Turpentine) are dressed rather strangely," Crapstone remarked. "Are you actors?"

"❶We are all actors," the highwayman said ❷philosophically. "But these people are foreigners who have come from afar to
5 experience the wonderful ❸things fair England has to offer," was Turpentine's ❹appropriate response, ❺for at that point, despite ❻the bizarre features of Spookfish and Suctrocious in particular, Captain Crapstone ❼flung the gates open wide and shouted "Welcome to Crapstone. Enjoy your stay. Oh, by the way, do you know where
10 the Stumble Inn is located?" Without waiting for a reply, he told the group to go straight down the main street, and they would find it on the right, after a five-minute walk.

The Tribe entered town ❽like weary gods into Valhalla, where they would ❾chow down on an 18th-century ❿chuck or some
15 other body part. ⓫It was not long before they arrived at their final destination, ⓬well not actually final ... their ⓭destination for a

---

❶ We are all actors: We は自分と the Tribe の一団を指すのではなく、人間み んなということ。

❷ philosophically: (哲学者のように) 達観した口調で

❸ things fair England has to offer: fair はほとんど意味のない枕詞。has to offer は「offer しなくてはならない」ではなく、「offer すべく持っている」。 *Listen to what I have to say.* (私の言わんとしていることを聞いて下さい) などと同じ。

❹ appropriate: 適切な、その場に相応しい

❺ for:「なぜなら」の意の接続詞で、次行末からの Captain Crapstone flung ... につながる。

❻ the bizarre features: 奇怪な諸特徴

❼ flung the gates open wide: 門を大きく開け放った

なかなかおかしな格好をしておるなあ」とクラップストーンは言った。「お前ら、役者か？」

「人はみな役者です」と追い剝ぎが達観した口調で言った。「ですが、この方々は異国の人で、麗しきイングランドの素晴らしさを体験なさるべく、はるか遠くからおいでになったのです」──この的確な返答のおかげで、とりわけスプークフィッシュとサクトローシャスはなんとも珍妙な見かけであるにもかかわらず、キャプテン・クラップストーンは門をパッと大きく開け、「クラップストーンへようこそ。楽しい時を過ごされますよう。あ、ところで、スタンブル・インの場所はご存じで？」と叫んだ。そうして返事も待たず、本通りをまっすぐ行きなさい、5分歩けば右手にあります、と一同に告げたのだった。

ヴァルハラへと入っていく疲れた神々もかくや、という趣で一同は、18世紀のチャックステーキだかどこかほかの部位の肉だかを食すことになる町へと入っていった。そしてまもなく最終目的地に着いた……いや、最終ではないのだが、とにかく誰一人忘れないであろう食事の目的地ではあった。

❽ like weary gods into Valhalla: ヴァルハラは北欧神話に登場する天上の殿堂。ワーグナーの『ラインの黄金』第4場「ヴァルハラ城への神々の入城」で知られる。weary: 疲れた
❾ chow down: がつがつ食べる
❿ chuck:（牛などの）首回りの肉。「肩ロース」に近い。
⓫ It was not long before ...: ほどなく〜した
⓬ well not actually final: いやまあ実は最終ではないが。今後まだ彼らの移動は続くので。
⓭ destination: 目的地

meal no one would forget.

Chapter 6 We Don't Sup on Cats

5 The Stumble Inn might be compared to one of those 21st-century
❶motel hells, you know, places with numbers for names — ❷Motel
88, Hotel 25¼ —the kind of place with ❸ razor-thin walls, ❹ odd
odors, and ❺ odder inhabitants, both human and insect, where
meals come out of vending machines or ❻taste like they have.

10   The Tribe, the Iep, and Turpentine took their seats around a
long wooden table.

   "You're an odd bunch," their 18th-century ❼ equivalent of a
waitress remarked.

   "And you're ❽a tidy wench," answered Turpentine, as he stared
15 at ❾the gravy stains on ❿her rarely washed dress.

   "I think I'll start with ⓫a side order of French fries," Squeezle

---

❶ motel hell(s): *Motel Hell* は 1980 年制作の、アメリカのホラー・コメディ映画のタイトルでもある（邦題は『地獄のモーテル』）。
❷ Motel 88, Hotel 25¼: たとえばアメリカの幹線道路 66 号線沿いには 66 Motel という名のモーテルがいくつかある。
❸ razor-thin: 剃刀の刃のように薄い、ぺらぺらの
❹ odd odors: 変な臭い、異臭
❺ odder inhabitants, both human and insect: inhabitants といっても人間だけじゃなく虫もいるぜ、というジョーク。
❻ taste like they have: taste as if they have come out of vending machines
❼ (an) equivalent: 等価物
❽ a tidy wench: 小ざっぱりしたねえちゃん

第6章　我ら猫を食せず

　スタンブル・インは21世紀によくあるモーテル地獄に比されよう。モーテル88とか、ホテル25¼とか、名前の代わりに数字があって、剃刀みたいに薄い壁、奇妙な臭い、もっと奇妙な居住者（人間・昆虫の両方）、食事は自動販売機から出てくる（あるいは出てきたような味がする）……。

　有象無象団の団員たち、レプ、ターペンタインは、細長い木のテーブルを囲んでそれぞれ席についた。

「あんたらおっかしな人たちだねえ」と、ウェイトレスの18世紀版が言った。

「で、君は清潔な娘だなあ」とターペンタインが、彼女のめったに洗濯しない服についた肉汁のしみに見入りながら答えた。

「まずはサイドメニューのフレンチフライをもらおうかしら」とスクイーズルが言った。

---

❾ the gravy stains: 肉汁の染み
❿ her rarely washed dress: p. 104, l. 5 で述べたように、dress はたいていの場合「ワンピース」と訳すのが自然で、「ドレス」と訳すことはあまりないが、ここはそのどちらでもなく単に「服」と訳すのがベストか。
⓫ a side order of French fries: 付け合わせのフライドポテト

said.

"❶Believe me, we'd all like to fry the French, but we can't do it here," replied the waitress. "What are you going to eat?"

"She wants a baked potato," Turpentine said helpfully. "And
5 we'll all have a piece of ❷that wonderful roast we smell cooking."

"We can do that for you. And to drink?"

Spookfish, knowing his history, decided to ask for ❸ cock ale. To which the waitress replied, "Okay, one cock ale. And the rest of you?"

10 Spookfish's request ❹ sparked a heated conversation about this drink of which no other member of the Tribe had heard. "It's a kind of chicken-soup-flavored beer," he informed them. "❺ It is very popular in this century."

"And what century are you from, ❻mirror man?" the waitress
15 asked sarcastically.

Wanting to avoid any ❼exploration of this ❽fascinating ❾can of

---

❶ Believe me, we'd all like to fry the French: この時代には French fries は まだ存在しないので（*Oxford English Dictionary* の初出用例は 1902 年、イ ギリスではどのみち chips と言いこの言い方は使わない）、フランス人をフライ にしろと言われたと思っている。

❷ that wonderful roast we smell cooking: We smell that wonderful roast cooking（あの美味しい肉が焼けている匂いがする）という文が元になっている。

❸ cock ale: 果汁・スパイス・雄鶏（cockerel）の出汁で味をつけた昔のビール。

❹ spark(ed): 〜を引き起こす

❺ It is very popular in this century: cock ale は 17、18 世紀によく飲まれた。

❻ mirror man: p. 194, l. 16 にあるとおり、頭に鏡がついているので。

❼ exploration: 探求

❽ fascinating: 実に興味深い

「いやそりゃあたしたちだって、フランス人をフライにしてやりたいわよ、だけどここじゃそれ、できないわよぉ」とウェイトレスは答えた。「で、何食べる？」

「この人、ベークトポテトがお望みなんだよ」とターペンタインが助け舟を出した。「で、俺たちみんな、たったいまもいい匂いで焼けてる絶品のローストを一切れずつもらう」

「それならできるわ。飲み物は？」

　歴史に詳しいスプークフィッシュは、コックエールを頼むことにした。するとウェイトレスは「オーケー、コックエールひとつね。ほかの人たちは？」と言った。

　スプークフィッシュがかように、団の誰一人聞いたことのない飲み物を注文したことで、侃々諤々(かんかんがくがく)の議論が始まった。「まあその、チキンスープ風味のビールだよ」とスプークフィッシュはみんなに説明した。「この世紀では非常に人気があるんだ」

「で、あんたは何世紀から来たの、鏡男さん？」とウェイトレスが辛辣な口調で訊いた。

　興味深くはあるが面倒なことになりかねないこの質問をかわそうと、ター

❾ can of worms:「芋虫の缶詰」とは、下手に手をつけるとひどく厄介になりかねない事柄や状況のこと。*I just don't know what to do – every solution I can think of would just open up a whole new can of worms.*（どうしたらいいかわからないよ——どんな解決策を思いついても、また新たに厄介ごとが山と生じてしまいそうなんだ。*Longman Dictionary of Contemporary English*） worms Turpentine quickly replied, "**❶**Bring us some mugs of your finest."

The waitress, not liking the appearance or attitude of her guests, remarked that that would be "inferior, more inferior, and
5 most inferior."

"We'll take the first-mentioned, if you don't mind."

"**❷**Not at all," the rather untidied wench replied, as she left to **❸**fill the order.

"Wait a minute," the Cold Duck said. "I'll have **❹** the birdy
10 brew."

"Okay, two chicken **❺**chug-a-lugs," **❻**she said rather cryptically, as the word "okay" had not as yet been coined.

A short time later the waitress reappeared **❼** with heaps of steaming meat, followed by mugs of **❽**nondescript brew, and two
15 mugs of cock ale.

❾ The diners **❿** dove into their dinners like **⓫** undernourished

---

❶ Bring us some mugs of your finest: 一番上等のやつ（ビール）をマグでくれ

❷ Not at all: I don't mind at all. 承知しました、はい喜んで

❸ fill the order: 注文に応じる、注文の品を出す

❹ the birdy brew: 鳥を使ったビール。Spookfish が注文した cock ale のことを、よくわからずにこう言っている。

❺ chug-a-lug(s): ぐびぐび飲む酒。つまりビール。

❻ she said rather cryptically, as the word "okay" had not as yet been coined: okay は 19 世紀に作られた（coined）言葉で、彼女が知っているはずはないので、cryptically（不思議なことに）と言っている。

❼ with heaps of ...: どっさり山と載せた〜を持って

❽ nondescript: ありふれた

ペンタインがすかさず「この店自慢のやつを何杯か持ってきてくれよ」と口
をはさんだ。

　客たちの見かけも態度もウェイトレスは気に入らず、「てゆうと『不味いの』
と『もっと不味いの』と『最高に不味いの』ね」と言った。

「じゃその最初のをいただこうかな」

「いいわよぉ」と清潔とは言いがたい娘は答え、注文の品を取りに立ち去り
かけた。

「ちょっと待って」コールド・ダックが言った。「私もその鳥ビールもらう」

「オーケー、チキングビグビ二つね」と相手は言った。謎の発言である──
「オーケー」という言葉はまだ作られていないのだから。

　少し経ってウェイトレスがふたたび、湯気を立てている肉が山盛になった
皿を手に現われ、どうという特色もないビールのマグいくつかと、コックエー
ルのマグ二つがあとに続いた。

❾ The diner(s):（食事をする）客
❿ dove into their dinners: dive into ... で「〜を熱心に食べはじめる」
⓫ undernourished piranhas: 栄養不良のピラニアたち

piranhas, all except the Cold Duck, who found the meat somewhat flavorless.

"Excuse me, wench," he said trying to get the waitress's attention.

5   "❶It's 'waitress' to you," she replied.

"Do you have any catsup?" using ❷that odd pronunciation of the word that some Americans employ.

"❸We don't sup on cats here. ❹You may want to try France for that," she quipped.

10   The Cold Duck ❺was tickled chicken over his cock ale. It went very well with the beef. ❻Fur and feathers trumps surf and turf ❼any day, he thought.

The visitors from the 21st century ❽were impressed with the quality of the meat. It was ❾succulent, flavorful, and had an 15 ❿honest-to-goodness beefy smell, so different from ⓫the grain-

---

❶ It's 'waitress' to you: wench (ねえちゃん) とぞんざいな呼び方をされたので、あんたにとっては wench じゃないよ、と言い返している。むろん waitress は当時まだ「ウェイトレス」の意味では使われていない (*OED* 初出は 1834 年) ので、この言い返しも一種のジョーク。

❷ that odd pronunciation of the word that some Americans employ: ケチャップ (ketchup) はアメリカでは catsup と綴られることもあり、発音もそのような音になる。

❸ We don't sup on cats here: ケチャップは 17 世紀末には東南アジアからイギリスに導入されているが、いまのようなトマトケチャップが広まるのは 19 世紀から。なので彼女はこれも、「猫 (cat) を夕食に食べる (sup)」と聞き間違えている。

❹ You may want to try France for that: p. 184, ll. 5-6 の "you don't want to let the big guy extend those arms" (この巨漢にフルスイングを許してはまずい) と同じような発想。「そんなゲテモノが欲しかったらフランス行ってみれば」

❺ was tickled chicken: 普通は was tickled pink で「大喜びしていた」だが、

　栄養の足りないピラニアのごとく、一同は食事にかぶりついた。ただしコールド・ダックは例外で、どうもこの肉、味気ないなあ、と評した。

「すまんが、君ぃ」と彼は、ウェイトレスの気を惹こうとして言った。

「あんた相手には『ウェイトレス』よ」と彼女は答えた。

「キャットサップはあるかね？」とコールド・ダックはケチャップのことを、一部のアメリカ人が用いる奇妙な発音で言った。

「ここじゃ猫を夕食にはしないわねえ。そういうのはフランスに当たってみたら」と彼女はからかった。

　コールド・ダックはコック・エールがいたく気に入った。ビーフと大変よく合う。やっぱり「海と山」より「毛皮と羽根」だよな、と思った。

　21世紀からの訪問者たちは、肉の質の高さに感心した。汁気に富み、風味豊かで、これぞビーフという香り。いつも食べている、穀物を食わされて

　“chicken-soup-flavored beer” を飲んでいるのでこのようにもじっている。

❻ Fur and feathers trumps surf and turf: surf and turf は一皿に盛った surf（波＝シーフード）と turf（芝＝ステーキ）、通常ロブスターとフィレミニョンのこと。これと対比すべく、通例「猟獣と猟鳥」の意で使われる “fur and feather(s)” という句を牛ローストとチキン風味ビールの意味で使っている。trump(s): ～をしのぐ

❼ any day: いつでも、決まって

❽ were impressed with ...: ～に感銘を受けた

❾ succulent: ジューシーな

❿ honest-to-goodness: 正真正銘の

⓫ the grain-fed stuff they were accustomed to: いつも食べている、穀物飼料で育てたやつ。stuff はここでも、p. 232, l. 6 の “enough time had been wasted on this stuff”（もうこの一件には十分時間を無駄にした）と同じく、言及している「もの」を軽視する響きがある。

fed stuff they were accustomed to, **❶**which often bore a disturbing resemblance to tuna. There was one problem, however, like most **❷**grass-fed beef, it did require a bit of chewing, which occasionally ended in failure. On those occasions, Turpentine, following the

5 advice of **❸**Desiderius Erasmus, who wrote a book on etiquette, would look behind his right shoulder, then behind his left, and if no one was there, would remove the piece of meat from his mouth and toss it behind him.

The Odd Duck noticed this, and when confronted with a piece

10 of meat that **❹**defied chewing, he decided to **❺**ape the highwayman. Unfortunately, he failed to **❻**take the necessary precautions and threw the meat in the direction of the waitress, hitting her **❼**squarely on the tip of her nose.

❽Anticipating the worst, Turpentine tried to excuse his

15 newfound friend's behavior by reminding the angry waitress that his friend was a foreigner, whose ways were different from theirs.

---

❶ which often bore a disturbing resemblance to tuna: しばしば（本当に牛なのかと）不安になるほどマグロに似た。bore <bear: ～を帯びる。(a) resemblance: 類似

❷ grass-fed:（人工飼料でなく）牧草で育てた

❸ Desiderius Erasmus, who wrote a book on etiquette: エラスムスはオランダの人文主義者（1466?–1536）。本当にエチケットの本を書いていて、ラテン語原題は *De civilitate morum puerilium*（1530）, 英語の直訳は "On civility in children's manners" だが 1532 年に出た初の英訳は *A Little Book of Good Manners for Children* と題されていた。

❹ defied <defy:（解決などを）許さない。*The scene defies description.*（その景色は筆舌に尽くしがたい。『コンパスローズ英和辞典』）

❺ ape: ～を猿真似する

育った、しばしば不気味なほどツナに似ている牛肉とは全然違う。ただし、芝を食べて育った牛の肉の常として、相当嚙まないといけない点が難であり、嚙みきれないこともしばしばであった。こうした場合ターペンタインは、エラスムスの著したエチケット本の教えに従って、右肩越しにうしろを見て、次に左肩越しにうしろを見て、誰もいなければ口から肉を出してうしろに放り投げた。

オッド・ダックがこれに目をとめ、嚙むことを受け付けない肉片に行きあたると、追い剝ぎを真似ることにした。あいにく、必要な用心を怠ったため、ウェイトレスのいる方向に肉を投げて、彼女の鼻先にもろにぶつけてしまった。

最悪の事態を予想したターペンタインは、この新たな友のふるまいを弁護しようと、カンカンに怒ったウェイトレスに、まあまあこの人は異国の人なんだから、やり方も私らとは違うんだよ、と取りなした。

❻ take the necessary precautions: 必要な用心をする
❼ squarely: まともに
❽ Anticipating the worst: 最悪の事態を見越して

"❶I'll say they are! If he does that again, I'll ❷tan his hide like we did that cow he is eating and ❸tossing around. ❹If a piece is not to his majesty's liking, tell him to leave it on the table, and I'll give it to ❺the spitdog after you leave," the waitress shouted.

5   "*Spitdog*?" they all said in unison, except for Uncle Rebus, of course, who tapped:

？ ？ ？

Spookfish, who knew his history and was not at all surprised, 10 and Turpentine, who, being from the 18th century, also knew.

"If you have ❻spitting dogs in your ❼establishment, I think you should ❽be closed down," said the Cold Duck angrily.

Chapter 7 The Saga of the Spitdog

15

"I can explain ❾the spitdog thing," said Spookfish.

---

❶ I'll say they are!: (こんな真似をするんだから) そりゃ違うんでしょうよ！
❷ tan his hide: 皮 (hide) を剝いでなめす
❸ toss(ing) around ...: 〜をそこらへんに投げ散らす
❹ If a piece is not to his majesty's liking: もし料理が陛下のお気に召さないなら。王・女王はこのように（書くときは通例大文字で）His Majesty, Her Majesty と呼ぶ。
❺ the spitdog: この時点では謎の呼び名。
❻ spitting dogs: 「焼き串」を意味する spit を、綴りも音も同じ「唾を吐く」の意味に勘違いしている。
❼ (an) establishment: 店
❽ be closed down: 閉店させられる
❾ the spitdog thing: そのスピットドッグってやつ

「違うでしょうよ！　もう一度やったら、そいつが食べて放り投げた牛と同じに皮剝いでやるからね。肉がお気に召さないんだったら、テーブルに置いとけって伝えとくれ、あんたらが帰ったらスピットドッグにくれてやるから」とウェイトレスはどなった。

「スピットドッグ？」と皆が一斉に叫んだ。ただしむろんアンクル・リーバスは例外で、「???」とタップしたし、歴史に通じていて少しも驚かないスプークフィッシュと、18世紀人なのでやはり知っているターペンタインも叫びはしなかった。

「この店、唾吐く犬がいるんだったら、閉店させられるべきだね」とコールド・ダックが怒って言った。

第7章　スピットドッグのサーガ

「スピットドッグのこと、私、説明できますよ」とスプークフィッシュが言った。

"No, Spooky, let's ❶get it from the horse's mouth," the Odd Duck replied, ❷referring to the waitress.

" ❸This guy is not going to last very long here," the waitress said ❹under her breath. "Well, it's very simple, really. You see
5 how your meat ❺is evenly cooked," she said pointing to one of the plates ❻laden with beef. "Well, that is the work of the dog, the spitdog, ❼the turnspit dog, ❽the kitchen cur. The spit here, you see, is ❾the horizontal rod on which we put the meat."

"It's like our present-day ❿rotisserie," added Spookfish.
10 "You have *dogs* cooking your meals?" the Cold Duck said even more angrily.

"We certainly do, and it saves us a great deal of money, too," the waitress replied.

The Odd Duck was becoming increasingly interested in this
15 topic. ⓫His ears pricked up when he heard "save," "great deal," and "money." "⓬How does it actually work, hon?"

---

❶ get it from the horse's mouth: 「本人・当事者から直接聞く」という意味の成句。*I had the information from the horse's mouth.*（その情報を信ずべき筋から得た。『研究社 新英和大辞典』）競馬で馬の歯を見て体調を推測することから。

❷ referring to the waitress: ウェイトレスのことを指して

❸ This guy is not going to last very long here: ここじゃ長く持たないね、そのうちぶっ殺されるね

❹ under her breath: 押し殺した声で

❺ is evenly cooked: むらなく焼けている

❻ laden with ...: 〜を山盛りにした

❼ the turnspit dog: 焼き串 (spit) を回す (turn) ために使われた胴長で短足の犬。

❽ the kitchen cur: 調理場で働く雑種犬

「いやいやスプーキー、ここは馬の口からじかに」とオッド・ダックが応じた。ウェイトレスから直接聞こうというのである。

「こいつ、ここじゃ長生きしそうにないね」とウェイトレスは小声で言った。

「すごく簡単な話よ、ほんとに。あんたたちの肉、むらなく火が通ってるでしょ」と彼女は言って、ビーフが載った皿のひとつを指さした。「これはね、犬の手柄なのよ。スピットドッグ、つまり焼き串回し犬、厨房の雑用犬。ここでスピットってのはね、肉を刺す水平の棒のことなの」

「現代で言う回転肉焼き器ですな」とスプークフィッシュが言い添えた。

「あんたら、犬に料理させるのか？」コールド・ダックがもっと怒って言った。

「ええもちろん、お金もすごく節約になるのよ」とウェイトレスは答えた。

　オッド・ダックがにわかに興味を示した。「お金」「すごく」「節約」と聞いて耳がピンと立った。「具体的にどうやるのかね、お嬢さん？」

❾ the horizontal rod: 水平の棹

❿ (a) rotisserie: 回転式肉焼き器

⓫ His ears pricked up: 耳がピンと立った

⓬ How does it actually work, hon?: actually は具体的に説明してほしいという響き。hon（/hʌ́n/）は honey の短縮形。

❶ Though not knowing exactly what "hon" meant, ❷ she assumed it referred to her and responded as follows: "Rather than explain it to you, I think it might be better ❸if you were to see it for yourselves. It is ❹a marvel to behold. Follow me," she said, and she

5 led them to the kitchen.

Upon entering the room, Squeezle immediately began to weep ❺uncontrollably. Other members of the Tribe were either disturbed by what they saw or by Squeezle's reaction to it. The Odd Duck, however, ❻was the odd man out, so to speak. He was ❼ecstatic.

10 The sight that ❽so upset Squeezle was that of a little dog with short legs inside ❾what appeared to be a very large hamster wheel, which was attached to a spit by a chain. As the dog ran, the spit turned the meat. The animal in the wheel was ❿filthy and ragged. There was a second dog, of the same type — ⓫stubby legs and long

15 body — sleeping in one of the corners of the room. "They ⓬ work in shifts," the waitress said, pointing to the sleeping dog.

---

❶ Though not knowing exactly what "hon" meant: hon も *OED* の初出例は 1896 年。

❷ she assumed ...: まあたぶん〜なのだろうと思った

❸ if you were to ...: 〜できるなら、〜してみれば

❹ a marvel to behold: a marvel to see/behold で一種の定型句。「大した見物」

❺ uncontrollably: 抑えがたく

❻ was the odd man out, so to speak: (odd のつく名だけに) まさしく仲間はずれ (the odd man out) だった。the odd one out とも言う。*I was always the odd one out at school.* (私は学校でいつも仲間はずれだった。*Longman Dictionary of Contemporary English*)

❼ ecstatic: うっとりして、恍惚状態で

❽ so upset ...: 〜をそれほどまで動揺させた

「ハン」とはどういう意味かいまひとつわからなかったが、まあ自分のこと
だろうと思ったので、ウェイトレスは答えた。「あたしが説明するより、自
分で見てみた方がいいと思うわ。なかなか見物なのよ。ついて来て」と彼女
は言い、みんなを厨房に連れていった。

　部屋に入ったとたん、スクイーズルは抑えようもなく泣き出した。ほかの
メンバーたちも、目にしたものに心乱されるか、あるいはスクイーズルの反
応に心乱されるかした。だがオッド・ダックだけはいわば仲間はずれだった。<ruby>仲間はずれ<rt>オッド・マン・アウト</rt></ruby>
心底魅了されたのである。

　スクイーズルの心をかくも乱したのは、足の短い小さな犬が、巨大なハム
スター回し車のごときものの中に入れられ、この回し車が、鎖で一本の串に
つながっている情景であった。犬が走ると、串が肉を回す。回し車の中の犬
はおそろしく不潔で、毛もぼさぼさだ。同じように足がずんぐり短く胴の長
い犬がもう一匹、部屋の隅で眠っていた。「交代で働くのよ」とウェイトレ
スが眠っている犬を指して言った。

❾ what appeared to be a very large hamster wheel: 下図はウィキペディア
英語版、Turnspit dog のページより。

❿ filthy and ragged: ひどく不潔で、毛はボロボロ
⓫ stubby:（切り株〔stub〕のように）太く短い
⓬ work in shifts: 交代で仕事する

"This is a splendid idea," observed the Odd Duck. "There's almost no ❶overhead—❷no pay, no ❸medical benefits, no holidays, no ❹labor unions! ❺Why our ❻captains of industry have been looking for something like this for years."

5   "❼*Captains*? More like buccaneers," Squeezle replied.

Rebus took out his tablet and ❽tapped:

10   "❾You bet," said Squeezle, as Suctrocious waved his tentacles over the Odd Duck's head and chanted:

Octopus, octopi, a misinformed person I descry
Suctorial power, remove the clutter
15   That has turned his brain into butter.

---

❶ overhead: 経費
❷ no pay: pay は「給料」
❸ medical benefit(s): 医療給付
❹ labor union(s): 労働組合
❺ Why: 本シリーズで何度か出てきたとおり、発言の最初に置かれる軽い「景気づけ」のような語。第4巻 p. 124, ll. 9-10: "The woman says Why sure, and suddenly she appears happier, so much more satisfied with everything."（あ、はい、もちろん、と女の人は言って、何だか急に嬉しそうな顔になり、何もかにもに満足した様子になる）
❻ captains of industry:「産業界の大立て者」に相当する定型句。
❼ *Captains*? More like buccaneers: captains（船長）というより buccaneers（海賊）に近い、という反論。

256

「実に名案だ」オッド・ダックが述べた。「経費はほぼゼロ——給料はなし、医療手当も、休暇も、労働組合もない！　我々の産業界の重鎮(キャプテン)たちも、長年まさにこういうのを探してたんだ」

「船長(キャプテン)？　てゆうより海賊でしょ」とスクイーズルが言い返した。

　リーバスがタブレットを取り出し、

犬たちを自由にしてやれますか？

とタップした。

「当然よ」とスクイーズルが言い、サクトローシャスはオッド・ダックの頭の上で触手を振り、唱えた。

　　　蛸よ、蛸たちよ、思い違いの人間がいたぞ
　　　吸引力よ、取り除け混乱を
　　　脳味噌をバターに変えた錯乱を。

❽ tapped: 下の WE の次の絵は "free"（自由にする）。K9s: canines（犬科の動物）
❾ You bet: もちろん

Squeezle got control of her emotions and approached the dog in the corner and gave ❶the sad cur a hug, perhaps ❷the first that he had ever had. She then took out her smartphone and ❸selfie stick and, not realizing the dog was ❹infested with lice, put her head next to that of ❺the pooch and snapped a photo. The waitress did not know ❻what to make of all of this but decided not to ask any questions, as she was beginning to feel that these visitors might be dangerous, and, as we shall see, she was right.

The group left the kitchen ❼disgusted, depressed, and deter- mined. They returned to their table, pushed their plates aside, and ❽plotted in hushed voices ❾the liberation of the kitchen dogs.

A whisper here, a whisper there, and Squeezle began to scratch uncontrollably.

"What's the matter with you?" Ver Dure asked, examining her head. "❿Why you have lice, my dear!"

"⓫She was always sugar and spice," the Cold Duck said. "And

---

❶ the sad cur: そのみすぼらしい雑種犬

❷ the first: the first hug

❸ selfie stick: 自撮り棒

❹ infested with lice: シラミにたかられて。lice はタイトルに既出。

❺ the pooch: 犬、ワンちゃん

❻ what to make of all of this: こうした一連の事態をどう捉えたらいいのか。 *What do you make of his behavior?*（彼のふるまいをどう思いますか。『コンパスローズ英和辞典』）

❼ disgusted, depressed, and determined: 嫌悪と、憂鬱と、決意を抱えて

❽ plotted in hushed voices ...: 声をひそめて〜をめぐる策略を練った

❾ the liberation: 解放

❿ Why you have lice, my dear!: ふたたび「軽い景気づけ」の why。

　スクイーズルは冷静さを取り戻し、隅にいる犬に寄っていって、その情け
ない駄犬をハグした。おそらくこの犬にとって、生まれて初めてのハグだっ
たにちがいない。それからスクイーズルはスマートフォンと自撮り棒を取り
出し、犬にシラミがたかっているとも知らずに、犬の顔の横に自分の顔を持っ
ていって写真を撮った。いったい何をやっているのか、ウェイトレスにはさっ
ぱりわからなかったが、どうやらこの訪問者たち、けっこう危険かもしれな
いぞと思いはじめていたので、余計なことは訊くまいと決めた。これからわ
かるとおり、彼女の勘は当たっていた。

　団員たちはみな、うんざりした、落ちこんだ、だが断固たる思いで厨房を
去った。食卓に戻ると、皿を脇へ押しやり、ヒソヒソ声で、厨房の犬たちの
解放策を練った。

　こっちでヒソヒソ、あっちでヒソヒソ。と、スクイーズルが痒くてたまら
ないという様子で体をぽりぽり掻きはじめた。

「どうしたんです」とヴァー・ジャーが訊きながら、彼女の頭を見てみた。「あ、
シラミがたかってますよ！」

「彼女、前々から『砂糖と香料と……』だったけど」とコールド・ダックが言っ

❶ She was always sugar and spice ... And now she's everything lice: p.
　194 でタイトルについて解説したとおり。

now she's everything lice," he added.

"Let's ❶concentrate on what we have to do, shall we?" Squeezle advised.

"I am the most qualified to free those animals," said Turpen-
5 tine. "I have a pistol and, after all, I am a highwayman."

They all agreed. They also agreed that the most difficult thing would not be liberating the dogs but making their escape.

Finally, the lep said, "I can help with that. You get the dogs, and I will create a rainbow of time. You can leave Crapstone
10 without passing through its gates. You simply ❷walk along the rainbow of time, and jump off whenever you like. The rainbow begins in this century and ends in yours — the 21st."

They all, with the exception of the Odd Duck, agreed that it was a wonderful idea. "Let's go," said Squeezle, ❸scratching her
15 scalp furiously.

---

❶ concentrate on ...: 〜に集中する
❷ walk along the rainbow of time: このように along は walk と一緒に使わ
  れると、「〜に沿って」というよりは「〜を」に近い。p. 128, ll. 8-9: "all the
  pickers had to do was walk along the field with powerful magnets" (こ
  れなら掘り手は、強力磁石を使って畑を歩くだけでいい)
❸ scratching her scalp furiously: 頭皮をぼりぼり掻きむしりながら

た。「これで『シラミなものすべて』になっちまったね」

「やるべきことに集中しましょうよ、ね？」とスクイーズルが促した。

「あの動物たちを自由にするのに、一番適役なのは俺だ」とターペンタインが言った。「ピストル持ってるし、なんてったって追い剥ぎなんだから」

　みんなも賛成だった。またみんな、一番難しいのは犬を解放することではなくここから逃げ出すことだ、という点も意見が一致した。

　やがてレプが言った。「私が手伝ってあげられます。あんたたちが犬を連れ出したら、私は〈時の虹〉を作ります。〈時の虹〉があれば門を通らずにクラップストーンから出られます。ただ単に虹の上を歩いていって、いつでも好きなときに飛び降りるんです。虹はこの世紀で始まって、あなた方の世紀で終わります——21世紀で」

　オッド・ダック以外、それは名案だとみな口々に言った。「さあ、行きましょ」スクイーズルが頭皮を猛烈に掻きながら言った。

"Why not?" replied the Cold Duck.

Chapter 8 ❶Spitdog's Set Free

5 The group, led by Turpentine, returned to the kitchen, where many of Stumble Inn's employees were working. The highwayman took out his pistol and shouted, ❷"Stand and dogliver, splatterers," screwing it up once again. The staff was puzzled by this and thought that he was referring to the roast that was slowly cooking
10 over the fire.

"Well, sure," one of them replied. "You can take it, but ❸it's not ready yet."

"No, I mean the dogs," Turpentine replied.

The staff did not put up a struggle, after all they were ❹under-
15 paid and ❺facing the wrong end of a pistol. "Take them," one of them said. At which point, Squeezle grabbed the two turnspit

---

❶ **Spitdog's**: Spitdog is
❷ "Stand and dogliver, splatterers," screwing it up once again: p. 222, l. 1 と同じように "Stand and deliver, travelers" という決まり文句を台なしにして (screw it up) しまっている、ということ。dogliver: 犬の肝臓。splatter(ers): バチャバチャはね飛ばす
❸ it's not ready yet: まだちゃんと焼けてない
❹ underpaid: (どうせ) ろくな給料をもらっていない
❺ facing the wrong end of a pistol: ピストルの間違った端に向きあって＝銃口を突きつけられて

「そうとも」コールド・ダックも応えた。

第8章　スピットドッグの解放

　ターペンタインを先頭に一同が厨房に戻ると、スタンブル・インの従業員の大半がそこで仕事をしていた。追い剥ぎはピストルを取り出し、「有り犬出せ、浴びせる者ども！」と叫んだ。またしてもヘマ。従業員たちは何のことかわからず、目下ゆっくり焼けつつあるローストのことだろうと考えた。「ええ、いいですとも」と一人が応えた。「持ってっていいですけど、まだ焼けてませんよ」
「違う、犬だ」とターペンタインは答えた。
　従業員たちは抵抗しなかった。何しろ給料は安いし、銃口を突きつけられているのだ。「持ってってください」と一人が言った。それを聞いてスクイー

dogs, and the group quickly left the inn. As they were doing so, Suctrocious caught a glimpse of **❶**a scold's bridle on a shelf. Believing it would **❷**come in useful **❸**with the Odd Duck, who **❹**despite his many chants had far too much butter left in his brain,

5 reached out with one of his tentacles and took it with his **❺**suctorial disks.

As soon as the group got outside, Ver Dure set to work preparing his rainbow of time. The lep **❻**employed one of his most powerful chants to **❼**conjure the magnificent rainbow: " **❽**Haughey,

10 Lynch, and Deva, too, the rainbow of time I give to you." **❾** And that being said, the rainbow appeared before all.

Chapter 9 On the Rainbow of Time

15 "I am going to **❿**say farewell to you here," the lep said. "It was my pleasure being your guide. Now my last responsibility is to

---

❶ a scold's bridle: p. 220, l. 9 に既出。

❷ come in useful: p. 16, l. 4 に出てきた come in handy とほぼ同じ: "My knowledge of biology came in handy, at this point." (ここで私の生物学の知識が役に立った)

❸ with the Odd Duck: the Odd Duck に対処する上で

❹ despite his many chants: あれだけ自分が何度も呪文 (chants) を唱えたにもかかわらず

❺ suctorial disks: 吸盤。p. 198, l. 7 に既出。

❻ employ(ed): ～を用いる

❼ conjure: (魔法で) ～を呼び出す、作り出す

❽ Haughey, Lynch, and Deva: いずれもアイルランドの首相の名。Charles Haughey (首 相 1979-81、1982、1987-92)、Jack Lynch (1966-73、

ズルが焼き串回し犬二匹を抱き上げ、みんな急いで店から出ていった。その最中、棚に〈ガミガミ女の轡（くつわ）〉が置いてあることにサクトローシャスが目をとめた。何度呪文を唱えてもまだ脳内にバターがありすぎるオッド・ダック相手に役立つかもしれないと思って、サクトローシャスは触手を一本のばし、吸盤で轡をつかんだ。

　みんな外に出るとすぐ、ヴァー・ジャーは〈時の虹〉の準備にかかった。壮大な虹を呼び出そうと、とりわけ効き目のある呪文を使った。「ホーヒー、リンチ、そしてディーヴァ、あなた方に〈時の虹〉を」。そう言うと、一同の前に虹が現われた。

第９章　時の虹に乗って

「ここでお別れしますよ」レプは言った。「皆さんのガイドをやれて楽しかっ

1977-79)、および Éamon de Valera (1937-48、1951-54、1957-59) の愛称 Dev を語呂に合わせて変えてある。
❾ And that being said: そう唱えるや否や
❿ say farewell: 別れを告げる

tell you how to use this thing that I just created. You get on here,"
he said pointing to the end of the rainbow that was nearer to the
group, "and you walk along it. Don't worry, you won't fall off. You
can travel to the other end, which will take you back to your time
5 period, or you can jump off it at any place in-between. If you fancy
❶1916, for instance, you can get off there. It is up to you. Goodbye and good luck," and with that he ❷disappeared as quickly as a
Celtic tiger.

Turpentine spoke first: "I'm going to stay in the 18th century.
10 I have a feeling that I will become a ❸well-respected and
significantly wealthy man. However, I must get out of Crapstone
safely, so I think I will take a few baby steps along the rainbow
and jump off into tomorrow or next week. Good-bye, my friends,"
and with that he took his baby steps, jumped off, and disappeared.
15 The Tribe, on the other hand, agreed to return to their time
period. Each walked onto the rainbow, but before doing so,

---

❶ 1916: 第一次世界大戦の真っ只中だが、当時まだ英国の支配下にあったアイル
ランドではイースター蜂起と呼ばれる大規模な独立闘争が起きた年で、これが
のちのアイルランド独立のきっかけとなった。

❷ disappeared as quickly as a Celtic tiger:「ケルトの虎」は 1990 年代から
急成長した（ケルト系の国である）アイルランドの経済を指す呼び名。2008
年以降、成長率は急激に落ち込んだ。

❸ well-respected and significantly wealthy: 人々に敬われる、立派に裕福な

たです。私の最後の仕事は、たったいま作り出したこいつの使い方をご説明することです。ここに乗るんです」と言って虹の、みんなに近い側の端を指さした。「で、そのまま歩いていくんです。ご心配なく、落ちやしません。向こう端まで行ってご自分たちの時代に戻ってもいいし、途中どこで飛び降りてもいい。たとえば1916年がいいなと思ったら、そこで降りればいいんです。みなさん次第です。ではさようなら、ご機嫌よう」そう言ってレプは、ケルトの虎のごとくあっさり消えた。

　ターペンタインがまず口を開いた。「俺は18世紀にとどまることにするよ。いずれここで、世間に尊敬される、相当裕福な人間になれる気がするんだ。とはいえ、クラップストーンから無事抜け出さないといけないから、この虹を軽く2、3歩歩いて、明日か来週に飛び降りようと思う。それじゃ、みなさん元気で」そう言って軽く2、3歩歩き、飛び降りて、消えた。

　一方、有象無象団は、自分たちの時代に帰ることにした。一人ひとり虹の

Suctrocious **❶**slapped the scold's bridle he had taken onto the Odd Duck's head. When the Duck tried to protest, he found it far too painful to utter a word.

As the Tribe **❷**made their way over the rainbow, Uncle Rebus 5 could not resist the temptation to push the Odd Duck off sometime in the 19th century, where he **❸**coincidentally landed in a debtors' prison, whose **❹**inmates **❺**were profoundly put off and puzzled by **❻**the stench coming from the seat of his pants.

The remaining members of the Tribe soon found themselves 10 back on the very pavement they were on when they were sucked by the vortex into the inclusion.

The End

Illustrations: © Satomi Shimabukuro

---

❶ slapped ... onto the Odd Duck's head: ～を the Odd Duck の頭にバシッとはめた

❷ made their way over the rainbow: 虹の上を進んでいった。along ではなく over になっているのは、虹が（たとえば峠などと同じように）「越えるもの」だという意識があるから。

❸ coincidentally landed in ...: 偶然～に落ちた

❹ inmate(s): 在監者

❺ were profoundly put off: ひどく気を悪くした

❻ the stench coming from the seat of his pants: ズボンの尻 (seat) から漂う悪臭。例の cow pie の威力がまだ衰えていない。

上に乗ったが、サクトローシャスがその前に、さっき取った轡をオッド・ダックの顔にガシッとはめた。ダックは文句を言おうとしたが、ものすごく痛くて一言も喋れなかった。

　みんなで虹の上を歩きながら、19世紀のどこかにオッド・ダックを突き落としたいという誘惑にアンクル・リーバスは抗えなかった。ダックは偶然、債務者監獄の中に墜落した。彼のズボンの尻から発する悪臭に、収監者たちはひどくげんなりし、かつ戸惑った。

　残りの団員たちは、まもなく、竜巻によって包有物の中に吸い込まれたとき立っていた、まさにその舗道に帰りついたのだった。

完

ちなみに

　著者の名 Jack Napes が「猿」もしくは「猿のように悪辣な人間」を意味する語 jackanapes に妙に似ていることはすでに述べたが、さらに補足するなら、15 世紀には jackanapes とは初代サフォーク公 William de la Pole のあだ名でもあった。これは公の紋章が猿の足枷と鎖であったことに由来していると考えられる。公はヘンリー 6 世の下で権勢を振るったがやがて失墜し最後は暗殺された。16 世紀のある時点では、jackanapes という語は十字架を意味した。19 世紀には炭鉱で石炭を引き上げるロープにつける滑車もしくはローラーを意味した。16 世紀末以来、サクラソウ科の花、プリムラ・ポリアンサの一種が "jackanapes on horseback"（馬の背に乗った猿）と呼ばれるようになり、この呼称はいまも流通している。jackanapes on horseback は可憐な花であり、猿を思わせるところはない。

授業後の雑談

　笑いは翻訳で一番失われやすい要素です。翻訳しているとしょっちゅう、原文なら誰でも笑う箇所が出てきて、ああここはほんとは原文を見てもらうといいんだけどなあ、と思ってしまいます。なのでこの本で、まさに「原文を見てもらう」ことを一番必要としている作品を並べることができて、大変いい気分です。

　全6巻、どの巻も入れたい作品は多く、ページ数を増やしすぎないようにするのに一苦労でしたが、「ユーモア」をテーマとしたこの巻はとりわけ入れたい作品が多く、結果的にやや厚めの一冊になってしまいました。どうかご容赦を。

　フィリップ・K・ディックの "The Eyes Have It" は、以前東京大学でみんなで教材候補を持ち寄って教科書を作ったときに、大堀壽夫さん（現・慶應義塾大学教授）が持ってこられて、さすがに言語学者は目の付け所が違うなあ、と感じ入ったことを覚えています。

　トマス・ハーディは本シリーズのどこかに入るとすれば、名作 "The Withered Arm" あたりが第5巻「怪奇に浸る」に入るのが順当だと思いますが、そうでないハーディの一面を見せることができて（もちろん "The Withered Arm" も素晴らしいのですが）嬉しいです。個人的な話ですが、ここに載せた2篇は僕の朗読会での定番で、何度読んでも楽しい（そして、

やがて哀しい）です。

　サローヤンはシンプルな英語で移民社会の空気をあたたかく伝えること
ができる人で、学部時代からすでに「ああ、いい文章だなあ」と実感でき
る実に有難い作家でした。あの嬉しさを多くの人が共有してくださいます
ように。

　レオノーラ・キャリントンの"The Debutante"はもともとフランス語
で書かれていて澁澤龍彦による邦訳もあるので、本来『英文精読教室』に
入れるのは遠慮すべきなのかもしれないのですが、最後にハイエナが捨て
台詞とともに窓から飛び出していくというくだりがあまりに好きなので、
入れてしまいました。まあ訳文については、著者（母語は英語）が監修も
しているということですし、読んでいて翻訳臭は感じられないと思います。

　ケン・スミスのこの"Casual Labour"が収められた作品集を買ったとき、
この人が1985年から87年にかけてWormwood Scrubs prisonという刑務
所でwriter-in-residenceだったと書いてあったので、そうか一服役しなが
ら書いてたのかすごいなーとひどく感心したことを覚えています（恥ずか
しい勘違いを活字にしなくてよかったです）。囚人たちに創作を教えた体
験はその後の詩集や散文集に生きています。なお、この作品の方言英語に
ついてはポリー・バートンさんに大いに助けられました。この場を借りて
お礼を申し上げます。

　スティーヴン・ミルハウザーをこの"Home Run"一作で代表させるの
は、彼の精緻で耽美的な作風を愛するファンからは叱られるかもしれませ
ん。でも彼を「言葉の魔術師」として見るなら、これはこれで大変ミルハ
ウザーらしい作品だと思います。

　この『英文精読教室』全6巻を、ジャック・ネイプス氏の作品で締めく

くれるのは僕にとって大きな喜びです。氏が画策中の、国際レプラコーン結社と河童同盟との提携が遠からず成立しますように。

　本を作るときはいつも多くの方々に助けられることは言うまでもありませんが、この6巻を作るにあたってはとりわけ多くの皆さんに助けていただきました。まず司令塔の、研究社編集部の金子靖さん。彼の無謀な企画力とタフな実行力がなかったらこのシリーズはとうてい成立しませんでした。古正佳緒里さん、山本太平さんは無茶苦茶なスケジュールの中で煩雑な組版・レイアウトを完璧にこなしてくださいました。高橋由香理さんと滝野沢友理さんは大半の作品に関し註釈の素案を作成してくださり、編者の無知を何度も救ってくださいました。各作品・註のゲラは何人かに見ていただき無数の誤り・矛盾・不適切な表現等々を摘発していただきましたが、中でも今井亮一さんと福間恵さんにはものすごくお世話になりました。
「はじめに」でも述べたとおり註には多くの辞書の例文を盛り込んでいます。『リーダーズ英和辞典』『コンパスローズ英和辞典』『新英和大辞典』『新英和中辞典』（以上 研究社）、『動詞を使いこなすための英和活用辞典』（朝日出版社）、『ロングマン英和辞典』（ピアソン・エデュケーション／桐原書店）、*Longman Dictionary of Contemporary English* (Pearson Education Ltd.), *The Dickson Baseball Dictionary* (W. W. Norton), *Oxford English Dictionary* (Oxford University Press) を作成された方々に深く深く感謝します。

　そして言うまでもなく、本は読まれてナンボです。この本を読んでくださるすべての方にお礼を申し上げます。Happy reading!

2022年5月

柴田元幸

編訳註者

柴田元幸（しばた もとゆき）

　翻訳家、東京大学名誉教授。東京都生まれ。ポール・オースター、レベッカ・ブラウン、スティーヴン・ミルハウザー、スチュアート・ダイベック、スティーヴ・エリクソンなど、現代アメリカ文学を数多く翻訳。2010 年、トマス・ピンチョン『メイスン＆ディクスン』（新潮社）で日本翻訳文化賞を受賞。翻訳に、『ハックルベリー・フィンの冒けん』（研究社）、シルヴィア・プラス『メアリ・ヴェントゥーラと第九王国 シルヴィア・プラス短篇集』（集英社）、マグナス・ミルズ『鑑識レコード倶楽部』（アルテスパブリッシング）、スティーヴン・ミルハウザー『夜の声』（白水社）、ブライアン・エヴンソン『ウインドアイ』（新潮社）など多数。編訳書に、『「ハックルベリー・フィンの冒けん」をめぐる冒けん』、レアード・ハント『英文創作教室　Writing Your Own Stories』（研究社）など。文芸誌『MONKEY』、および英語文芸誌 MONKEY 責任編集。2017 年、早稲田大学坪内逍遥大賞を受賞。

挿画
島袋里美

編集協力
滝野沢友理・髙橋由香理・今井亮一・福間恵
坪野圭介・鈴木孫和・麻畠徳子・青木比登美
平野久美・中野真紀・大光明宜孝
Polly Barton

組版・レイアウト
古正佳緒里・山本太平

社内協力
三谷裕・髙見沢紀子・三島知子・鈴木美和・松本千晶・星野龍

英文精読教室

第6巻

ユーモアを味わう

● 2022 年 6 月 30 日　初版発行 ●

● 編訳註者 ●
柴田元幸

Copyright © 2022 by Motoyuki Shibata

発行者　●　吉田尚志

発行所　●　株式会社　研究社

〒 102-8152　東京都千代田区富士見 2-11-3

電話　営業 03-3288-7777（代）　編集 03-3288-7711（代）

振替　00150-9-26710

https://www.kenkyusha.co.jp/

KENKYUSHA

装丁　●　久保和正

組版・レイアウト　●　渾天堂

印刷所　●　図書印刷株式会社

ISBN 978-4-327-09906-0 C1082　Printed in Japan